Rebellion in Missouri: 1861

Nathaniel Lyon and His Army of the West

Previous Books by the Author
ADMIRAL THUNDERBOLT
KEEPERS OF THE LIGHTS
EDDIE RICKENBACKER

With Charles A. Lockwood, Vice Admiral, USN, Ret.
TRAGEDY AT HONDA
THROUGH HELL AND DEEP WATER
ZOOMIES, SUBS AND ZEROS
HELLCATS OF THE SEA

Lyon on His Dappled-Gray Stallion Portrayed with Colonel Frank P. Blair, Jr., First Missouri Regiment of Volunteers. (Painting by George Caleb Bingham. From the original in the collection of Mrs. Frank Rollins, Columbia, Mo.)

Rebellion in Missouri: 1861

Nathaniel Lyon and His Army of the West

HANS CHRISTIAN ADAMSON

The Rise of
Brigadier General Nathaniel Lyon, USA,
Who Saved Missouri from Secession
in the Civil War

CHILTON COMPANY · BOOK DIVISION
Publishers
PHILADELPHIA AND NEW YORK

Published in Philadelphia by Chilton Company
and simultaneously in Toronto, Canada
by Ambassador Books, Ltd.

Library of Congress Catalog Card Number 61-6725

Designed by William E. Lickfield

Manufactured in the United States of America
by Quinn & Boden Company, Inc., Rahway, N. J.

To
HELEN LYON ADAMSON
as well as
MELVILLE AND RUPERT LYON
plus
THE CUBS IN THE LYON'S DEN
In Memory of
ALBERT AND MAUDE LYON

Foreword

The story of General Nathaniel Lyon, whom the author aptly calls a "Missouri Yankee," is a drama of stirring political-military events breaking on the Western Border in the spring of 1861. In exactly 90 days, Missouri was forever lost to the Confederacy.

The Lyon story is high tragedy staged at the sanguine second battle of the American Civil War—Wilson's Creek.

There should be no finis to the Lyon story without an inquiry into the might-have-beens but for his tragic, heroic election to play the role of a captain of infantry and thereby sacrifice himself that torrid August 10, 1861, at Wilson's Creek.

Colonel Hans Christian Adamson in *Rebellion in Missouri* combines all the necessary elements in the dramatic story. He expertly re-examines Lyon's generalship of the Union Army of the West. He ably reflects upon the significance of the Battle of Wilson's Creek now, a century later, in the light of all the evidence. Moreover, he brings to us, during the centennial year of Lyon's death, a monumental biography of Lyon. The others are eulogistic and written in the stilted and artificial speech of the eighteen sixties.

In early 1861 Missouri was a large slaveholding State with a government indicating strong Southern sympathies and a plan to co-operate with the other Southern States. To this end, Governor Claiborne F. Jackson called the State Militia to assemble at Camp Jackson in Saint Louis.

In the pro-Union city of Saint Louis, Lyon, a militant Unionist and commander of the Arsenal, allied with Congressman F. P. Blair, Jr., in the interest of stamping out the secessionist movement headed by Jackson and General Sterling Price.

After Lyon captured Camp Jackson, he took command in the field. The State Troops under Price and Jackson withdrew to Cowskin Prairie in the southwest corner of the state.

Some believed that Lyon did not plan to fight; however, this belief quickly disappeared when Lyon wrote Colonel Francis Sigel from Huffman's Crossing on the Osage River just above the mouth of Sac River on July 10, 1861: "Hang on Jackson's flank or rear if he advances to meet me." This is evidence that Lyon moved toward southwest Missouri to fight. In fact, Lyon appeared so anxious to fight that he forced one of the severest marches in the annals of warfare from the Grand and Osage River crossings to Springfield. By the 20th of July, Lyon was firmly encamped at Springfield, with 6,000 troops consisting of the 1st, 2nd, 3rd, and 5th Missouri, the 1st Iowa, the 1st and 2nd Kansas, and several companies and batteries of regulars from Fort Leavenworth.

In the meantime, Price had been given command of all the Missouri Militia, numbering 5,000 troops, now drilling and recruiting on Cowskin Prairie. On July 28, General Bart Pearce, with over 2,000 Arkansas troops, and General Ben McCulloch, with about 3,000 Confederate troops, including Colonel J. D. Walker's "Texas Rangers," and Colonel Louis Hébert's Louisiana "Pelicans," united with Price, now removed to Cassville, Missouri, about 60 miles southwest of Springfield. On August 1, these combined forces began their approach march eastward, their objective being to capture Lyon's army at Springfield, and to regain control of the State Government. On August 6, most of the Southern forces reached Wilson's Creek and went into camp along its banks close to the ripening corn in the bottom land, 12 miles southwest of Springfield.

On the morning of August 9, Lyon, still at Springfield, called a council of war and said: "I propose to march this evening with all our available force . . . and marching by the Fayetteville road, throw our whole force upon the enemy at once and endeavor to rout him before he can recover from his surprise." The plan was accepted, but the single-pronged assault idea was canceled.

At the insistence of Sigel, the battle plan was changed and the force divided into two columns with a lack of communications and a divided command. The substitute plan was a departure from accepted principles but agreed to by Lyon because of Sigel's supposedly great military ability and wide experience.

Thus did the final plan prescribe a desperate thrust in the face of an order from the Western Department in Saint Louis by his superior, General John C. Frémont, directing a withdrawal to Rolla. What compelled Lyon to override Frémont and to execute instead this substitute plan of a divided attack on his adversary whom he believed to hold a numerical superiority of five to one?

On the night before the battle on the road to surprise the Confederates at Wilson's Creek, Lyon en bivouac shared a rubber coat with his Chief of Staff and spoke clearly of his responsibility to the citizens of southwest Missouri. John M. Schofield, later to be General of the Armies, says: "This night Lyon was oppressed with the responsibility of this situation, with anxiety for the cause, and with sympathy for the Union people of that section, when he should retreat and leave to their fate those who could not forsake their homes."

On the Saturday morning that followed between daybreak and 10:30 o'clock, more than 15,000 troops were engaged on a field of battle comprising about two sections of land. The casualty list exceeded 2,500—one in six. Few battles in history disclose an equal percentage of dead and wounded, considering the number engaged and the time spent in fighting.

Some conclude that the battle was drawn, others that it was a Confederate victory tragically dissipated because McCulloch, despite Price's prodding, chose not to follow the Union Column after it withdrew from the field. Seemingly, the classic test of which side wins a battle is determined by which side is in control of the battlefield after the battle is over. At least this is a simple rule if not always a realistic one. Perhaps Wilson's Creek is an exception.

From battles, many important lessons usually are learned and ofttimes valuable tactical experience is absorbed to be applied in battle another day. Occasionally a battle bears significantly on the outcome of the war. Of the many important lessons learned at Wilson's Creek, the foremost was that the rigors of frontier life developed outstanding courage and endurance and marksmanship in the private soldiers of the new West. Witness the performance of the volunteers from Missouri, Arkansas, Kansas, Iowa, Louisiana, Texas, and Illinois. Of equal importance is the fact that the young and inexperienced company and field grade officers under their first real test of fire on August 10, 1861, soon became good general officers. Witness the names of Schofield, Granger, Sturgis, Steele, Carr, Major, McIntosh, Hébert, and Gilbert—all graduates of the United States Military Academy.

However, the real significance of the battle is twofold: (1) The Lincoln government, through Lyon's decision to fight, kept faith with those Missourians who were loyal; (2) Price's drive to the Missouri and the Mississippi rivers was obliquely blocked. Thus the most important Border State was saved to the Union, forty years from the very day of its admission.

Lyon's initiative and decisiveness, his drive and daring against orders, and uneven odds, won the fight for Missouri.

Soon the way was cleared for the South's loss of Kentucky. Mississippi and Tennessee followed. . . . Finally Sherman's March. . . . After the loss of the Mississippi Valley, Appomattox was inevitable. Perhaps it is best expressed by Pulitzer Prize historian Bruce Catton who boldly asserts, "The final doom of the Confederacy was written in the West rather than the East."

Of the many brilliant generals in that war, Lyon ranks high on any list; however, his fate remains as a classic example of one who elected to give his life and thereby to lose military and/or political immortality.

It should be remembered that Lyon was a well-rounded officer. He was a lover of Shakespeare, yet his favorite study was Alexis de Tocqueville's *Democracy in America.*

Lyon vigorously opposed war with Mexico; yet, when war came, he fought gallantly under General Winfield Scott in and around Mexico City.

Once in a Manhattan, Kansas, paper, Lyon, discussing the "Kansas Question," dared to call President Buchanan a "Blue-eyed old hypocrite."

Assuming that the "Missouri Yankee" had lived to direct the withdrawal of his army to Saint Louis, would not Lyon, the career general who fought, have received the opportunity that went to the obscure volunteer general, U. S. Grant? And in such event, would not Lyon have moved south as did Grant, perhaps even more expertly?

One cannot read Colonel Adamson's moving story of the "Missouri Yankee" without feeling that Lyon as a national military hero would have been eminently qualified to seek his nation's highest office, perhaps with success.

JOHN K. HULSTON

Springfield, Missouri

Introduction

I first became aware of Nathaniel Lyon's place in history during summer visits to Cape Cod in the 1930's. My mentor was my father-in-law, Albert W. Lyon. A former member of the Massachusetts House of Representatives, a World War I officer, and, finally, a retired lawyer, he had, with typical New England instinct, turned to a study of the deep roots and wide branches of his family tree as an avocation.

Thus I learned about the Connecticut farm boy, born in 1818, who dreamed of serving his country in his own generation even as his forebears had served the young colonies in the French and Indian and Revolutionary wars.

Nathaniel Lyon rose like a roaring rocket in the Western skies. And, like a rocket—expended after its flash and flare—he plummeted after his death in battle into dark but undeserved oblivion. In the course of three brief months, Lyon staged an offensive within Missouri that made Saint Louis secure for the Union, chased Governor Jackson and his henchmen out of their capital, made the Missouri, Ohio, and Upper Mississippi Union rivers, and served to keep Missouri and Kentucky in the realm of the North.

At a time when most Northern leaders seemed as lethargic as steers in a slaughter pen, Lyon took the offensive. He operated not only brilliantly but so swiftly that he was, among other things, called "The Whirlwind in Pantaloons." His spectacular exploits began with the capture of Camp Jackson in Saint Louis on May 10, 1861, and ended when he fell in the

Battle of Wilson's Creek on August 10, 1861. In this sanguinary contest—one of the bloodiest in the Civil War—there was no real victor, but Lyon fought against odds of four to one.

In his day, Brigadier General Lyon was a national hero. But his appearance on the scene of the Civil War occurred too early and too briefly in the holocaust of conflict to be long remembered. Now that the nation commemorates the passing of a full century since the launching of the War Between the States, and reviews anew the heroes and their deeds in those bitter battles, I thought that it was timely to revive memories and restore recognition to Nathaniel Lyon.

Not that he has been completely forgotten. In California, a mountain peak and a valley were named after him. In San Francisco a street bears his name. In Saint Louis his equestrian statue stands in Lyon Park, once part of the old U. S. Arsenal grounds. In the spring of 1960, Congress enacted and the President signed a measure that made the battlefield of Wilson's Creek a national park.

Elsewhere I have listed persons, institutions, and other sources to whom I owe debts of gratitude for their help in collecting material pertinent to the life and acts of Nathaniel Lyon. They were all gallantly patient and dedicated. However, among those whose patience I could have worn painfully thin were Miss Dorothy A. Brockhoff, Reference Librarian, Missouri Historical Society, St. Louis; Miss Dolores Cadell, Reference Librarian, San Francisco Public Library; Richard Dillon, Sutro Librarian, California State Library; George Goldfine and Mrs. Ripley, research librarians, Sixth Army Reference Library, Presidio, San Francisco; and, at the top, my dear friend and companion Vice Admiral Charles A. Lockwood, USN, who during World War II was Commander, Submarines, Pacific. Although he left his hometown, Lamar, in Barton County, Missouri, in his late teens to go to Annapolis, he has never lost his love for, interest in, or knowledge of Missouri and her people.

A particular debt is owed to Mr. John K. Hulston, who has written the Foreword. Mr. Hulston, who practices law in

Springfield, has had a lifelong interest in the Civil War in the West. Following his return from World War II—which he entered as a private and ended as a major—he began a concentrated study of Nathaniel Lyon's position in Missouri's Civil War history. He has written widely on the subject and significance of the Battle of Wilson's Creek, one of his best-known compositions being a monograph on "West Pointers at Wilson's Creek." Mr. Hulston was chairman of the steering committee organized in Missouri to have Congress pass the now-enacted bill creating a National Battlefield Park at Wilson's Creek. He is also a member of the Civil War Centennial Commission for Missouri, appointed by Governor James T. Blair, Jr., of that state.

Last come my beloved wife and respected critic, Helen; and Mrs. Hugh W. Davies of Los Gatos, whose gift for deciphering manuscript verges on the border of black magic.

A word may be appropriate here on the subject of footnotes. In the interests of narrative and readability, they have been left out, but it is hoped that the Bibliography will be comprehensive enough for those who pursue detailed research.

HANS CHRISTIAN ADAMSON
Colonel, USAF, Ret.

The Francesca, Nob Hill
San Francisco, California

Contents

Rebellion in Missouri: 1861

Nathaniel Lyon and His Army of the West

Chapter 1

Rebellion in Missouri

———◆———

Lincoln's Demand for Troops Angers the Governor

The usually pale and passive face of Claiborne F. Jackson, Governor of Missouri, flushed with anger and froze into lines of wrath as he read the telegram handed him by Thomas L. Snead, his executive secretary and political counselor. The message was from Washington and signed by Secretary of War Simon Cameron. It asked the Governor—in line with President Lincoln's April 15th proclamation for 75,000 troops —to have the State of Missouri furnish the Union Army with four regiments of 90-day enlistees.

Jackson, whose tall, well-set-up figure made him appear younger than his 55 years, slammed his desk with flat palms. Clenching and unclenching his hands, the Governor walked up and down the floor of his office in the capitol of Missouri in Jefferson City. Snead followed his friend and superior with speculative eyes.

Both men were ardent believers in, and supporters of, the cause of Southern Rights, the institution of slavery, and the peculiarly "sacred" but inhuman property rights that went with it. Both wanted to drive Missouri into the ranks of seceded states. As of this date—April 17, 1861—these included Mississippi, Florida, Alabama, Georgia, Louisiana, and Texas. On that very day—although Jackson and Snead had no knowledge of it at the time—the Virginia legislature passed a secession referendum.

1

But, much as Jackson wanted to array Missouri on the Southern side, he knew that her pro-Southern citizens—a virulently aggressive minority—were not adequately armed. In addition, Jackson wanted his secession-minded legislature to assume the responsibility for tossing Missouri's chestnuts into the rebel fire. Less than a month earlier, a State Convention, created by Jackson to have Missouri throw in with the South, had backfired. It voted overwhelmingly against Missouri quitting the Union at that particular time (March, 1861).

Since then, momentous events had happened. In South Carolina, Beauregard had fired on Fort Sumter and the great bastion in Charleston's harbor had fallen. While hostilities between North and South had not been formally declared, the hissing of the fuse, soon to explode the powder keg called the United States into fragments of fierce hatred, could be heard in every corner of the land.

Out and out Slave States had little difficulty in lining up with the Confederacy. But border commonwealths, such as Kentucky and Missouri—although harboring the institution of slavery—contained heavy percentages of pro-Northern sentiment. Because of its strategic position on two vital waterways, the Missouri and the Mississippi rivers, Jackson knew that his State was vital not only as a fortress on a flank but also as a source of manpower and matériel. Even in 1861, Missouri was well on the way toward the development of her industrial and natural resources. He who held Missouri held a high trump in the game of war. Jackson was resolved that it should fall into the hands of the Confederacy.

Lincoln's Administration was now, so to speak, forcing Jackson's hand. And yet this was not the moment to play it. He needed time. But, being a clever strategist, the Governor saw how he could use Cameron's request for troops as a means of displaying himself in a mantle of neutrality—while still putting in a crafty word for the South.

Running a strong, long-fingered hand over his smooth-shaven mouth and jaw, Jackson continued pacing up and down the floor while he and Snead composed a reply. At last Jackson had it as he wanted it. The telegram sent to Secretary of War Cameron read:

Sir: Your dispatch of the 15th instant, making a call on Missouri for four regiments of men for immediate service, has been received. There can be, I apprehend, no doubt that the men are intended to form a part of the President's army to make war upon the people of the seceded states.

Your requisition, in my judgment, is illegal, unconstitutional, and revolutionary in its object, inhuman and diabolical and cannot be complied with. Not one man will the State of Missouri furnish to carry on any unholy crusade.

With the message on its way, Jackson and Snead discussed the steps that lay immediately ahead. To be sure, Jackson could always call an extra session of the legislature and cajole it into overriding the State Convention's decision to remain in the Union. However, lack of weapons among Southern sympathizers might make realists among the lawmakers hang back.

The Missouri State Militia was neither numerically strong nor was it armed with up-to-date weapons. Hence, no military force could be mounted with the militia as a nucleus. However, several Southern states—Louisiana, for instance—had seized and raided well-stocked Federal arsenals with most encouraging results. Missouri had two such repositories. A large one in Saint Louis and a smaller one in Liberty, near Kansas City. The idea of taking the Saint Louis Arsenal was not a new one for Jackson. He had played with the idea since the hour he became Governor at the turn of the year. But his desire to cloak his secesh activities in the garments of legitimacy had prevented him from putting any seizure project into action.

Now, he and Snead began to regret that they had not taken control of the Saint Louis Arsenal—with its thousands of guns, vast stores of ammunition, and tons of gunpowder—earlier in the year. The then commandant had been willing to recognize

3

the authority of the State and to open the Arsenal's doors for the asking. Brigadier General Daniel M. Frost, commander of the Saint Louis Militia District, had made all the necessary arrangements. But Jackson had remained indecisive. Meanwhile, leaders of the strong Union element in Saint Louis had learned about the plot. They had the commandant relieved, and companies of the city's Union Guards kept unofficial but vigilant eyes on the Arsenal's conspicuously under-garrisoned defenses.

That had been in January. Now in April the Arsenal complement of Army regulars had been increased materially. In command of the troops was Captain Nathaniel Lyon, who, in Southern eyes, was a horse-stealing damn Yankee and a nigger-loving abolitionist. All chance of taking the Saint Louis Arsenal by stealth had vanished. And, while its defenses were not strong, it would require a well-organized and well-equipped military force either to take it by storm or to starve it into surrender.

After discussing the pros and cons, Jackson and Snead decided to go by train to Saint Louis. There they would go into executive session with the Governor's secret board of strategy. This included Brigadier General Frost as well as Captain Basil W. Duke, Company C, and Captain Colton Greene, Company E, Second Regiment of Frost's Brigade.

Duke and Greene—both under thirty—are worth knowing and remembering. The former was born in Kentucky. In addition to being a lawyer with an affluent practice, he was also head of the Saint Louis Police Authority created by the Governor to keep militant Saint Louis Union organizations in check. In time, Captain Duke was to become second-in-command of Morgan's Raiders and commander of a Confederate cavalry brigade. Colton Greene was a South Carolinean. Despite his youth, he had accumulated a sizable fortune in merchandising and he was eager to give himself, his time, ability, and money to the cause of the South.

However, Brigadier General Frost was by far the most

4

violent Southern Righter of the trio. Strangely enough, his pro-Southern patina was completely acquired. Frost was born in Schenectady, New York, at a time when that city at the eastern end of the Mohawk River boomed into becoming an important terminal on the State's new Erie Canal. His father, a self-made canaler, swore that his Dan'l should become a gentleman. As a step in that direction, he obtained an appointment for the boy to West Point. When Second Lieutenant Frost graduated in 1844, he stood fourth in his class. With his commission, Frost also had acquired a decidedly Southern accent because of the extent to which he had cultivated the friendship and aped the manner of those classmates who were lighthearted, horsy aristocrats from below the Mason-Dixon line. Like other members of his class, Frost went off to the wars in Mexico. He was brevetted a first lieutenant for gallantry under fire in the Battle of Cerro Gordo. He resigned in 1853 to enter business, matrimony, and the *chivalry* of Saint Louis. The upper strata of society in the lovely old city on the Father of Waters was, in those halcyon days, uncontaminated by Yankee notions such as freedom and other human rights for Negroes. Hence, the former barge canal boy of upstate New York grew into a full-fledged Missouri reactionary.

Having an orderly and excellent mind, Brigadier General Frost had a complete and workable program of aggression to place before the Governor when they met across the conference table in Saint Louis on April 18. The brigadier was raven dark, ramrod stiff, and spoke with a carefully cultivated Louisiana drawl.

First of all, he urged the Governor to place the Missouri Militia divisions under arms in encampments within their respective districts. In this connection, Basil Duke reminded Jackson that he had the power to do so under a law of 1858. It authorized the Governor to call the militia into training camps for six days on May 6 of each year. That date was still about three weeks away.

5

By calling the militia out, ostensibly for peaceable purposes, the division Frost commanded could be encamped at Lindell Grove, within the very limits of Saint Louis. Frost, therefore, would be in a fine position to swoop down on the Arsenal.

But, the Governor objected, how would the militia, although superior in numbers, be able to take the Arsenal by force with inferior arms?

Longheaded Frost also had thought of that. If the Governor would write an appeal for assistance to President Jefferson Davis, of the Confederate States of America, Captain Greene and Captain Duke would take it to Montgomery, Alabama.

What kind of assistance? Jackson wanted to know.

Frost explained that the Louisiana patriots who seized the Baton Rouge Arsenal a little while back had found it well supplied. The Confederacy, considering its interest in the Saint Louis Arsenal, could well afford to give them muskets, artillery, siege guns, and appropriate ammunition. He promised the Governor that it was safe to assume that, if they captured the Arsenal, they would be in a position to take Missouri out of the Union.

The upshot of the meeting was that Jackson wrote a letter of appeal for help to Jefferson Davis. To insure its safe delivery, the note was to be taken south by Duke and Greene. At the same time, the Governor agreed to call the legislature into special session early in May so that the timing of the taking of the Arsenal would percussion the lawmakers into giving Jackson special military and executive powers. As for the Liberty Arsenal, in western Missouri, local secessionists would be urged to seize its 1,500 muskets and four light fieldpieces at the earliest opportunity.

The certainty with which Jackson regarded the outcome of the forthcoming Missouri rebellion is reflected in a secret note he sent to David Walker, president of the Arkansas State Convention which on May 6 was to push Arkansas into the Confederate ranks. Dated April 19, it read:

6

Missouri will be ready for secession in less than thirty days. And [she] will secede if Arkansas will only get out of the way and give her a free passage [to the Southern states].

Nathaniel Lyon Enters Upon the Scene

Brigadier General William S. Harney—after 40 years of active campaigning in Seminole and Mexican wars, as well as on the wide and turbulent frontiers of the West—had been put to pasture in Saint Louis by friends in the War Department. The white-haired, elderly cavalryman was a person to conjure with in a situation that called for military sagacity. But any kind of job that took him into civilian or political relations put him at a disadvantage. The brigadier general's current assignment, as Commander of the politically sensitive Department of the West, with headquarters in Saint Louis, was one for which he was wholly untrained. With countless friends in the upper strata of the city's social and financial circles, the general saw the complex situation in Saint Louis through their ultraconservative eyes. Not because he was disloyal to the Union. He was not. But his contacts with friends who leaned toward the South provided Harney with blinders that limited and obscured his range of vision. By marriage, he was connected with high Creole society. His two daughters had married into the French nobility abroad.

In absolute contrast to Brigadier General Harney stood Captain Nathaniel Lyon. He had arrived in Saint Louis from Kansas with his Company B, Second U. S. Infantry, some two months earlier (February 6) to reinforce the Arsenal garrison. The slim, rather slight, infantry officer had clear-cut opinions against the South, against slavery in general, and against proslavery Missourians who had tried to extend slavery into Kansas in particular. He had served in Kansas during the bloody days of 1854–1856 when Claiborne Jackson, then a State Senator, and other Missouri slaveowners had led Border Ruffians by the thousands from western Missouri into

7

eastern Kansas. Their mission was to stuff ballot boxes at gun point to insure the election of a proslavery Territorial Legislature. The mission was accomplished. At that time, Lyon had served under Harney and had been compelled to carry out orders to punish, restrict, and suppress free-soil Kansans.

In those days the South was in the saddle in Washington. Slaveowning bigwigs controlled both the Congress and the White House. In fact, Jefferson Davis, as Secretary of War, set the tune for the Army in Kansas. Much as he hated it, Lyon had to dance to the slave-state piper. He described Davis as a "heartless villain."

By 1856, the captain was so fed up with making life unbearable for innocent settlers, who did not adjust from ballots to bullets, that he was ready to quit the Army. Just as he was about to frame his resignation, Lyon was ordered on frontier duty against Indians in Nebraska. He did not resign. Fighting Indians was quite all right. In the early 1850's, during the harsh and ruthless push of westward expansion, the land claims of Indians were brushed aside. Those who tried to resist the white tide were simply swept under.

Lyon had the strong sense of justice and the lively feeling of fair play toward the underdog so characteristic of his Puritan forefathers. And yet—those attitudes did not extend toward Indians. Even to this day his name is associated with the bloodiest "massacre" of Indians ever staged in California. It was enacted on an island in Clear Lake, about 100 miles north of San Francisco, on May 19, 1850.

Captain Lyon, heading an expedition of one company of cavalry and three companies of infantry, was sent into northern California to avenge the murder of several whites, including Captain W. H. Warner of the Army's Topographical Engineers. The crimes had been committed in the fall of 1849 by a confederation of natives with whom the Clear Lake Indians were in league.

Before the punitive mission left Benicia, it was learned that the natives, expecting reprisal, had taken refuge on an island

8

in the northern end of the lake beyond musket range. The only vessels on the lake were tule rafts built by the Indians. Some way had to be found to reach the marauders. Three large Army transport wagons were stripped to their frames and three 10-oared whaleboats were roped into place. To take the Indians by surprise, Lyon avoided established trails and placed a backbreaking burden on horses and men as the heavy wagons were hauled up and down mountainsides until they reached the southern end of Clear Lake. This was about 29 miles by water from the island where the Indians had sought shelter.

Lyon sent the dragoons, commanded by Lieutenant Davidson, to take positions on the shores that faced the island. This was both to prevent the natives from escaping and to create a diversion so that the whaleboats, loaded with infantrymen, might sneak up on the island unobserved. The plan worked so well that Lyon's men were in firing position before the Indians were aware of their presence. With only bows and arrows, the Indians put up but feeble resistance. Soon, to escape bullets and bayonets, they sought shelter in the heavy stand of tule that grew in the water on the shoreward side of the island. Lyon ordered his men to sling their ammunition around their necks and give pursuit. In a report to Brigadier General Pulsifer Smith (who gave him a warm commendation), Lyon wrote:

The tule was thoroughly searched with severe and protracted efforts, and with most gratifying results; the number killed, I confidently report, at not less than sixty, and doubt little, extended to a hundred and upwards.

An entirely different Nathaniel Lyon is brought to light in two incidents that took place in 1854 in Fort Riley, Kansas. Lyon's Second Infantry was stationed there under Colonel William R. Montgomery, a browbeating martinet who ran the regiment with highhanded arrogance. A major came to Fort

9

Riley with his family from the East. His wife brought along as upstairs maid a young girl whose name was Sarah Ahren. Corporal Allender of Lyon's company fell in love with her, proposed marriage, and was accepted. The major was furious. He had brought Sarah west at his own expense, and now she was marrying out of his household. Pulling rank, he forbade Lyon to consent to the marriage. He placed the case before Montgomery who informed the chaplain that the marriage had his disapproval.

One would think that against such obstructions, even Love could not find a way. But Lyon had read enough military law to realize that the colonel had no such authority. He knew an injustice was being perpetrated and decided to set things aright. In asking Dr. William Hammond, the regimental surgeon, to serve as a marriage witness, Lyon said—as Hammond recalled:

"Certainly, I'm going to perform the ceremony! Marriage is a civil contract. I shall read them a chapter from Blackstone, make them a short address, ask them some proper questions and make them man and wife. Then we'll see what Old Montgomery will do!"

When Montgomery heard about the marriage, he placed Lyon under house arrest and threatened dire consequences. But the choleric colonel soon found that he had no case. The matter was forgotten, or so it seemed.

Fort Riley was bordered by land that had been set aside for Pawnee, the planned Territorial capital of Kansas. In 1854, the area was swept by a cyclonic land boom. Montgomery, seeing a chance to line his own pockets, arbitrarily and without authority, extended the western limits of the Army Reservation to include some highly desirable lands that had been settled by two brothers named Dixon and their families. Later on, he intended to rescind the seizure and sell the land.

When the Dixons defied the order to vacate, the colonel resolved to have Lyon do the dirty job or put his neck in a noose. The peppery little captain had not bothered to mute his voice in claiming that Montgomery had no right to dispossess the settlers. On the other hand, the vengeful Montgomery knew that Lyon had no right to refuse to obey the order. But he was gambling that the captain would let his heart dominate his head.

In obedience to orders, Lyon, much as he resented the illegal assignment, marched on the Dixon houses. He put the brothers and their families off the land and pulled their houses down. Montgomery, who had been ready to prefer charges of disobedience against Lyon, was stricken dumb when the captain reported that his orders had been executed. In all likelihood, Montgomery would have been completely befuddled had he known that Lyon went straight to his quarters, wrote out charges of corruption and other crimes against his superior officer, and forwarded them to Fort Leavenworth. Early in 1855, Montgomery was tried on these charges before a General Court-Martial and dismissed from the service.

Lyon's raid on the Clear Lake Indians reflected a conspicuous lack of sympathy with the natives. Similarly, his action against Colonel Montgomery revealed strong resentments against highhanded treatment of antislavery Kansas settlers. However, there is nothing in his record that actually shows Lyon extending a helping hand to the Negro. The closest episode to such an incident was reported to have taken place at Fort Riley in the late 1850's.

One night in the officers' mess, so the story goes, Lyon and a fellow officer, who had strong Southern leanings, became involved in an argument over the rights and wrongs of slavery. Lyon, in condemning the inhuman treatment of slaves, used language which his opponent considered insulting. The Southerner challenged him to a duel. Soon after, a second called on Captain Lyon at his quarters to make the proper arrangements. Lyon said that he would not need a second. As the challenged party, he had the right to select weapons. He picked service revolvers. When the second inquired as to the distance between combatants, Lyon laconically replied: "Three."

"Three paces?" exclaimed the astounded second. Even ten paces would have been close range.

"No, three feet," Lyon is said to have answered. "Your principal will sit on one side of a table. I will sit on the other. We will point our Colts at each other and fire at the count of three."

The challenge was withdrawn.

The son of Amasa and Keziah (Knowlton) Lyon, Nathaniel was born in Eastford, Connecticut, on a typical New England farm of rocks, rills, and ridges in 1818. From the time he was old enough to think about his future, the boy was imbued with the idea that he wanted to be a soldier. His paternal and maternal forebears had fought in the French and Indian War as well as in the American Revolution. Determined to march in their patriotic boots, Nat's wish was fulfilled in 1837 when he became a plebe at West Point. Four years later, as a second lieutenant, he was assigned to the Second U. S. Infantry and sent to the Seminole wars. After a brief interlude of peace, he went with the Second Infantry to fight in the Mexican War. He was wounded in the taking of Mexico City and brevetted a first lieutenant for conspicuous bravery in capturing a section of enemy artillery.

With the ending of the Mexican War, Lyon's Army assignments took him on frontier duties against Indian raiders from California to the Great Plains. In that era the Indian policies of Uncle Sam were mainly forged into the steel of bayonets or molded into the lead of musket bullets. As captain of Company B, Second Infantry, Nat acquired a well-earned reputation for turning bad Indians into good Indians. The latter being dead ones.

Captain Lyon and his Company B, Second Infantry, returned to Kansas in July, 1859. The three years had brought a decided change. The free-soilers not only had learned to defend themselves against Missouri raiders, they actually had assumed the offensive. Now they were taking more than an eye for an eye and more than one tooth for a tooth during sweeps into the Missouri counties adjacent to the Kansas border. Under the leadership of such violent zealots as James H. Lane, Captain James Montgomery, Charles R. "Doc" Jennison, and, last but not least, John Brown, the Missouri proslavers had been given massive doses of their own bitter medicine. When Missouri bushwhackers invaded Kansas to spread unspeakable terror, Death now rode at the head of Kansas jayhawkers, equally intent on murder, mayhem, and arson in Missouri.

In the warfare between the two regions—one free and one slave—Lyon saw a miniature of what was to come: the war between the North and the South. He wanted to be in it to fight for "the triumph of my principles," as he wrote in a letter dated January 27, 1861, from Fort Scott, Kansas; he closed the sentence by adding: ". . . in which I certainly expect to expose and very likely lose my life."

The Situation in Saint Louis, April, 1861

Lyon had come to look on slavery as a killing cancer that had to be removed if the nation were to survive. When, in January, 1861, he received orders to take Company B to Saint Louis to reinforce the Arsenal garrison, Captain Lyon saw a wonderful opportunity to help uphold the strong, but unorganized, Northern sentiment that prevailed in that city and throughout the State. This Connecticut Yankee's mission at King Cotton's Court—as he saw it—was to keep Missouri in the Union at any cost. He knew that he would not have much to do it with. The North was timid and it was ruled by middle-of-the-roaders who sought peace at any price. Buchanan was still in office. But in a few weeks President-elect Abraham Lincoln would take over. Lyon fervently hoped that this event would change the situation.

War, as Lyon saw it, was inescapable. A campaigner of long standing, he knew that the fortunes of war favor those who take the initiative. From occasional assignments of fairly long

13

duration the captain was thoroughly familiar with the situation in Saint Louis. He knew it to be a tinderbox that could flare into flame on easy provocation. Roughly, the town was divided into two camps. Arrogant and aggressive were the pro-Southern Minute Men, totaling some 700 members. They were divided into companies and most of them were armed. The Minute Men were composed mainly of the scions of fine old plantation or commercial families, many dating back to the days when Saint Louis was French. They were known as the "cavaliers." At the other end of the city's proslavery spectrum were the river rabble, poor white trash and men so low that they could only find stature by having someone like a slave to look down on.

The Northern element in Saint Louis, at least so far as organization was concerned, consisted of the Union Guards. Most of them were Germans (or their sons) who had come to this country on the heels of the great middle-European revolution in 1848. Regarding slavery with distaste, these Saint Louis Germans had turned toward Frémont, the first Republican Presidential candidate in 1856 and had voted almost solidly for Lincoln in 1860. Similarly, they helped elect Frank Blair, Jr., to the Congressional seat he once had occupied as a Democrat. Blair had earned this support from the politically "radical" German element because of his early and steady advocacy of free soil, free men and free labor, first in the Missouri Legislature, later in Congress. Also, he had a friendly attitude toward immigrants (as opposed to the Know-Nothing faction) and their numerous integration problems in a society that regarded white labor as degrading. The Germans were particularly indebted to him for his vigorous opposition to legislation that would extend residence requirements for citizenship from 5 to 21 years.

Unlike the Minute Men, who were in favor with the Jackson administration and had access to the State Adjutant General's military stores, the Union Guards had few weapons. This posed a serious problem to Frank Blair and the city's unofficial board of Northern strategy, namely the Union Committee on Public Safety of which Oliver E. Filley was chairman. Thanks to the sharp eyes and ears of the secret agents employed by the Safety Committee, its members were well informed about the various schemes entertained by the Minute Men for the seizure of the Arsenal. Luckily, the plans had never matured because of Governor Jackson's political timidity. Had the secessionists attacked the Arsenal prior to Lincoln's April 15th proclamation, there was nothing the Union men of Saint Louis could have done about it. Mere mortals cannot stand up against muskets with wooden drill guns; and, at that time, that was virtually all the numerous companies of Union Guards would have had to fight with.

One reason why the early organized Union defenders of Saint Louis were overwhelmingly German was that they were not only Republicans but also had, for years, been unified into Turner Societies or Turnvereins. These German clubs— devoted to singing, beer drinking, athletics, social events, and marching—had the ready-made leadership to turn them into militant patriotic groups. Soon after the Minute Men sprang into being, the Turner Societies converted themselves into military units and set up small-arms drill with wooden weapons. Members who had served in European armies acted as instructors.

There were exceptions to the general lack of armament. The *Schwarze Jaeger,* being mainly hunters and sportsmen, were well armed. Some Union companies had a few rifles or muskets owned by individuals or bought surreptitiously by public-spirited sympathizers. Once about 100 up-to-date rifles were smuggled into the hands of Saint Louis Union men. Packed in boxes labeled "plaster casts," they had been part of a shipment of statuary from New York to be placed on temporary public exhibit.

From this it will be seen that the Union element moved and acted with great concern, like an elephant worried by a mouse, in order to avoid open conflict with the proslavery minority. The secessionists had no such civic scruples. They displayed side arms, from light pistols to heavy revolvers, with strutting arrogance. And their headquarters in the Berthold mansion on Pine Street was a veritable arsenal of rifles, revolvers, muskets, and hand grenades.

The Stars and Bars of the Confederacy waved flauntingly above the Berthold mansion. But the very Union men who hated the sight of the Southern ensign were fearful lest the appearance of Old Glory should arouse explosive wrath. Hence the national emblem was kept under wraps. It should be made clear that while all Republicans were pro-Union not all Democrats were for secession. Once the bonds were cut, Douglas Democrats by the tens of thousands flocked to the Northern cause—some as Unconditional Union men, who would remain with Lincoln at any cost, others as Conditional Union men. Many of the latter would stay with the Union short of coercing the seceded states back into the Union by force.

President Lincoln's April 15th proclamation for 75,000 three months' enlistees and Cameron's request for four Missouri regiments were read eagerly by John M. Schofield, a youthful instructor in physics at Saint Louis' Washington University. He at once wired Governor Jackson and offered his services as mustering officer. There was no reply. After reading Jackson's answer to Cameron in the press, Schofield hurried to the downtown departmental offices of Brigadier General Harney. He identified himself as a first lieutenant of artillery, USA, on extended leave of absence. Again he offered his services as mustering officer.

General Harney listened wearily, wiped his handsome white mustaches with a snowy handkerchief, and observed that he had no authority to swear in troops without direct orders from Washington.

Taken aback by this wholly unexpected attitude, Lieutenant Schofield reminded Harney that it was common gossip in town that Jackson and his henchmen were plotting to capture the Arsenal with an armed force under the guise of the Missouri Militia. Harney, with the naïvete that characterized him in dealing with nonmilitary affairs, observed:

"Why, the State has not as yet passed an ordinance of secession; she has not gone out of the Union."

Lyon Is Ready to Defy Harney's Authority

In 1861, the Saint Louis Arsenal covered an area of 56 acres in the form of a rough rectangle that ran between Carondelet Avenue and the Mississippi River in the southern section of the city. The Arsenal was situated on low and level ground that was faced by hills to the south and southwest. On its three land sides, the area was enclosed by massive limestone walls ten feet high and three feet thick. A substantial fence ran along the river front. In the center of this fence was an opening known as the water gate. It opened on a landing large enough to accommodate an average-sized river packet.

Within the walls were, in addition to workshops, warehouses, foundries, laboratories, powder magazines, and barracks for personnel, four large two-story stone buildings with slate roofs. The largest of these housed about 30,000 rifles, carbines, and muskets. Also in storage were 150,000 ball cartridges; scores of fieldpieces; dozens of siege guns; heavy supplies of cannon ammunition; about 50 tons of gunpowder; and machinery for making shot, shells, bombs, canister, and other ammunition. To be sure, some of the muskets were so worn by usage that their bores were oversized. They could not shoot straight and, being equipped with flintlocks, were not adapted for percussion caps.

Next largest structure in the Arsenal was the administration building, which also included quarters for some of the officers. In mid-April, 1861, the entire garrison consisted of 9 officers and 430 enlisted men. While he was not in command of the Arsenal as such, Lyon's authority extended over the officers and men who in an emergency would constitute the defending forces. Against mere small arms, the hardy regulars could probably hold their own, even if assaulted by superior numbers. But if the Arsenal were attacked by artillery and siege mortars, the defenders soon would be reduced to cannon fodder.

After his disheartening interview with Brigadier General Harney, young Schofield caught a horsecar that took him to the Arsenal. There he called on Captain Lyon, whom he had never met before. As the older officer rose from his desk to greet him, Schofield saw a man who was as sharp, straight, and ready as Caesar's sword. Five feet, seven inches tall, Lyon looked as if he had been forged in the fires and hammered on the anvils of endurance. His strongly muscled body was slim, but that slimness was all coil and cable. His face, deeply creased, tanned by sun, and weathered by wind, was set in a frame of unkempt sandy hair and a sparse fringe of reddish whiskers. It could be said that Lyon had an almost comical appearance until one caught a look of the mouth that held the quality of a bear trap, and gazed into eyes that were as blue and cold as newly chilled steel. There were in the set of Lyon's features—his mouth, his eyes, his sharp, slightly bent nose, shaped like a Yankee clipper's cutwater—an implacability of purpose that could be winning or repelling. He was, obviously, a man who was not to be taken lightly, nor one who looked on life from its lighter side.

From his neck down, Lyon's appearance was almost as unique as it was from the neck up. His long-skirted Army coat revealed signs of long wear. In fact, it was faded to a point where it showed a bit green around the gills. His belt buckle was quite off-center, and, of the eight brass buttons designed to hold the top of the single-breasted garment in place, only one—the second from the top—was in position. Lyon's white neckband was clean but crumpled. The silver thread of which his captain's bars were fashioned was tarnished. The sword that hung at his side was a regulation, highly serviceable dragoon saber and no kin to the lighter, dressier infantry officer's sword. His trousers, wrinkled as his coat, terminated in a pair of sturdy cavalry boots. They were clean, but no blackening agent had been used to hide the scuffs and scars of heavy usage.

It could be that Nathaniel Lyon's disdain for well-policed uniforms on his own part, although he demanded military neatness among his subordinates, dated back to Mexican War days. He had served under Brigadier General Zachary Taylor, whom he worshipped as an immortal luminary. Old Rough-and-Ready—in rumpled linen dusters and fray-brimmed straw hats—had a gift for looking like an animated scarecrow at parades, inspections, and on the field of battle. In this he was a pronounced contrast to his colleague, Brigadier General Winfield Scott. The latter's spic-and-span concepts radiated from himself throughout his entire staff. Scott, it was said, would never dream of entering on a battle scene unless all requirements of military protocol were met. This earned him the nickname of Fuss-and-Feathers as well as the dislike of officers like Nathaniel Lyon, who loved Taylor for his unpretentious bravery as against Scott's pompous bravado.

From the day he left West Point to the time when he took protracted leave, young Schofield—he was now 32 years old—had learned enough about the Army to recognize a tough and tried campaigner when he saw one. Also to recognize the authoritative voice of command when he heard it. What he saw in Lyon, he liked. Somehow, the feeling of having the props swept from under him that had burdened Schofield on leaving Harney's office vanished before this strange little captain's air of steely confidence.

Schofield's story did not surprise Lyon. Harney was acting according to his creed: do nothing, say nothing that would rile the Southern Rights firebrands. Lyon went on to brief Schofield on the situation. The captain spoke slowly as he pressed home his points. His voice never had lost its Yankee twang and he slurred his *r* sounds so that *Harney* became *Hahney*. In effect, he stated that he discovered that some sort of plot was brewing to get him out of Saint Louis and away from

19

his command early in April. At that time, he received orders to report at Fort Leavenworth to attend a Board of Inquiry that was to start on April 15. From past experience, Lyon knew that such a board might sit for many weeks. On concluding that someone in Harney's headquarters had pulled strings for ulterior purposes, Lyon pulled a few of his own. The result was that the orders were canceled by the Adjutant General of the Army in Washington. From the howl that went up in Saint Louis among outspoken secessionists and lukewarm Union men, it was plain that persons with devious motives had been at work. In fact, before the orders were canceled, some loudmouths even bragged that they had had a hand in shunting Lyon out of Saint Louis.

Captain Lyon's failure to understand Brigadier General Harney's trend of thinking had been increased when he was summarily ordered to discontinue patrols outside the Arsenal because they were provocative and could stir up trouble. These patrols had served a double purpose. First, to keep unruly mobs from staging demonstrations in the Arsenal area; second, to give trouble-hunting cavaliers and their ruffians pause for thought at the sight of well-drilled soldiers with loaded rifles and fixed bayonets.

As he saw the situation, Lyon believed that the cause of peace was best served by impressing potential troublemakers with the Arsenal's armed strength. Although this key point had pitifully few defenders, the resourceful little captain resorted successfully to tricks making his forces appear larger than they were. He would, for instance, sneak whole companies of infantry—in full field equipment—out of the Arsenal in covered wagons during the small hours of the night. They'd take to the road halfway down to Jefferson Barracks and come morning they'd march back into town in tempo to their drums. Soon word would go the rounds that the Arsenal had received additional reinforcements. The result was that no one on the outside was quite sure how many men Lyon had at his disposal.

These and many more things, Lyon told Schofield on that first day of their meeting. Also, in the anticipation that—Harney or no Harney—steps would soon be taken to raise Union regiments in Saint Louis, Lyon assured the younger man that he would be most acceptable as a mustering officer when time for mustering arrived.

So far as anyone knows, Schofield's visit was the first intimation Lyon had that the Department Commander would not take the initiative in meeting the President's appeal for soldiers. The strongly partisan little Yankee captain was worried. Matters were taking a turn that could lead to a Union disaster throughout the State if the Arsenal fell into secessionist hands.

Major Peter V. Hagner, Commandant of the Arsenal, had hindered Lyon at every point in setting up defenses on the walls and inside the grounds. If it came to a showdown, Lyon knew that he might be unable to protect the weapons, especially the rifles and muskets, the Jackson-Frost forces were so eager to obtain. The President's proclamation had lifted Saint Louis hotheads into combative moods; Governor Jackson's hostile reply had fanned the fires of dissension even higher. In the last few days, since the patrols had been withdrawn by Harney's order, steadily growing crowds had been milling around the Arsenal's main gate. At first, they were merely noisy; then they became ugly; now it was almost impossible to worm one's way through the swarming mobs to enter or leave the Arsenal.

There is that old maxim in the Army which has guided commanders for better or for worse since the Army was born:

"One does the best he can with what he has!"

That is the Army way. And it was Lyon's way. In the past, he had found that it worked rather well. Now he was to put it to the test again.

Boiled down to its essence, the situation was that the weapons must not fall into secessionist hands and the devil take both Harney and Hagner. One way of preventing that would be to destroy the guns. But total destruction was too uncertain and also too time consuming. It was a course of last resort.

What then?

Then Lyon saw it—the solution.

Illinois, as solidly pro-Northern as Lincoln himself, was just across the Mississippi River. Her Governor, Richard Yates, was a true-blue supporter of the President. With his help, the muskets and rifles Lyon would not need, after he had armed his own contingent—Cameron had asked for 4,000 men, 123 officers and one brigadier general—could be shipped to Illinois for safekeeping.

After spending several hours thinking the matter through, Lyon outlined his plan in a letter to the Governor and sent it to Springfield, Illinois, with a trusted messenger. The first step would be for Yates to have the War Department issue a secret order to him, Yates, for the withdrawal by the State of Illinois, of 10,000 rifled muskets from the Saint Louis Arsenal. That would be the key to unlock and empty the treasure chest the Southern Righters plotted so eternally to grab.

At this same time, Brigadier General Harney wrote a letter to Lieutenant General Winfield Scott saying that "the Arsenal buildings and grounds are completely commanded by the hills immediately in their rear, and within easy range." He added that he had information that Governor Jackson sought to place batteries on these hills and that he would "in the event of Secession of the State from the Union demand the surrender of the Arsenal." In conclusion, the general asked for instructions. Evidently Harney was firmly committed to the belief that no overt acts would be committed by the Governor and his followers until after formal action for seceding had been taken. These beliefs were not shared by Captain Lyon, Frank Blair, or the latter's pro-Union associates.

Frank Blair Returns from Washington

Congressman Francis P. Blair, Jr., was a veritable colossus in Missouri politics. Born in Lexington, Kentucky, in 1821, he was the younger son of Francis Preston Blair, Sr., famous newspaper editor and a member of Jackson's Kitchen Cabinet. His older brother, Montgomery Blair, was a Washington barrister of national repute. Both were among the ultraprogressives. For that reason, they had left the Democratic fold for Republican ranks to wage all-out war on slavery. Montgomery Blair had pleaded the case for Dred Scott—the *cause célèbre* of a runaway Negro who sought freedom—before the United States Supreme Court. Frank Blair, from the time of Lincoln's election, in November, 1860, to his inauguration in March, 1861, had led the fight to stem the aggressions of secessionists in Saint Louis and throughout the State. He was, indeed, the forceful leader, the master strategist to whom all Union men turned for advice and confidence during those dark months of mounting turmoil and oppressive fears.

Because of the major position he occupies in the shaping of national as well as Missourian political and military events, Frank Blair is, of necessity, a character of great eminence in any story that deals with our period in the saga of Missouri. So, for that matter, are his father and his brother, Montgomery. Together, in the stormy era that preceded the Civil War, they were three terrible thorns in the sides of the hidebound proslavery faction of the old-line Democratic Party.

To segregate Frank from Francis and Montgomery Blair is difficult indeed. They thought, fought, and acted as one. If the older Blairs had a separate purpose it was to someday put Frank in the White House. The latter stood then as now diagonally opposite Blair House on Pennsylvania Avenue in Washington, D. C.

Frank attended Princeton but he did not graduate. He was not exactly kicked out, but the high-spirited young man was asked to close the door behind him as he left. After graduating from and studying law at Transylvania University, young Blair, at Montgomery's invitation, headed for Saint Louis where the latter had taken up law after he resigned from the Army in 1837. Montgomery had gone in for politics and was, at the time of Frank's arrival in 1843, Mayor of Saint Louis. A place had been made for young Blair in the law office of Thomas H. Benton who for decades was a towering power in the Democratic-controlled United States Senate. The Senator was also the father-in-law of Lieutenant John C. Frémont, then building up his fame as the Pathfinder of the West.

Benton developed a deep liking for young Frank who not only had a good legal mind but also a flair for politics. When the war with Mexico broke out, Frank enlisted as a private. However, he came to the notice of Brigadier General Philip Kearney, the nemesis-to-be of John C. Frémont as the first Governor of California. Kearney made Frank Blair Attorney General of the eastern portion of the Territory of New Mexico. He held that office until 1847 when, due to a misunderstanding, Brigadier General Sterling Price, of whom much more later, bounced him out of office.

Before he returned to Missouri, Frank went to Kentucky where he married his childhood sweetheart "Apo" Alexander, short for Appoline. It was to be an ideally happy marriage. Besides becoming the mother of eight children and mistress of a large household, "Apo" was also a valuable counselor to her husband in public affairs and political frays. Frank's first venture into practical politics was his election, as a Democrat, to the 1848 Missouri State Assembly. When the solidity of the Democratic state organization was splintered by the drastic Jackson Resolutions—"Claib" Jackson was then a State Senator—Blair sided with the faction which under Benton's leadership opposed the resolutions. The proposals would have Congress cede to the settlers of the new U. S. Western territories the right to vote on slavery issues—objective: the extension of slavery. David R. Atchison, Missouri's junior U. S. Senator and a fervid proslaver, led the proponents of the measures.

In the ensuing intraparty warfare, bitter, protracted, and calamitous to long-range Democratic unity, Blair fought savagely and effectively for the Benton cause. The Senator

24

named him The Lesser Ajax, because to him Blair's courage and capacity seemed second only to that of Achilles himself. A measure of Blair's personal strength in his district was that he was the only free-soiler elected to the 1850 Legislature. For his times and class, Frank was unique. He was a strong and outspoken champion of labor, of human rights—a "radical" of the purest water.

From the legislature, Frank went on to Congress. Because of his leanings toward Frémont's Republican Presidential candidacy in 1856, Blair was labeled a "Black Republican" by his former Democratic associates. Even so, he won repeated reelections to the House. On the other hand, the sun of Senator Benton, the Old Roman of the Senate, had set. He not only had lost his Senate seat, but, as the years drifted on, he sank into deeper and deeper political oblivion. While the stature of Benton declined, that of Blair increased. In the early days of the Civil War, he was not only a power in his city and State, but also a force in the nation. In Congress he was chairman of the key House Committee on Military Affairs; in political inner circles he was a member of the influential trio constituted by himself with Francis and Montgomery Blair.

But the strength of Frank Blair politically was not reflected in his financial status. In an era when corruption was brashly open in politics, the Blairs were above reproach. As Frank gave more of his time to politics, his law practice suffered. He was badly hit in the 1857 depression and the start of the 1860's saw him in debt to the tune of $100,000. He was saved from utter financial ruin only by the assistance of his father and by Franklin A. Dick, a famous Saint Louis lawyer, former law partner of Montgomery, and a staunch Union man. Mr. Dick took Frank's affairs in hand. The latter did not lose his comfortable Washington Avenue home, but the fine horses and glittering carriages that had formed part of the Congressman's Saint Louis household had to go. This was a great personal loss to Mrs. Alexander, the blind and widowed mother of "Apo" who lived with the Blairs. Over the years, she had acquired the habit of taking daily rides through the city in a handsome barouche. However, Franklin Dick compensated for this loss by placing his own carriage and coachman at Mrs. Alexander's disposal.

In 1861, Blair was just entering his fortieth year. There was a youthful swing to his stride, his presence was commanding, his voice decisive. In the manner of most politicians of his time, he was hard hitting, hard drinking, and had a hearty room-filling laugh. While he loved a fight, he was also open-hearted and generous to a fault.

By now, tall, thin, and pinch-faced, Montgomery for some seven years had been practicing law in Washington and gathering formidable laurels through his legal talents. As Postmaster General in the first Lincoln cabinet, he pulled a heavy oar aboard the craft of privileged influence. An Old Grad of West Point (1835), he also had unusually good connections in the War Department. Francis Blair, Sr., who, too, had turned his back on the slave oligarchy, occupied a position of commanding dominance in the Washington of the early months of Lincoln's Administration.

Frank, who had been in Washington attending to Congressional affairs, left the Capital just before the issuance of President Lincoln's proclamation. Knowing that the Governor's sympathies were with the South, he knew that Jackson would not take any steps to support the Union. Following his arrival in Saint Louis on the evening of April 17, Blair was in conference with Captain Lyon. After a brief discussion of the situation and a review of Harney's baffling attitude, Blair produced a War Department order that authorized the issuance of 5,000 stands of arms from the Arsenal to Saint Louis residents who enlisted in the Home Guards. This order bore no relation to the request that called for the raising of four regiments of infantry for Federal service. The weapons were to be placed in the hands of patriotic Union men who were ready to defend the city and their homes in case of a secessionist uprising. Lyon was not enthused. He observed that

Harney would have to clear the order and predicted that nothing would come of it. He held that even if Harney should permit the enrolling of Home Guards, "the news would leak out before it became public. As a result, the Arsenal would be surrounded by a wall of secessionists so thick that few Union men would dare to try to push through."

Before Lyon completed his remarks, Blair had moved to a desk in the center of the study. Swiftly, he scribbled a message and passed it on to Lyon. It was a telegram to the Secretary of War.

Our Governor will not meet your request for volunteers. Will you accept independent companies and regiments from Missouri? If so, please order Captain Lyon to muster them into service.

While Lyon read the wire, Blair wrote another, somewhat longer, message to Montgomery Blair. In it he recommended the removal of Brigadier General Harney because he

. . . at the instance of secessionists, obstructs the orders of the government. We also want an order for Captain Lyon to swear in the four regiments assigned to Missouri. If you will send General Wool or someone who is not to be doubted, to take command of this district and designate an officer to swear in our volunteers and arm the rest of our people, who are willing to act as Civil or Home Guards, I think we shall be able to hold our ground here.

Since telegraphers in Saint Louis were not regarded as "reliable," Blair had the two messages taken to East Saint Louis in Illinois where a Union operator forwarded them to Washington. The next day brought news of the raid on Liberty Arsenal. The seizure had been a walkaway. It was also learned that a bribe, in the amount of $25,000 in gold, was to be offered the Commandant of Fort Leavenworth, Kansas, to surrender to secession. Discreet preliminary inquiries were, however, so thoroughly rebuffed that the offer was never actually extended.

Up to now, Lyon, with the meticulousness of a well-trained officer, had gone through channels in his efforts to place the Arsenal in a defensive position. He announced to Blair that, orders or not, he would start fortifying the area at dawn the next day.

"What'll you do if Major Hagner kicks up a row?" asked Blair doubtfully. He knew the Army.

"I'll pitch him into the river," replied Lyon with conviction. Now Blair also knew Lyon.

Early the following morning, Lyon set the execution of his fortification plans into motion. Miraculously, an order arrived from Harney that instructed Hagner to give Lyon all the help and material needed for the defense of the Arsenal. William Tecumseh Sherman, who then ran a horsecar line in Saint Louis, visited the Arsenal that afternoon. On a later occasion he expressed amazement over the speed and efficiency with which loopholes were cut in the walls, banquettes raised, and batteries of cannon and mortars placed in position. The main handicap was that not enough men were on hand to man the walls, occupy the banquettes, and handle the cannon.

Based on the rising tremors within the local situation, as well as the expanding pattern of trouble throughout the State, Lyon renewed his plea, in a strongly worded message to Harney, for permission to enroll volunteers. Harney, to say the least, was consistent. In a letter of the morning of April 21, he had his adjutant write Lyon as follows:

Sir: Your two communications of this date, one asking for authority to accept the services of volunteers, in the defense of the Arsenal, have been laid before the Commanding General who deems it inexpedient to approve the recommendations contained in your communications.

Meanwhile, the patience of many members of the Union Guards was wearing thin. The continuing timidity in giving them a chance to arm themselves against secessionist onslaught had awakened resentment. If these Unionists could

28

not fight for their country in Missouri, they would journey across the river to Illinois and enlist in the regiments Governor Yates was raising.

In the late afternoon of April 21, some 300 members of three Turner Societies met at Flora Garten, a beer garden at 7th Street and Geyer Avenue, to discuss the question and reach a decision. The younger men were all for boarding ferries and going off to enlist in Illinois. Older men tried to persuade them to wait just a little longer. Arguments ran back and forth when Blair rushed into the center of the crowd and demanded silence:

"I have just received a telegram from the War Department," he shouted as he waved a piece of paper over his head. "It is authority to enlist four volunteer regiments at the Arsenal in Saint Louis."

Thunderous cheers greeted this statement. To a man, they wanted to march on the Arsenal at once to enlist in the service of the Union. However, Blair explained that that would never do. If the secessionists were alerted to what was going on, the situation might slip beyond control and Saint Louis could be caught in the grip of riots. Finally, it was arranged that beginning about midnight the men, singly, not in groups, would go to the Arsenal. Each man would present a card with the word "Saxton" written on it. On seeing the cards, the sentries would let the bearers enter the premises.

Acting on their own initiative, Oliver Filley and John How, of the Union Committee on Public Safety, set out to locate Lieutenant Schofield to have him report at the Arsenal as mustering officer. Later, on entering Lyon's office, Schofield stated his errand. Lyon reluctantly called the lieutenant's attention to Harney's explicit order against enlistments.

Lyon felt as one who was perched on the horns of a dilemma. Either way, he had a difficult choice. If he armed the Union Guards against orders, he could be court-martialed and shot. If he did not arm the Union Guards, he ran the risk of turning the city, and thereby the state, lock, stock, and barrel

29

over to secession. He knew that on that very evening, there had been a stormy meeting of Minute Men in their headquarters on Pine Street. The majority had demanded action against the Arsenal then and there. Only the intervention of Mayor Daniel Taylor, a Conditional Unionist—a classification that disguised many secretly active secessionists—prevented the attack from being launched then and there. In fact, when Schofield entered the Arsenal that night, he found it in a virtual state of siege. Loopholes and banquettes were manned, but the lines of sentries were, perforce, thinly drawn. In anticipation of a showdown that might go against him, the captain had even gone to the extent of mining all the buildings. His plans were to blow the structures sky-high—but only after the Minute Men had entered them in force.

Following a few explosive puffs on his cigar, Lyon placed it in an ash tray on his desk. Next he turned to Schofield and told him, decisively, that while Blair had authority from the War Department to enroll four regiments, Schofield as mustering officer, had no authority to arm or equip them. Nor were there any instructions about the location and disposal of these troops.

Schofield understood. In the Army, he was a channel swimmer in good standing. Lyon went on to explain that, without the consent of the Commanding General, execution of the order could lead to serious consequences. He said that he was not governed by personal fears in taking this attitude but that he did not want to jeopardize the objective. He suggested that Blair and Schofield should call on the Department Commander and make fresh representations of the situation. Off the record, Lyon told the young lieutenant that he would play along even if he incurred the general's wrath to a point where Harney ordered his arrest.

In line with Lyon's proposal, Blair and Schofield called on Harney who unequivocally declined to change his orders. There would be no mustering of troops at this time so long as he, Harney, had anything to say about it. Blair wondered why in blazes it took Brother Montgomery so long to get Harney's removal order approved and executed as he and Schofield headed toward the Arsenal. There they found Filley, How, and Broadhead in conference with Lyon. The latter, on hearing Blair's report, announced that he would be responsible for the enrollment of volunteers regardless of cost to himself.

It was agreed that the 300 Turner members assembled at Flora Garten were to enter the Arsenal by way of the river path and through the water gate as soon as the night grew dark enough to hide their movements. Prior to that, their officers would come one by one through the main Arsenal gate and proceed directly to the water gate so as to identify their respective members as they sought admission. Lyon wanted to be absolutely sure that no secesh spies or saboteurs slipped by in the rush.

It was late in the evening when the last man stepped forward, presented his card of admission with the word "Saxton" written on it, and was recognized. As the clusters of volunteers grew larger, Lyon's worries as to what might happen from Harney's direction grew apace. Any moment might bring an order to place Lyon under arrest plus instructions to disarm and disband the volunteers.

The Union Scores in the Struggle for the Arsenal

Whatever anxieties Lyon may have felt about his drastic decision to disregard orders were dispelled about midnight. A grinning clerk handed him a telegram which came like a gift from heaven. Signed by the Adjutant General of the Army, the wire gave Washington's full and official blessing to the undertaking Lyon had launched. Not only that, but Harney, the stumbling block, was removed from the path of Union mobilization. Addressed to Lyon, the message read:

General Harney has this date been relieved from his command. The Secretary of War directs that you immediately execute the

31

order previously given to arm the loyal citizens to protect the public property and execute the laws. Muster four regiments into service.

First to enter the Arsenal were the three Turner Societies that had assembled at the Flora beer garden. They were organized into three companies headed by Captain Rufus Saxton, Lieutenant L. M. Lothrop, and Lieutenant George H. Stone, all of the Second U. S. Infantry. Without taking time out to muster them into the service, the men were given muskets, 40 rounds of ammunition, percussion caps, and bayonets. Thus equipped, they were rushed to the walls of the Arsenal to bolster the thin line of defense. Mustering and other red tape niceties could be dealt with when the anxieties of the moment had been reduced to lesser pressures.

Before the night was over, 700 men had entered the Arsenal. Some 600 were received on April 22; 700 on the following day. By the middle of the week, 2,100 had been received, sworn in, and armed. Day by day, volunteers by the hundreds streamed into the Arsenal. The First Regiment Missouri Volunteers, Colonel Frank Blair, commanding, was up to strength. Two other regiments were approaching their full complements; a fourth was better than half formed. These units were about 80 per cent German or of German descent; 12 per cent native American, and 8 per cent French, Irish, and Bohemian.

Meanwhile Brigadier General Harney, naturally perturbed by his sudden removal from command, had taken a train to Washington to learn the reason for this action and to see what could be done to have it rescinded. In his own eyes, the old Indian Fighter believed that he had acted correctly in maintaining peace in Saint Louis. He felt, and with some justification, that his years of loyal and efficient military service entitled him to less summary treatment than that which he had received. He had many friends in the War Department, from Winfield Scott down. And in Congress, now that Kansas was a state, were men he had known intimately during his years of service in Kansas Territory.

In departing from Saint Louis, Harney did not place Major Peter V. Hagner, Commandant of the Arsenal and senior to Lyon, in temporary command of the department. And Hagner, who had been bypassed by Blair and other pro-Union leaders because of his indifference to the defenses of the Arsenal, meekly let matters ride. Thus Lyon, a mere captain, actually performed the duties and held the responsibilities of a brigadier general. Still, although his position was exalted, it was far from comfortable.

With each new company of volunteer infantry under arms, Lyon felt a little more secure. Yet, he knew that Jackson and Frost still posed extremely serious threats. There were almost daily disturbances in downtown Saint Louis. They ranged from shouted obscenities and curses to the swinging of clubs and the throwing of stones. Known Union men were attacked on streets and in public places. Blair's home was stoned so seriously that he moved his family out of town. Lyon's insecurity grew when he heard about the reply President Jefferson Davis of the Confederacy had sent to Jackson's appeal. To be sure, the new Departmental Commander had no knowledge of the actual contents of the letter, but he was well aware that it had been favorable. From the day he put foot in Saint Louis, Lyon had co-operated with the Union Committee on Public Safety in setting up a system of spies and security agents in the service of and paid by the committee. These secret eyes and ears were effective in penetrating the secesh organizations as well as in discovering leaks within the Union setup. By way of these agents, it was known that a shipment of muskets, cannon, and ammunition would arrive by river boat in Saint Louis at the time Brigadier General Frost's command would be encamped in Lindell Grove—half a dozen miles west of the Arsenal.

As already established, the contents of the Davis letter were not known to Lyon at the time. However, here is the text as preserved in Confederate War Department records:

After learning as well as I could, from the gentlemen accredited to me, what was needful for the attack on the Arsenal, I have directed that Captains Greene and Duke should be furnished with two 12-pounder howitzers and two 32-pounder guns, with the proper ammunition for each. These, from the commanding hills, will be effective against the garrison and break the enclosing walls of the place.

I concur with you as to the great importance of capturing the Arsenal and securing its supplies, rendered doubly important by the means taken to obstruct your commerce and to render you unarmed victims of a hostile invasion. We look anxiously and hopefully for the day when the star of Missouri shall be added to the constellation of the Confederate States of America. With best wishes, I am, very respectfully yours, Jefferson Davis.

There were also rumors that Jackson would order several thousand militiamen to Saint Louis from western and northern counties and place the cannon seized at Liberty on the hills that overlooked the Arsenal.

As against these gambits, Lyon felt that he had a checkmating move up his sleeve in his plan to shift his surplus muskets to Illinois, if it succeeded. Or he could blow the secessionists heaven high by exploding the buildings if they stormed the walls and took the structures by force.

On April 24, Captain James H. Stokes, late of the United States Army, now Military Adviser to Governor Yates of Illinois, arrived at the Arsenal. Although he was in mufti, he had—being a stranger—a difficult time cajoling himself through the crowds of secessionists that milled around the entrance to the Arsenal. Stokes had an order from the War Department that called for the delivery of 10,000 weapons to the State of Illinois. He also had, at Alton, upriver on the Illinois side, the steamer *City of Alton*. Her captain, Samuel Mitchell, was standing by for orders until further notice. But, as Stokes observed to Lyon, how in the world were they going to get that many weapons out of the Arsenal with such a hostile mob in the offing?

Lyon admitted that it was a problem. He added that he thought he had found a way to make a feint that would serve to divert the enemy's attention. The brisk Yankee told Stokes that he would show him and invited his visitor to come along.

Leading the way to the main Arsenal building, Lyon showed Stokes several heavy wooden crates. They were superabundantly girded by flat, wide sheet metal bands. On the sides of the crates, in huge capital letters, appeared: "Department of the Ohio, USA—Springfield Rifled Muskets, 1860."

Lyon explained that the boxes actually contained about 1,000 useless old-time flintlock muskets that had been gathering dust for years as they stood, forgotten, in storage.

As Stokes wondered what bearing these boxes could have on the success of his mission, Lyon disclosed that they were to serve as bait in luring the attention of secesh spies around the Arsenal from the dangerously exposed principal undertaking. To create this essential diversion, the crates were to be loaded into transport wagons and, at the proper time, sent up to the levee as if they were to be shipped by steamer to Cincinnati. To create an impression, the worthless muskets would be as well guarded en route as if they were priceless rifles.

Lyon was ready to gamble that the secesh spies would summon their ruffians from nearby river-front bars and attack the wagons. With this in view, the armed escort had been instructed not to put up a fight but to retreat. With the crates in their possession, the attackers would be bound to celebrate and defer the opening of the crates. All this would take time. The opening of the iron-bound hardwood crates would take even more time, for they would be tough nuts to crack. Meanwhile, the Illinois-bound muskets would be placed aboard the *City of Alton.* And the steamer would be well away up the river before the truth was known.

Captain Stokes agreed heartily that this seemed a capital idea. Certainly, nothing was lost by trying it. After further conference, Stokes sent a telegram to Alton directing that the packet be ready to tie to at the Arsenal landing at midnight on the following evening, April 25. No whistles were to be blown. All lights were to be doused.

The trick worked as planned. Departure from the Arsenal of a line of covered wagons was reported by Minute Men spies shortly before midnight. Most of them ran off to collect assistance in capturing the wagons and collecting the boxes. The latter were stacked high in the street outside an ornate saloon and remained there while the brave attackers bragged about how they drove off a Federal patrol and captured a wagon train of real, honest to Hank, Springfield rifled muskets. Just wait until they turned their own guns on the Damn Dutch and that crafty little blue-bellied Yankee.

Much, much later, after laborious hewing, hammering, and sawing, the heroes discovered that their loot added up to hundreds of absolutely worthless muskets. But by then the *City of Alton* had long departed with more than 20,000 muskets, 5,000 carbines, 500 revolvers, 100,000 cartridges, and much miscellaneous equipment. The secesh spies who had remained at the Arsenal as their colleagues ran off never had a chance to report the arrival and departure of the packet. They had been swept up by the retiring wagon guard—split so that it swooped down on the watchers from two side streets. The prisoners were placed in the guardhouse and held incommunicado until daylight, when they were released. In the Arsenal there now remained just enough muskets to meet Lyon's demands in the foreseeable future.

As expected, the incident inflated Union morale and took a lot of wind out of the arrogantly set sail of the cavaliers and their cohorts. Now Lyon felt reasonably secure. This feeling of solidity increased when Captain James Totten rode into the Arsenal grounds ahead of Company F, Light Artillery, USA. The doughty captain, sensing that Arkansas was swinging toward secession, had rolled out of Little Rock with his half-dozen 6-pounders without asking by your leave. He had learned what had happened to loyal Federal troops in other Southern States, and he would have none of it.

The limbered guns, caissons, and baggage train—drawn by four to six beautifully matched bays—emerged from the Arsenal gate into the parade straight as a string. Burly, full-bearded Captain Totten wheeled his horse, gave a quick glance up and down his outfit, and barked at Lieutenant T. P. Immels:

"Take over, God damn you, sir!"

Totten was not angry. Totten was just Totten. And cussin' was just Totten's way.

On April 29, Jefferson Davis issued his Proclamation of War in Montgomery, Alabama.

The same day, Nathaniel Lyon received an order from Washington that extended his authority and increased his armed forces to 10,000. This instrument of power is unique in American military and civil procedures. It follows:

The president directs that you enroll, in the military service of the United States, the loyal citizens of Saint Louis and vicinity not exceeding—with those heretofore enlisted—10,000 in number for the purpose of maintaining the authority of the United States and for the protection of the peaceable inhabitants of Missouri; and you will, if deemed necessary for that purpose, by yourself and Oliver D. Filley, John How, James Broadhead, Samuel D. Glover, J. J. Witzig and Francis P. Blair, Jr. proclaim martial law in Saint Louis.

On the back of this document, in an oldish, rambling hand, was written: "It is revolutionary times and therefore, I do not object to the irregularity of this. Approved. W. S." (Winfield Scott).

Beneath the general's initials were the words, black with heavy ink: "Approved. A. Lincoln."

The effect was that, on or with the advice of the Union Committee on Public Safety, Nathaniel Lyon had powers to maintain the authority of the United States not only in Saint Louis but also throughout Missouri. He was the man of the hour.

His acceptance as such was by no means universal. In a letter from a friend, Mr. Broadhead of the Public Safety Committee was upbraided for being associated with one "whom all honest Missourians curse with a deep and bitter hatred."

Chapter 2

The Capture of Camp Jackson

Lyon Moves to Check Frost's Gambit

The week that began on Monday May 6 was to build up mounting tensions and cast increasingly darker shadows of uncertainty over the Union cause not only in Missouri but throughout the country. News came to Lyon, by Government telegram, on May 6 that Arkansas had joined the Confederacy. A lesser shock, but nonetheless a significant one, were the tidings that during the night 50 armed men had broken into the Army storehouse at Kansas City and stolen scores of muskets, carbines, pistols, and sabers as well as 34,000 rounds of ammunition.

The following day, as Minute Men in Camp Jackson and secessionists throughout Missouri celebrated the unfurling of the Stars and Bars over Arkansas, came the news that Tennessee had gone South. Lyon, who had sharp hunches and gave them due heed, felt that given the slightest chance Missouri could be tilted in the same direction. Further food for thought came in the form of information that Captain Joe Kelly of Company E, First Regiment, Missouri Militia, had taken 200 rifles, 70 tons of gunpowder, and a quantity of camp equipment, purchased secretly in Saint Louis by the State Militia Quartermaster, to Jefferson City.

Lyon felt it in his bones—something fateful and sinister was coming to a head. Every instinct told him that the Arsenal was in grave jeopardy; that it was only a matter of time until

Jackson and Frost believed that they were strong enough to mount an attack. In fact, Brigadier General Frost had that very day given Lyon a glimpse of his hand when he sent his aide-de-camp William D. Wood to the Arsenal with a somewhat peculiar message. He said that the general was anxious to give his pioneers (engineers) some practical experience in the building of fortified positions. To that end, he was planning to move his pioneers—some 40 men under the command of First Lieutenant William H. Finney—to the bluff just south of the Arsenal.

Thinking fast, Lyon concluded that Frost's real scheme was to plant guns in positions that commanded the Arsenal. He sent Frost his compliments and added: "If any one not authorized by me stuck a pick or a spade into the top of that bluff—or any other spot within shelling range of the Arsenal —I'd turn my guns on him and salute the enterprise with the music of whistling shells."

Hardly had the door closed on the heels of nattily uniformed Lieutenant Wood than one of the principal undercover agents of the Union Safety Committee was ushered into Lyon's office. He had just arrived from Cairo on a fast packet. There he had confirmed the suspicion that the steamer *J. C. Swon*— coming up from Baton Rouge on a fast run and putting in at Cairo for fuel—carried the guns, cannon, and other sinews of war donated by Jefferson Davis. The matériel was packed in huge crates marked Tamaroa marble or in great barrels said to contain ale. The steamer, reported the agent, would probably reach Saint Louis the following morning, meaning May 8.

Acting on this information, Lyon sought and obtained a meeting of the Safety Committee. Some of the members favored seizure of the shipment as soon as the *Swon* tied up. But the majority sided with Lyon's belief that it would be best to let the boxes and barrels be picked up and follow them to their destination. And that destination, Lyon predicted, would be Camp Jackson. In those crates, he argued,

40

were the heavy cannon which Frost had hoped to emplace on the bluff near the Arsenal.

If Lyon guessed right with respect to the nature of the goods in the shipment, he would have a legitimate excuse to invade Camp Jackson. To march against the camp merely to beat Frost to the draw against a potential attack on the Arsenal was one thing. But to catch him and his secesh militia red-handed, with stolen Federal weapons and munitions in their possession, that was positive proof that the encampment was an actual menace to the peace and security of the State, a definite link between the militia and the South.

While the meeting was in progress, Captain Cavender, who served in Colonel Blair's First Missouri Volunteers, was admitted to the room. He informed his colonel that the train for Jefferson Barracks, where the regiment was quartered, was ready to depart. As he left, Blair informed Lyon that he concurred in advance with anything the captain wanted to do with respect to Camp Jackson. When, somewhat later, the meeting ended, it had been agreed that the agent of the Security Committee would keep constant watch at the berth of the *J. C. Swon* and report directly to Lyon on all activities with respect to the movements of the suspected shipment.

As the members of the committee left his office, Lyon placed a detaining hand on the arm of Franklin A. Dick. As rapidly as he could—and in a voice so low that it could not reach across the room—Lyon asked for Dick's co-operation in staging an ingenious but dangerous plan if the *J. C. Swon* shipment was actually taken to Camp Jackson. Briefly, Lyon planned to conduct a one-man reconnaissance of the encampment disguised as Mrs. Alexander, "Apo" Blair's blind and widowed mother. Frank Blair had left the meeting too hurriedly to give Lyon a chance to discuss the idea with him. But since Dick was an intimate friend of the entire family, he did not hesitate to lay the matter before the lawyer. Besides, Lyon, in his guise as Mrs. Alexander, would need the barouche Franklin Dick placed at her disposal for rides about town. In addition to

41

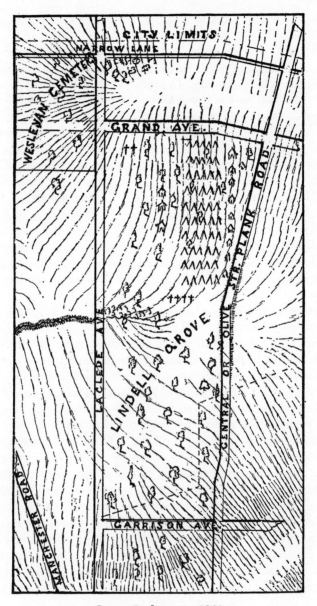

Camp Jackson in 1861

42

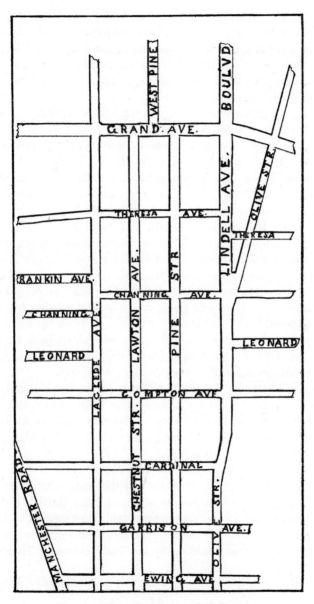

Camp Jackson's Present Subdivision

43

providing the carriage, horses, and Old Peter, Dick's somber liveried coachman, the lawyer was requested to obtain Mrs. Alexander's consent. If he received it, the lawyer was to borrow the widow's black, long-sleeved bombazine gown, lace mitts, heavy widow's veil, and huge bonnet she always wore on her daily rides around the city.

A boyish grin spread across Franklin Dick's face from ear to ear. It was an audacious scheme, but it had the merit of being workable. Mrs. Alexander was a Juno who had grown to greater stature over the years. Small, slim Lyon could easily get into her clothes. A popular and familiar figure in Saint Louis and a firmly placed local institution, Mrs. Alexander was known to young and old, to people of high and low degree alike. Being blind, she covered her face with a heavy veil. When anyone greeted her in passing, she never answered but merely nodded her head. Old Peter, the long-freed, venerable white-thatched coachman who drove her, was a constantly bubbling well of information. His was a running commentary as to what was going on, who was passing by, and with whom. Old Peter saw all and told all from his high seat of the low-slung carriage with its calash folded back on fine weather days. Facing forward from the back seat, Mrs. Alexander always sat stiffly erect in solitary majesty.

While Dick saw the perils of the plan—he knew that Lyon would never leave Camp Jackson alive if he were discovered by Southern zealots in the ranks—he also realized its basic merits. He was for it, and certain, as well, that Mrs. Alexander would favor the masquerade.

Lyon reached out his hand and they sealed the bargain with a warmhearted handshake. On the assumption that the "ale" and "marble" would be removed from the levee after dark on the day of the steamer's arrival, Dick agreed to have the garments and the carriage at the back entrance to the Arsenal's ordnance building in the early hours of Thursday afternoon.

As expected, the *J. C. Swon* arrived on Wednesday, May 8.

44

Despite her mysterious cargo, she looked blandly innocent as she made fast at the levee while her officers and roustabouts went about the task of getting her heavy and cumbersome freight ashore. The great boxes marked "marble" were so heavy that one could not be placed on top of another.

Inconspicuous Union agents kept the vessel and its shipment under surveillance all day. In the late afternoon, a horseman rode up, sought the *Swon's* captain, delivered a message, and cantered off. The sun set and evening spread its shadows. Still, nothing happened. Then, very late in the night, at an hour when the levee was virtually deserted, a long train of drays drove up, accompanied by Colton Greene's Minute Men in mufti.

One by one, amid much groaning and cursing on the part of the inexpert stevedores, the boxes and barrels were lifted on the drays—half a hundred of them. Then the long caravan rumbled slowly westward through the streets of the sleeping city until it reached Camp Jackson. There, the materials were unloaded and stored in a fairly thick stand of trees near General Frost's headquarters tent. Every foot of the way, from the levee to Lindell Grove, Union spies, like flittering shadows, had followed the slow-creeping procession. In compliance with orders, some of them reported to Captain Lyon as soon as the unloading had been completed and the empty drays returned to town. Others took observation posts in Wesleyan Cemetery to rush information to the Arsenal if immediate steps were taken to unpack the boxes and barrels. Such an act, Lyon believed, would signal plans for the immediate seizure of the Arsenal by force. However, once the shipment was unloaded, Camp Jackson returned to its slumbers.

A Disguised Lyon Scouts Camp Jackson

The morning of May 9 dawned with overcast skies. But as the day grew older, the threatening clouds drifted off and the mild spring sun shone forth in full brilliance. At Camp Jackson,

Lyon learned, through virtually continuous reports, that all ran according to routine. There had been the usual morning and forenoon drills; marching and countermarching, blaring of bands, blasts of bugles, and roll of drums. But no uncrating of boxes nor opening of barrels.

At noon, all hands had turned toward dinner in high good fettle. There was the usual flow of the stuff that cheers, from vintage wines to 40-Rod whiskey: so named because it was guaranteed to strike a man down at that distance. Beer and such—even "ale"—was disdained by true Missourians as something that was swilled only by the Damn Dutch. Toasts, cheers, and exuberant shouts rang high. The secession of Arkansas and Tennessee was regarded as a sign on the road along which Missouri soon would travel. Toasts for Jefferson Davis. Hurrah! Shouts for General Beauregard. Yippee!

In the early afternoon hours came the daily inflow of relatives of the militia men—mothers, aunts, cousins, sweethearts, wives, and sisters. Besides being a military encampment, Camp Jackson was also a highly popular and well-attended social affair, which reached its daily zenith at the time of the inspiring afternoon parade, and ended with the boom of the sunset gun. As General Frost commented, rather floridly, in a newspaper interview on some later and less happy day:

It was a very attractive encampment because it was filled with the fairest of Missouri's daughters who, from morn to dewey eve, treaded its mazes in company with sons, brothers and lovers.

Captain Lyon dined early and alone that Thursday noon after informing Chester Harding that he would not be available until later in the day. The yard was empty as the captain made his way to the ordnance building. There, he waited in a small room, smoking a cigar with quick, impatient puffs as his eyes constantly ranged through the window across the yard to Arsenal gate. Soon he saw what he was waiting for. A black barouche, whose body gleamed like ancient onyx, wheeled lightly through the portal, drawn by a span of coal-black geldings. On the box, perched Old Peter, regal as a king. On the back seat of the vehicle—called a "Jenny Lind" because it had been popularized by the famous Swedish song-bird—sat Franklin Dick in evident enjoyment of his post-prandial cigar. The barouche flashed out of sight as it vanished around a corner that took it to the rear entrance of the ordnance building.

A few moments later, there was a tap on the door. Dick entered. He carried a rather bulky package which he placed carefully on the table. Then he wished the captain luck and left as quickly and quietly as he had arrived.

When the door swung shut, Lyon unwrapped the bundle and a pile of woman's clothing came to sight. He removed his coat, took off his stiffly starched collar, and pushed the bottoms of his trouser legs into his boots. Then he donned the bombazine dress. It fitted him generously. On went the bonnet. As expected, it covered his entire head and neck. Its sweeping brim left little of his face to be seen. A thick, black veil fell from the bonnet to his chest and shoulders like a veritable curtain. No one could possibly see through it. Even Lyon's keen blue eyes had to peer sharply in order to penetrate its billowing folds.

Just before he left the room, Lyon took two heavy Colt revolvers from a cupboard. He twirled their chambers to make sure that they were fully loaded. Lyon intended to hold the weapons ready under the cover of the lap robe in the carriage. He did not expect to use them. Still, some overzealous sentry, who did not know Mrs. Alexander, could challenge him. And that heavy veil could serve as an invitation to some country yokel, with a drink too many, to yank it off. Lyon had no illusions as to what would happen if he were unmasked. But if a secesh mob sent him to the happy hunting grounds, Nathaniel Lyon was firmly resolved that he would not go alone.

He left the room and stepped into sight of Old Peter whose wrinkled face rippled into wide smiles as he beheld the new

Mrs. Alexander. Even the terse little Yankee, whose own grin was a bit slow on the trigger during those trying days, could not repress an answering chuckle.

Drawn by the high-stepping span, the barouche rolled rapidly over the few miles of streets that separated the outlying area from the heart of Saint Louis. Sitting stiffly and primly, in an apt imitation of Mrs. Alexander, the captain saw Lindell Grove come into view. In the foreground there was a large expanse of grassy meadow. To the west, north, and south stood a wide fringe of well-spaced shade trees still clad in the soft greens of early spring.

While some tents had been pitched in among the trees, the great majority of them stood along neatly arranged company streets in the western portion of the meadow. Running down the centers of those canvas-lined thoroughfares were straight-as-string stacked arms. Four 6-pounder cannon were placed in the meadow across a path that later became Channing Avenue. Two additional pieces, really small brass saluting guns, were poised near Brigadier General Frost's headquarters tent and between two flagpoles at the tops of which the Stars and Stripes and the State flag of Missouri fluttered lightly in the gentle breeze.

According to orders given him by his passenger on the way out to the camp, Peter chattered away about the interesting sights on either hand as was his wont. It would have given rise to suspicion, indeed, if a wordless coachman had been sitting on that box. But Lyon paid no attention to Peter's flow of words. Despite the thickness of the veil, his sharp, almost photographic eyes, took in every detail as he passed. He noticed a distinct variety in uniforms.

The First Regiment wore the old State Militia uniform. So did some of the companies of the Second Regiment. But most of the latter, officers and men alike, and all members of the newly enlisted companies of Minute Men, were conspicuously resplendent in Confederate gray. No doubt as to

48

where those lads stood on the paramount issue. To Lyon, the mere fact that the Minute Men were allowed to wear such uniforms proved that General Frost and Governor Jackson were prepared to insure the solidity of their pro-Confederate position. From the stacked muskets and rifles—as well as the numbers of men milling around in company streets, on the meadow, and among the trees or grouped around their tents—Lyon clearly saw that Frost had enough men under arms to put two full regiments into the field. He also guessed that there would be enough men left over to form a third regiment if he could arm them. Any doubt about Frost being able to do that would probably vanish with the opening of the boxes from Baton Rouge.

Up and down company streets, Peter drove. The two main thoroughfares met in the shape of a capital *T* right before the headquarters of the Commanding General of the First Division of the Missouri State Militia. In those days, Missouri Militia brigades were called divisions. Two huge signs stood where the two streets met. One bore the legend: Beauregard Boulevard. The other read: Jefferson Davis Avenue.

Lyon took it all in. Now and then, a voice would be heard over the general murmur, shouting greetings to Mrs. Alexander. In acknowledgment of these salutations, the captain gracefully bowed his head. But below the lap robe, his hands held the two loaded six-shooters in firm grips.

After driving around the camp for about half an hour, during which he made a mental map for his plan of attack, Lyon ordered Peter to return to town. Back at the Arsenal, the captain stepped out of his borrowed finery and shrugged into his own old, faded, and service-worn uniform coat. Out of long-established habit, he did not bother to button other than the tarnished brass button under the rim of the collar. Then, placing his floppy-brimmed black felt hat over his unruly mop of hair, Lyon left his hideaway and returned to his office. There, through Harding, he issued an express notice to Frank

49

Blair and all the members of the Safety Committee to attend a secret, emergency meeting in his office at the Arsenal at 5 o'clock that afternoon.

The Safety Committee Endorses Drastic Action

The committee was called to order at the designated hour by Chairman Oliver D. Filley. All were on hand—John How, Samuel Glover, Julius J. Witzig, and James O. Broadhead— as well as Frank Blair.

Without wasting time on polite or parliamentary preliminaries, Captain Lyon took the floor and bluntly stated that the meeting had been called to act on his proposal to march against Camp Jackson the following day. One by one, he stated his reasons for the proposed seizure. In this presentation, Nathaniel Lyon employed his great ability to place his train of thought on a straight and single track. And to make the train run firmly and steadily on rails of argument that were nailed down with spikes of fact.

Only two members held back from endorsing the proposed invasion of Camp Jackson—Samuel Glover and John How. They argued that the encampment had a legal standing under the laws of Missouri. As for the weapons stolen from Baton Rouge, Glover argued, the way to recover them was through a writ of replevin to be served by the United States Marshal. Law was law.

Lyon replied that this was no time to rely on Mr. Blackstone. He re-emphasized that the camp was a "nest of traitors." He reminded his listeners that the legislature could be in secret session in Jefferson City that very minute to enact military laws that would endanger the Union and its supporters. He recounted the fact that news from all over the State revealed that secession sympathizers were becoming increasingly threatening to the lives and property of Union men and their families. The time was past for arguments and writs.

They listened; even Glover and How seemed visibly impressed. Then Lyon threw in the clincher he had been holding in reserve. He had received word from the Adjutant General's office in Washington that Harney had been reinstated as Commanding General of the Department. More than that, he was at that very moment aboard a train that would reach East Saint Louis, on the Illinois side of the river, on Saturday, May 11. If Camp Jackson were to be taken at all, it had to be taken at once.

The news that Harney had been reinstated was indeed disturbing to men who had believed him to be well out of the way. Just how it came to pass never became known. However, educated guesses ran along the lines that friendships of long standing with Lieutenant General Scott and other high-ranking Army officers could be partly responsible; also that Attorney General Bates, a power in Missouri politics and closely associated with a group of ultraconservative Republicans who sought to maintain peace in the State at almost any price, had taken a hand in overcoming President Lincoln's lack of confidence in Harney.

Incidentally, an episode that took place in Virginia while the general was en route to Washington could have had some influence in this matter. The train was stopped at Harpers Ferry by a troop of horsemen. Going through the cars, they discovered the identity of General Harney. He was taken prisoner and herded with some fellow passengers to Richmond. In that bustling pro-Southern city, Harney was treated with great courtesy and allowed to continue on his way to Washington. It was said at the time that Southern leaders secretly entertained high hopes that their unwilling guest, being a son of the South, would cast his lot with "his own people." In that they were thoroughly disappointed. Harney might have been too politically naïve to be an efficient buffer between clashing civil forces, but he never turned his back on the Union he had served so well as a soldier. While it is true that many Southern officers resigned and returned to their home states when the states seceded, it is equally true that their numbers were not nearly as large as popularly believed.

51

About one half of Southern-born West Pointers remained, like Harney, faithful to the Union.

Now Harney was returning to his position of power in Saint Louis. And dangerous as the consequences of Lyon's proposal might be—so ran the thinking of the members of the Safety Committee—even greater disaster might befall Saint Louis, Missouri, and the Union if the handling of the problem were placed in Harney's hands.

Result: The committee voted in favor of Lyon's plan to capture Camp Jackson.

When Glover questioned whether the newly organized Volunteer and Home Guard regiments could stand up effectively against the many militia veterans in Frost's First Division, Lyon quoted Josh Billings, the Will Rogers of that era, who held that "thrice armed is he who has his quarrel just, and four times he, who get his work in fust!" At the same time, Lyon reminded his friends that he held a strong hand in the 400 infantry regulars at the Arsenal; not to overlook Captain Totten and his six-gun battery of light artillery.

As the meeting broke up, Blair warned all not to speak a word about the impending attack. Lyon added that with the exception of Colonel Blair and a few staff officers not even the regimental commanders would know what was afoot on the morrow until it was time to march.

As the men left, one by one to avoid the rousing of suspicion, Lyon pulled Filley aside. He wanted to know if Oliver and his brother Giles could secretly procure some 40 horses and have them at the Arsenal in the morning. Filley winked an eye and allowed that he thought they could.

In making this request of Oliver Filley, instead of through Major Justus McKinstry, the departmental quartermaster, Nathaniel Lyon added fuel to the fires of envy and dislike toward him in the heart and mind of McKinstry. The latter was a small-minded, career-conscious spit-and-polish soldier with the soul of a bookkeeper. Promotion was slow in the Quartermaster Corps and he was jealous because Lyon—below him in rank and seniority—had been placed in a post of prominent command. On the other hand, Lyon felt that he could not rely on McKinstry to furnish the horses he needed on such short notice. Nor could he be certain that word would not get out before nightfall that a large number of horses were wanted at the Arsenal. There were bound to be speculations and someone could come up with the right answer. Secrecy was the watchword.

This is not to imply that McKinstry had rebel leanings. Much worse, as time would soon reveal, he was a loyal Union officer who let his personal jealousies influence his official acts. In a few weeks he was to place Lyon and his entire Army of the West in grave and mortal jeopardy. But of that, more at the proper time.

Lights burned in the offices of the Arsenal commander until far into the night. Lyon, Blair, and Harding—with the aid of Lieutenant Schofield, Captain Totten, and Captain Sweeny, three regulars and trained campaigners—drew up the invasion plans. They knew that the march of a half-dozen miles from the Arsenal to Lindell Grove, in daylight over populated streets, would preclude any kind of surprise attack. A good time for a sudden raid, so far as noninterference by street crowds went, would be the morning. But that was also the time when the militia would be in ranks, commanded by officers and under arms, and most able to put up a show of resistance that could allow rebel sympathizers in town to arm themselves and attack the Union forces in the rear and on the flanks.

No! Much better to stage the march in the afternoon during the encampment's convivial hours of eating and drinking and before the heavy influx of women visitors, who might really clutter up the proceedings. The hour set for the invasion of Camp Jackson was 2:30 o'clock.

With that in mind, orders were drawn whereby various Union units would march over paralleling streets so as to reach Lindell Grove on the stroke of the clock. Each man would carry 40 rounds of ammunition. The two batteries of artillery —Totten's regulars and Bischoff's volunteers—would be prepared to fire grape and canister.

All in all, if compelled to take Camp Jackson by force, Lyon would show General Frost, Governor Jackson, and their pro-Southern associates, that he was acting in deadly earnest. If they wanted war, they could have it. However, he hoped that Frost, a West Pointer and once a professional soldier, would have the good sense to see that he was in a hopeless position and yield without putting up a fight.

That night, not long before sunrise, when all preparations had been completed, Nathaniel Lyon thoughtfully penned a letter to General Frost. He planned to have it delivered to his adversary as soon as the camp had been surrounded. Without equivocation, but rather with the thin shadow of a threat, Lyon demanded that Frost lay down his arms unconditionally within half an hour following the dispatching of the letter. The missive follows:

Your command is regarded as evidently hostile towards the government of the United States.

It is for the most part, made up of those secessionists who have openly avowed their hostility to the General Government, and have been plotting at the seizure of its property and the overthrow of its authority. You are openly in communication with the so-called Southern Confederacy, which is at war with the United States, and you are receiving at your camp, from the said Confederacy and under its flag, large supplies of the material of war, most of which is known to be the property of the United States. These extraordinary preparations plainly indicate none other than the well-known purpose of the Governor of this State, under whose orders you are acting, and whose purpose recently communicated to the Legislature, has just been responded to by that body in the most unparalleled legislation, having in direct view hostilities to the General Government and cooperation with its enemies.

In view of these considerations, and of your failure to disperse

54

in obedience to the proclamation of the President, and of the eminent necessities of State policy and welfare, and the obligations imposed upon me by instructions from Washington, it is my duty to demand, and I do hereby demand of you an immediate surrender of your command, with no other conditions than that all persons surrendering under this demand shall be humanely and kindly treated. Believing myself prepared to enforce this demand, one-half hour's time before doing so will be allowed for your compliance therewith.

Volunteers March on the Militia Camp

Early in the morning, orders were received by the regimental commanders of the Volunteer and Home Guard Infantry to report to the Arsenal for orders. The secret of the impending movement had been so well guarded by the few in the know that no inkling of it had reached even the high levels of colonels in command of regiments. In a few brisk words, and without waving a single verbal flag, Lyon outlined the operation. With the aid of a wall map, he defined the routes to be followed by the various regiments and the hours at which the units were to march. To insure proper timing, all regiments were to proceed at route step. During the night, Blair, Lyon, and Schofield had worked out marching routes and time-tables which, if adhered to, would bring about the complete encircling of Camp Jackson within minutes. The distance from the Arsenal to Camp Jackson was about six miles, give or take a few rods.

Among the horses secured for the Arsenal by Oliver and Giles Filley was a beautiful, high-spirited dappled-gray stallion. It had been tagged by the brothers for Nathaniel Lyon's use. Having been used to horses since boyhood and having learned horsemanship at West Point, Lyon knew a strong and splendid riding horse when he saw one. He was, as the saying goes, pleased as Punch, but in a reserved New England way.

The first column to march was headed by Captain Lyon

on his high-stepping charger. Behind him came Sweeny with two companies of regulars, Totten's artillery and Blair's First Regiment Volunteers which had marched up from Jefferson Barracks. These units left the Arsenal, moved north on Seventh Street, and westward over Chouteau Avenue toward Lindell Grove. Colonel Henry Boernstein led his Second Regiment Volunteers from the barracks at Marine Hospital, marched over Broadway to Pine and then swung westward. Colonel Francis Sigel—he had changed his native Franz to a less Teutonic variation—led Bischoff's artillery and his own Third Regiment Volunteers up Broadway from the Arsenal and out Olive Street to the camp. On the heels of Sigel came Colonel Nicholas Schuettner with the Fourth Regiment Volunteers. By way of Market Street and Laclede, his troops followed the beat of their drums.

Although barely organized, the Home Guards had not been left out of the planning. Commanded by Lieutenant Colonel Robert J. Rombauer, the First Battalion of Colonel Henry Almstedt's First U. S. Reserve Regiment marched from Jaeger's Garden on Tenth and Sidney Streets to Camp Jackson by way of Jefferson Avenue to stand in support of Bischoff's artillery. Following Rombauer's Battalion to the same position, came the First Battalion of Colonel Herman Kallmann's Second U. S. Reserve Regiment led by Lieutenant Colonel John T. Fiala. This unit fell in at Soulard Market and moved over Olive Street to its objective. Turner Hall, at Third and Walnut Streets, was the point of departure for Colonel John McNeil's Third U. S. Reserve Regiment which marched to its designated position by way of Pine Street and Clark Avenue. The Fourth U. S. Reserve Regiment, commanded by Colonel B. Gratz Brown, headed toward the Lindell Grove encampment by way of Morgan.

In mounting his attack, Lyon had not failed to foresee the possibility that Frost might learn of the Union plans not only in time to move out of Camp Jackson but also to stage a surprise assault on the Arsenal. To forestall the success of such a turnabout, Lyon left his two remaining companies of U. S. Infantry Regulars in command of Captain Saxton on guard at the Arsenal, as well as the half-dozen companies of Colonel Charles E. Salomon's Fifth Regiment Volunteers which, so far, had been mustered in. The Second Battalions of the First and Second U. S. Reserves—under Majors Phillip Brimmer and Julius Rapp, respectively—blocked the streets to the Arsenal with orders to let no one pass. Sharpshooters among the regulars were placed on the roofs of nearby buildings. Lyon was the last man in the world to underestimate Daniel Frost as a resourceful opponent. He would be well prepared to meet any overt act with snipers or grenade throwers.

Naturally, Lyon knew that the wholesale mobilization of his entire force, once begun, would be time consuming and attract wide attention. As soon as men under arms began to gather at the various staging points, and stood in ranks with bayonets fixed and their cartridge boxes filled with 40 rounds of ammunition, Southern supporters rushed the news to Brigadier General Frost. Definite proof that Frost now knew what was going on came to Captain Lyon at the Arsenal about noon in the form of a letter—redolent with innocence and sweetness—from the militia commander. It read:

I am constantly in receipt of information that you contemplate an attack upon my camp, while I understand that you are impressed with the idea that an attack upon the Arsenal and the United States troops is intended on the part of the Militia of Missouri. . . . I would be glad to know from you personally, whether there is any truth in the statements that are constantly poured into my ears.

So far as regards any hostility being intended toward the United States, or its property or representatives, by any portion of my command, or, as far as I can learn, and I think I am fully informed, of any other part of the State forces, I can say positively that the idea has never been entertained. . . . I trust that, after this explicit statement, we may be able to fully understand each other, and to keep far from our borders the misfortunes which so unhappily afflict our common country.

The messenger was informed that there would be no reply to this olive branch. Promptly at the hour designated, amid a chorus of shouted orders, clatter of weapons, blaring of bugles, beat of drums and the cadence of booted feet, Lyon swung into his saddle and led the way. The only concession in dress he had made to the occasion was that all the brass buttons on his coat were not only in place but actually polished. His long, heavy dragoon's sword, a favorite sidearm of many campaigns, hung on his left. He also displayed two holstered Colt revolvers. Riding behind Lyon, at proper distances, were his two adjutants, Major Chester Harding and Lieutenant John C. Schofield; also his aide, Major Horace Conant. At first—perhaps even at last—blush, it may seem a bit strange that a mere captain should have a major as an aide. Or, even stranger, that a captain should command regimental staff and field officers of higher rank than his own. But, until his election to Brigadier General of the Regiments of Missouri Volunteers had been approved by the War Department he was, for all military purposes, still a captain. To be sure, his volunteers addressed him and regarded him as their general, but that was a title conferred only by courtesy.

Although there were neither bands nor drums to herald their coming, the brisk cadence of their steps drew wide attention along the various routes. The appearance of soldiers tramping into and out of view of residents, who crammed into open doorways and windows, gave life to all sorts of wild rumors. As the columns approached their objective, men, women, and children—in steadily swelling hundreds and thousands—moved along in front, to the rear, and along their flanks like living streams. Hundreds of men with rebel leanings grabbed hunting rifles, ancient muskets, pistols, or whatever firearms they could lay their hands on and rushed toward the camp through alleys and side streets. Behind the marching columns, veritable maelstroms of traffic were formed by all sorts of vehicles—overcrowded with entire families—from

58

wagons to carriages, buggies to carts, and even hearses; men on horses, mules, and shanks' mare. All jockeying for position; all bent on beating each other to whatever might be going on. If this was war, the crowd wanted to make a truly Roman holiday of it even if rifles cracked and cannon boomed. The thought of death reaching in among them evidently never entered anyone's head. But Death was there, quietly in the boisterous processions.

Promptly, at the appointed hour, Lyon's column reached Lindell Grove. From the vantage point of his horse he observed widespread but somewhat disorganized activity among the militia troops. It was quite evident that so far no orders had been issued by General Frost for the defense of the camp. Lyon also noted, with approval of their excellent timing, the emergence of his five remaining columns from their respective streets.

Purposefully and without delay, followed by his staff, Captain Sweeny and his regulars, Totten and his artillery, Blair and his First Regiment Volunteers, Lyon moved across the center of the open portion of the meadow. As the infantry stepped up to the double-quick, Totten's mounted cannoneers changed the pace of their horses from a walk to a jog. In short order, all were on the western edge of the camp in a narrow lane that ran northward. Simultaneously, like long mobile walls, the other regiments marched over their appointed routes. Within moments the camp was enclosed by a wall tipped by bayonets that gleamed coldly in the sunlight. When the infantry drew to a halt, Totten's battery swung smartly out of column. As their riders urged them on, the horses at a gallop hauled the guns to the top of a nearby bluff. Unlimbered, the pieces were pointed so that they dominated the entire camp. The crews of each gun stood at their prescribed positions, alert for the order to go into action.

Meanwhile Lyon had turned to Captain Sweeny and called his attention to the four-gun militia battery on the meadow.

The guns were surrounded by a steadily growing group of men. Evidently the artillerists who served them, under the direction of Lieutenant Guibor, were at a loss what to do.

"Watch those men," clipped Lyon. "If they take steps to serve their pieces, deploy your leading company as skirmishers. Charge the battery and take it."

Without awaiting confirmation, Captain Lyon turned to Lieutenant Schofield, handed him the letter that demanded surrender, and instructed him to deliver it to General Frost in person.

Hardly had Schofield dashed off on his errand than three ringing cheers were heard from the camp of the militia men. Captain Sweeny had heard cheers like that before, usually from the throats of men about to go into battle and eager for the fray. As a precaution, Sweeny ordered the men of his two companies to move their cartridge boxes—which usually rode on their belts over the small of their backs—to the fore. Any seasoned soldier knew that this was a promise the shooting was about to start.

The order had been executed, and the men were again leaning on their arms, when Schofield returned at a rapid trot. He handed Lyon a note from Frost. It read:

I never for a moment conceived the idea that illegal and unconstitutional demands, as I have just received from you, would be made by an officer of the United States Army.

I am wholly unprepared to defend my command from this unwarranted attack, and shall, therefore, be forced to comply with your demand.

Nodding his head soberly, as if in serious agreement with the wisdom of the action taken by General Frost, Lyon took steps to call a meeting with his staff officers as well as those of the nearby First Regiment Volunteers, including Colonel Blair. The next moves would be to march the prisoners back to the Arsenal, guard the camp, and take possession of the illegally acquired pile of war materials sheltered in the woods.

Since his thoughts moved quickest and best when he was on his feet, Lyon dismounted and started to pace up and down on the greensward. This brought him into too close range of Major Conant's horse. It lashed out with a hind leg and a hoof hit the captain a heavy blow in the stomach. He slumped to the ground wholly unconscious. Dr. Florentz Cornyn, surgeon of the First Regiment Volunteers, went to work on Lyon. He brought him around slowly, while a ring of deeply worried officers surrounded their stricken commander.

Lyon was still unconscious, as Lieutenant William Wood, Frost's aide-de-camp, rode up and inquired for Captain Lyon. Thinking quickly, Sweeny decided that this was no time for the surrendering enemy to know that the Union force was without its head. He informed Wood that he had been authorized to receive communications from General Frost and to act on them. Like Lyon, Thomas Sweeny was a fast worker when it came to shouldering responsibility. Answering the Irishman's inquiry as to the nature of the message, Wood replied:

"General Frost sends his compliments to Captain Lyon and wishes to know if the officers will be allowed to retain their sidearms. Also, what disposition shall be made of government property, and if a guard will be sent to relieve his men now and take possession of everything when the camp shall be evacuated?"

Sweeny, after a brief consultation with Lieutenant Schofield, replied that the officers would be allowed to retain their sidearms; that all public property, such as arms, ammunition, and military equipment, would be confiscated to the United States; that private property would be collected and guards detailed to protect both. As a token of courtesy, he sent Lieutenant Schofield back with Lieutenant Wood to deliver the message. A small but interesting incident took place when Wood and Schofield reached Frost's headquarters' tent. Lieutenant Colonel John Knapp, commanding the First Regiment, had not anticipated such courteous treatment as officers being allowed the retain their swords. To avoid such surrender, he had broken his saber and thrown the pieces on the ground rather than surrender it to the much hated Nathaniel Lyon.

Meanwhile, Lyon's recovery from the blow in the stomach proceeded at a slow pace. About half an hour passed before he was able to resume command and start the machinery of evacuation and taking possession.

The "Massacre" at Camp Jackson

Approving the initiative taken by Captain Sweeny, Lyon ordered the former and his two companies of regulars to take possession of the camp and to request General Frost to march his two militia regiments—some 700 men in all—off the encampment grounds. At the same time, orders were issued to Colonel Blair to have his regiment open ranks on each side of the street and have the men face inward in two files. The purpose was to have Frost march his disarmed soldiers between the two lines of infantry, who would act as a guard and an escort.

The half-hour delay caused by Lyon's temporary disablement—plus the even longer wait incurred while the militia companies in Camp Jackson fell in and made ready to march off the field—gave a huge mob of spectators time to assemble around the First Missouri and the waiting regulars. This boisterous assembly of curious or angry citizens contained a large element of armed ruffians. They were in search of thrills and trouble and many of them were drunk.

After an overture of curses and shouts—hurrahs for the South and jeers for the North—things began to fly. Stones, clumps of dirt, chunks of wood, even bricks were hurled at the Union ranks. And with them came staccato fusillades of obscenities, insults, and challenges. Some of the more daring demonstrators pushed through the frontal fringe of the crowd to wave revolvers, even shotguns, at Blair, Lyon, and their subordinate officers. Recovering their senses or finding that the troops could not be intimidated or drawn into a row, the inciters to trouble transferred their attention to Company F, Third Regiment Volunteers, commanded by Captain Constantine Blandowski. The infantrymen took the abuse stolidly until a heavily built rowdy, crazed by alcohol and red with rage, attempted to force his way through the ranks. He was pushed back. As he staggered on his heels, the man pulled a revolver and fired point-blank at Captain Blandowski who fell to the ground, seriously wounded. Now, thoroughly roused, a ragged volley was fired by some of the men in Company F. It was prevented from spreading by orders for the column to move forward.

Last to be heckled by insults and exposed to rocks, dirt, and bullets was the company of volunteers commanded by Lieutenant Rufus Saxton. It marched at the rear of the First Regiment Volunteers which guarded the prisoners on the march to the Arsenal. Pushing forward and surging back like angry seas on a lee shore, the rioters drove on the troops from both sides of the column. Some of them, screaming like maniacs, shot at the troops with various types of firearms. Driven to exasperation, more natural than justified, the troops fired back. Some soldiers shot into the air in the hope of scaring their attackers off. Others, less steady, shot wildly into the crowds. As if by chain reaction, the shooting spread down the line. For a few moments, it looked as if the stage had been set for a truly wholesale slaughter. Then the firing on both sides stopped as suddenly as it had begun.

When the casualties were counted, 28 in the crowd had been killed and 10 wounded. Several soldiers were wounded, one was killed, and Captain Blandowski died later of his wounds.

The early part of the route back to the Arsenal ran through a part of town heavily inhabited by the pro-Southern element. The doors and windows of homes along these thoroughfares were no longer crowded by gaping spectators. The former were closed and the latter shut in stern disapproval of the sei-zure of Camp Jackson and the "massacre" that crowned its capture. Although a flood of humanity nibbled noisily, even angrily, at their heels, the foot-weary, hot and hungry soldiers showed neither interest nor irritation. It had been a long day. Most of them had stood under arms since early-morning hours. They were tired. At the same time, they carried a certain air of satisfaction and self-confidence. For the first time, as military units, the regiments had been called on to show how well they had learned their lessions of drill and discipline, and, with some obvious exceptions, they felt they had done rather well. However, the abusive elements in the human flood began to thin out when the regiments reached the pro-Union section of Saint Louis and its quickly thickening rows of spectators. There were cheers, loud and lusty. Women waved handkerchiefs and screamed joyously. Wonder of wonders, the American flag, Old Glory, not exposed to public view in Saint Louis for many months, actually waved from scores of windows.

By the time the regiments turned toward the Arsenal on Carondelet Avenue, the sidewalks overflowed and the streets were thronged by cheering, shouting, and singing thousands of people. Houses were decorated with flags and bunting and on the roof of the small Anheuser Brewery, near the Arsenal, a German band was playing Vaterland marching songs. The weary foot soldiers straightened their backs, raised their heads, and put more swing into their strides. They sang, and singing, marched through the tunnel-like portal that led into the Arsenal.

Whatever elation Lyon and Blair may have felt over the capture of Camp Jackson was completely extinguished by the harrowing results of the rioting. Feeling that the public was entitled to an official expression, Lyon issued a statement of explanation that ended with the comment:

"The sad results are much to be lamented. The killing of innocent men, women, and children is deplorable; there was no intention to fire upon peaceable citizens. The regular troops were over in the camp beyond the mob and in range of the firing. The troops manifested every forbearance, and discharged their guns simply obeying the impulse natural to us all in self defense. If innocent men, women, and children, whose curiosity placed them in a dangerous position, suffered with the guilty, it is no fault of the troops."

Chapter 3

Violent Reactions to Seizure

———◆—————

Weapons Traced to the Baton Rouge Arsenal

That night, the nation's telegraph wires hummed with the news of the taking of Camp Jackson. The grimly desperate atmosphere of Washington was considerably brightened by this wholly unexpected stroke of success against the South. Northern newspapers printed every detail they could get about the action and heralded Nathaniel Lyon as the hero of the hour. After all, they pointed out editorially, had he not been the first leader of Union forces to take action against the South which up to then had held the initiative? Here was a pay-off in kind for the seizures and lootings by secessionists of U. S. fortifications and arsenals.

The reception in Montgomery and throughout the South of this, the first sizable Union action in the Civil War, was, naturally, wholly different. Lyon's invasion was labeled a scoundrelly act and a stain on the honor of the Union. Southern newspapers referred to the incident as a "cold blooded and deliberate massacre."

One of the questions that pressed hardest on Lyon's mind was: Had he been right or wrong in assuming that the shipments from Baton Rouge were arms?

Any worry on that score was removed early in the evening, when Lieutenant L. P. Immels, of Totten's Battery, handed him a list of weapons and ammunition that had come up the river on the *J. C. Swon* in the guise of marble and ale.

A large quantity of mortar bombs and shells had been found in the barrels. The great wooden crates disgorged a hefty store of rifles, muskets, guns, and mortars. Even three massive 32-pounders. Checking the list, item by item, there was no longer any doubt in the captain's mind that a contemplated sneak attack on the Arsenal had been snuffed out in the proverbial eleventh hour.

Here is the itemized list, as prepared by Captain Sweeny, of the "Tamaroa marble" and "Baton Rouge ale" that reached Camp Jackson from Jefferson Davis:

Three 32-pounders, three mortar beds, six brass fieldpieces (6-pounders), 25 kegs of powder, 39 heavy bomb shells, 300 light bomb shells, six light brass mortars, one heavy iron mortar, three light iron cannon, five boxes of canister shot, and eight chests of new rifled muskets.

As the news of the seizure of Camp Jackson flashed through every section of Saint Louis—and filtered into the great country residences, farm dwellings, and shabby cabins beyond its suburbs—the downtown streets and those around the Arsenal literally boiled with swirling masses of Southern sympathizers. The crowds included a fairly large number of Conditional Union men who were opposed to any kind of coercion toward the South. From that night on, the line of demarcation between Conditional and Unconditional Union men was no longer a matter of degree but one of widening cleavage.

In the Arsenal extraordinary precautions had been taken against overt acts from within by captured militia men, or from without by hotheaded cavaliers or trouble-brewing ruffians. Every sentry post along the walls had been doubled. Fully manned guns, ready for firing, faced the weaker portions of the Arsenal as well as the buildings that housed the prisoners.

From the street beyond, over the hubbub of ranting voices, jeers, and catcalls, came explosive cheers for Jefferson Davis and exaggerated groans for Abraham Lincoln, Frank Blair, and Nathaniel Lyon.

Seemingly accurate and tautly written coverage of the events of that Friday evening in Saint Louis appeared in the next day's issue of *The Republican,* a strong proslavery newspaper. It read in part:

It is almost impossible to describe the intense exhibition of feeling which was manifested last evening in the city. All the most frequented streets and avenues were thronged with citizens in the highest state of excitement. Loud huzzahs, and occasional shots, were heard in various localities. There was very little congregation on the street corners. Everybody was on the move and rapid pedestrianism was turned into account.

Thousands upon thousands of restless human beings could be seen from almost any point on Fourth Street, all in search of the latest news. Imprecations, loud and long, were hurled into the darkening air and unanimous resentment was expressed on all sides at the manner of firing into the harmless crowds near Camp Jackson. . . .

All the drinking saloons, restaurants, and other public resorts of similar character were closed by their proprietors almost simultaneously at dark; and the windows of private dwellings were fastened in fear of a general riot. Theaters and other public places of amusement were entirely out of the question and nobody went near them. Matters of grave import were occupying the minds of our citizens, and everything but the present excitement was banished from their thoughts.

Crowds of men rushed through the principal thoroughfares bearing banners and placards suited to their general fancies and by turn cheering or groaning. Some were armed and others were unarmed. . . . A charge was made on the gun store of Dimmick on Main Street. The door was broken open and the crowd secured 15 to 20 rifles before sufficient police could be collected to stop the proceedings. Squads of armed policemen were stationed on several of the most public corners, and the offices of the *Missouri Democrat* and the *Anzeiger des Westens* (both devoted to the Union cause) were placed under guard for protection.

The prisoners at the Arsenal were crowded into three of the main buildings and guarded by companies of Blair's First

Regiment Volunteers. There was scant comfort for the captives and no ready acceptance on their part of the humiliating conditions imposed on them, which was not surprising. When supper, in the guise of coffee, hardtack, and bacon, was offered, they poured the coffee on the ground and threw the food out of the windows. Later, many of the prisoners claimed that the mudsills had refused to give them food. "Mudsill" was a term of opprobrium heaped on whites who performed manual labor by cavaliers, gamblers, gunslingers, and other professional idlers who regarded work as degrading. (A mudsill is the lowest sill in a structure, usually placed in or on the ground.) As the night passed, tempers cooled and, by morning, all but one officer signed parole papers. These included sworn allegiance to the United States and a solemn oath not to bear arms against it in the Civil War. The total captured amounted to threescore officers and 710 enlisted men.

With a show of wholly unexpected thoughtfulness, Lyon arranged to have the discharged prisoners picked up by a packet at the Arsenal landing to be disembarked in a pro-Southern section in an upriver part of town. This measure was taken to avoid unpleasant incidents as the disarmed militia marched through the streets around the Arsenal with their overwhelmingly German populations. In appreciation, released prisoners gave three rousing cheers for Jefferson Davis as soon as their vessel pushed off.

Brigadier General Frost, who also had taken the oath of allegiance, remained in Saint Louis for several months acting, it was said, as a Southern spy-master. Then he vanished and was heard of shortly after as a brigadier general in the Confederate Army. For reasons unknown, he resigned his commission in 1863 and moved to Canada. There he was joined by his family and did not return to Saint Louis until after the close of the Civil War. As for other members of Frost's Division, Missouri State Militia, most of them disregarded their oath. Asserting that it was given under duress, they joined the Confederate Army where many of them fought with great distinction and gallantry.

But, to measure the far-reaching events staged in Saint Louis that afternoon of May 10, the focus of attention must swing from the city on the Mississippi to Jefferson City, some 130 miles inland on the Missouri River, and the capital of the State. News of the Camp Jackson "massacre" reached Governor Jackson late in the afternoon in a series of telegrams sent to him by Deacon Tucker, editor of the violently rebel *Saint Louis State Journal.* In blow by blow accounts, Editor Tucker unfolded the entire story in a graphic and inflammatory style.

At first, Governor Jackson was shocked by the wholly unexpected turn of affairs. He had been looking forward to tidings of the fall of the Arsenal with General Frost in full control. Now Frost and his men were in the Arsenal, to be sure; but as prisoners, not victors. However, after the initial shock, Jackson's nimble mind—which was always in pursuit of the main chance—discovered a bright silver lining in the clouds over Saint Louis. Even if Frost had taken the Arsenal, there was always a doubt that the Legislature would lend a hand toward overriding the decision of the State Convention to remain in the Union. But now, with Camp Jackson taken by force of arms, spectators killed and wounded, and the forces of Missouri humbled and humiliated, he knew that he could mold the lawmakers to his will.

Before the night was over, he swore, Missouri would move in the direction of the rebellion. It was victory! Victory! Handed him on a silver platter by that low-down abolitionist Nathaniel Lyon.

From his executive office, Jackson ran to the Assembly. This body was in special session to debate the controversial Military Bill, a measure which would make the Governor an absolute dictator. There were numerous companion bills for the draining of millions of dollars of State funds into the military chest, as well as for the imposition of new taxes.

Fifteen minutes after Jackson had delivered the news in a

fiery harangue, the Military Bill and its companion measures were passed by both Houses without debate. Then and there, Jackson signed the measures.

The secessionists in and out of the legislature could now drop their masks of hypocritical neutrality.

Missouri was heading South. What with Arkansas having joined the Confederacy earlier that week, a tactical obstacle had been removed. Now, Missouri secessionists not only had free access to the Land of Cotton but could hope to receive military assistance from the Gulf States. To be sure, the legislature had not seceded from the Union. However, it had given Jackson the go-ahead that could lead the State out of the neutral ranks when he thought that the time for doing so was at hand.

The legislature adjourned, after much fire-eating, about 9 o'clock that Friday evening. Armed with his new powers, Governor Jackson set himself to the task of establishing his army. The new law created nine military districts. To these, he named the following commanders with rank of brigadier general: A. W. Doniphan, Monroe M. Parsons, James S. Rains, John B. Clark, M. L. Clark, N. W. Watkins, B. Randolph, William J. Slack, and James H. McBride. To head up the new organization—which could not be designated a National Guard since it was not sponsored by the United States—he named Sterling Price as major general. The army was to be known as the Missouri State Guard.

As the Governor worked, John Sappington Marmaduke, a West Pointer and recently resigned Army infantry officer, was elected colonel of a brand-new volunteer regiment formed that night in Jefferson City by several companies of volunteers from Jefferson City, Cooper, and Callaway counties. They also included the boys of Captain Joe Kelly's Company E from Saint Louis. They had escaped the fate of their brother Minute Men by having been assigned to escort Adjutant General James Harding's military purchases from Saint Louis to Jefferson City.

71

Young Colonel Marmaduke, still in his late twenties, was an offspring of two old-line Missouri families of great political and plantation prominence. He was also by marriage a nephew of Governor Jackson.

The humble beginnings of the latter started in Kentucky in 1806. "Claib" Jackson came to Missouri in his teens and obtained a job in a country store. Soon he struck out for himself and did so well in business that he was able to retire at the age of 30. At that time, he also made his first martial foray into the wealthy and powerful Sappington family. He wedded one of the three daughters of Dr. John Sappington, Missouri's patent medicine mogul. When his wife died, Jackson married a second daughter. When she passed on, he married the third and last. At that time, Dr. Sappington was reported to have ruminated: "Reckon Claib'll come back next for the old woman!" A virulent nullificationist, Jackson was for slavery as a national institution. To do him credit, he never sailed under false colors.

Personally, he was thin and tall, held himself rigidly erect, and was extremely dignified of bearing. One might say that he had the appearance of a Shakespearean actor. His long, slightly wavy black hair was parted in the center and hung almost shoulder-length over his ears. He was smooth shaven. His wide but rather thin-lipped mouth was highly mobile; his nose was strong, and there was an almost hypnotic look in his large dark deep-set eyes. They could gaze on the world broodingly or flare to life with the flames of fanaticism. Jackson's voice was low and vibrant, and he could play it with all the theatrical tricks of an Edwin Booth. Jackson knew politics. He had a poker-playing, horse-trader's knowledge of men and his devotion to the cause of the South amounted to an all-consuming obsession.

The naming of Sterling Price to the post of Major General of the Missouri State Guard was, politically and otherwise, one of the smartest moves Jackson could have made. Up to the time of the taking of Camp Jackson, the middle-of-the-road Chairman of the Constitutional Convention, an ardent Democrat and a strong Southern Rights man, had been a Conditional Union man. Price's stand had been somewhat shaken by the outbreak of hostilities, because he was opposed to coercion. On the other hand, he hoped to keep Missouri out of the war. However, with the taking of Camp Jackson, Price, who was in Jefferson City at the time, let it be known that he had come to a parting of the ways with the Union. Hearing this, Jackson invited Price to head up the State Guard. Price accepted at once.

In "Pap" Price, the Governor had a powerful trump card. He was, by the widest of margins, the most popular man in Missouri. He had been Governor, Congressman, and Legislator. In Missouri, "Pap" Price could run for any office, even on a Republican ticket, and win in a walk. His capacity to soften harsh partisan tempers and bring order out of political chaos was demonstrated in 1852 when the warring Benton and Jackson factions united in electing him Governor. But Price was also a warrior. As a soldier, he had built a spectacular record in the Mexican War. Resigning his seat in Congress in 1844, he formed the soon to become famous Second Missouri Mounted Volunteers. Promoted from colonel to brigadier general, he participated in and won numerous engagements. His most brilliant act was to put down an uprising of Pueblo and New Mexican Indians and hang the murderers of Governor Bent of New Mexico. Another feather in his cap was his victory at Santa Cruz de Rosales.

Statesman and soldier! The phrase, trite but true, fitted Sterling Price from the tips of his immaculately polished boots to the stubby gray hair that grew on his head six feet, three inches above them. Price, 52 years old in 1861, was a native of Virginia where he had studied law. He settled in Chariton County, Missouri, in 1831 and engaged in farming. His easy ways, sincere cordiality, and benevolent disposition earned him the nickname "Pap." At the outbreak of the Civil War he looked somewhat older than his years. Time had put

73

flesh on his heavy frame and jowls beneath his florid face. But he had the energy, experience, and popularity to build and lead an army. There is no doubt that Sterling Price's far-reaching influence on Missourians in all walks of life caused many self-proclaimed Conditional Union men to face toward the South because "Pap" Price set them the example to do so.

It is impossible to write an account of Nathaniel Lyon's fight to keep Missouri in the Union without bringing Sterling Price, who fought to keep it out of the Union, into sharp and prominent focus. While Jackson held the limelight as rabble-rouser and emissary to Confederate States, it was Price who built Missouri's State Guards out of willing but untried material. Price, not Jackson, was Lyon's real opponent. And but for one man, Brigadier General Ben McCulloch of the Confederate Army, Price could have succeeded in destroying all Union strength in the State and in placing the South in a controlling position. Such a victory in 1861 would not only have cost the North dearly but it could have materially affected the outcome of the war.

The Bells of Alarm Toll in the Capitol

As Governor Jackson worked diligently and profitably that night of May 10 at his executive offices, the hour of midnight signaled the start of a new day. It was heralded by heavy rains released to the accompaniment of crashing thunder and flashing lightning that ripped the silence and the darkness of the night. Amid this performance by the elements, the bells in the capitol's church spires were set ringing. And, as the weary legislators knew, it was for them that the bells were tolling—an emergency session at the capitol. Almost simultaneously, rumors mushroomed that Lyon and his Federals were en route to Jefferson City by train and could be expected almost any hour.

At that time, James Peckham, one of the few loyal Union men in the legislature, was a member of the House. In his book: *General Nathaniel Lyon and Missouri in 1861*, he describes the drama in the House when the midnight session convened in the expectation of Federal invasion. He wrote:

Nearly every individual was armed, some with many more weapons than others. Members in their seats were surrounded by guns of every description, some leaning against desks, some against chairs, some held between the knees, some leaning against the walls, some laying on the floor and some across desks.

Many members had belts strapped around their waists and from one to three pistols or bowie knives fastened to them. The scene in the House, particularly, was exeedingly grotesque and ludicrous. Many [members] showed faces pale with fear; others exhibited the anxiety natural in any crisis; a few sought to impel the movement of the doubtful into secessionist ranks while the leaders proposed drastic measures for adoption and dared opposition.

Before the night session ended, two things had happened:

First, Colonel Claiborn and Captain Kelly were given authority to commandeer a locomotive and crew to ride the rails down toward Saint Louis in order to determine the progress of the enemy and then to telegraph their findings. Claiborn and Kelly rocketed at full speed nearly all the way to Saint Louis without discovering a single troop train. Had they met one, their orders were to destroy the bridges across the Osage and Gasconade rivers.

Second, a bill was passed that gave the Governor absolute control over Saint Louis and also handed him dictatorial powers in dealing with and crushing Union sentiment in other parts of the State. A significant feature of the new law, hewn to the line of States sovereignty, prescribed that members of the Missouri State Guard must swear fealty to the State of Missouri as "first and supreme."

Naturally, news of these activities sped over the telegraph lines. In the Arsenal, Lyon and Blair watched the developments at Jefferson City with intense and speculative interest. Either or both would have given their good right arms to defer the return of General Harney to Saint Louis, if only for

24 hours. With the arrival of the general during the late hours of Saturday afternoon, the command of the Department of the West would automatically revert to Harney. Lyon would no longer have authority to order movements of troops.

Blair and Lyon knew now was the time to march on Jefferson City. If this could be accomplished without delay, and before Jackson and Price could set up their defenses, the drifting of Missouri toward secession could be stopped before it even made headway. But Nathaniel Lyon, daring as he was, did not feel justified in taking such drastic action, knowing that he would not be in command long enough to see it to its conclusion. There was, decided Lyon, nothing to do but wait and hope that Harney would be returning from Washington with a clearer viewpoint of what the situation demanded than the one he went away with.

Turmoil and Terror in Saint Louis

By Saturday morning, the hot tempers among Southern Rights leaders in Saint Louis had begun to cool. It actually seemed as though calm would be restored to the riot-ridden city. However, all hope of this vanished when rumors of impending trouble spread with the speed of light throughout the town. The Germans were said to be organizing in the southern wards, armed to the teeth and resolved to avenge the deaths of four Germans who had been murdered by ruffians during the night. Then in the early forenoon it became known that a fifth German had just been attacked and kidnapped by a raging mob on Market and Ninth Streets.

Much to the relief of vigilant and able Police Chief McDonough, no other open clashes occurred during daylight hours. Unknown to him, however, a gang of irreconcilable secessionists met secretly to plan a coup that would bring death to innocent persons and plant deeper seeds of ill feeling between the so-called "American" population and the "Damn Dutch."

Just about sunset, the Fifth Regiment, U. S. Reserve Corps —by now identified generally as the Home Guard—was marching under the command of Lieutenant Colonel Robert White, from the Arsenal to the home wards of its almost wholly German membership. The Fifth was the last Home Guard outfit to be organized in Saint Louis under the 90-days enlistment clause. It had been mustered in by Lieutenant Schofield that very day and received arms, accouterments, and ammunition. These would be housed in various company headquarters, which were always patrolled by heavily armed sentries.

By means that have never been disclosed, the gang of irreconcilables learned the time and route of march of the newly organized Fifth Home Guard Regiment. Equipped with firearms, bricks, stones, and other missiles, they established an ambush on both sides of the intersection of Walnut and Fifth Streets. Some hid in alleyways, others behind the pillars of the Presbyterian Church that stood on the corner; still others lay in wait behind windows in houses that faced the street.

The first companies of the regiment had crossed the intersection when the self-appointed avengers of the Camp Jackson "massacre" attacked. First, there were shouted curses and obscenities. Then, from both sides of Walnut Street, a rain of stones and other heavy objects pelted the Home Guards who continued their march. Suddenly, above the noise, cracked six angry blasts of a revolver. In the ranks of the Home Guard, a soldier fell dead. Seconds later, two rifle shots barked from a window on the opposite side of the street. Two soldiers were wounded.

Some of the soldiers, raw volunteer recruits, in spite of orders, had marched out of the Arsenal with loaded muskets. Now, panicky and disregarding orders of their officers, men in the leading companies came to a stop, swung about, and fired wildly down the street in the direction of the shots. So scattered was their aim, that musket balls peppered the church, houses on both sides of the streets, and, worst of all, struck many spectators. By the time command had been restored, the blood of dead and wounded ran red on the white crushed limestone of Walnut Street. Of the six who died, four were Home Guards, three killed by their own fire; the other two were either participants or spectators. The number of wounded was never ascertained.

This second attack on German troops, the impending death of Captain Blandowski, the assassination of five Germans and the maltreatment of dozens more by cruising gangs of plug-uglies, drove the Germans to greater heights of fury. Even the Home Guards clustered in street groups and swore loudly of swift and thorough retaliation. On the other hand, Fourth Street, especially the portion that fronted the Planter's House, was thronged with seething secesh crowds. They were made up mainly of the youthfully arrogant and hot-blooded cavalier fraternity and they swore dire threats against all and sundry submissionists, abolitionists, and disruptionists.

While these widely separated hubbubs were in full-throated uproar, a ferry from East Saint Louis pulled into its landing place. Among its passengers was Brigadier General Harney who, the moment he stepped ashore, again became Commander of the Department of the West. Harney was met on the levee by several of his closest Southern Rights friends. Even before he had a chance to enter the carriage that would take him home for a welcome rest after his wearying train ride, Harney had received a thorough briefing of the Saint Louis situation as seen from a Southern view. Among those present was Mayor Taylor. As reported at the time, General Harney's first promise—after listening to the outpourings of woe and criticism by the Mayor and other complainants—was that he would either remove or disband the Home Guards. This happy news was publicly proclaimed by Mayor Taylor without loss of time.

Later that evening, Colonel Blair informed General Harney that, under the orders issued by President Lincoln, the general had neither the authority to disband the Home Guards nor power to send them out of town for "safekeeping." In a final attempt to carry out his promise, Harney called a meeting of the commanders of the Home Guard regiments at 8 o'clock that evening at his home. Only one of the five Home Guard colonels put in an appearance. He was Colonel John McNeil of the Third. From him the old Indian fighter learned, in coldly spoken words, that the entire Union population of Saint Louis would regard the disarming of the Home Guard as an act of treason.

On Sunday morning, Harney sent word to Mayor Taylor to the effect that he had "no control" over the Home Guards. This information was taken to mean literally that the Home Guards, as threatened, had passed beyond General Harney's control and that the well-armed Germans would soon be on the rampage. This alarming news flew fast on the wings of fear. One rumor said Home Guard companies were assembling at their various company headquarters. Another had it that the guards were actually preparing to debouch from the First and Second Wards to march on the heavily "American" Fifth, Sixth, and Ninth Wards. Those were the wards in which the Minute Men had been ruling the roost during their now-ended days of armed strength. That Sunday forenoon, instead of arming for defense, the secessionists flew as stormy petrels delivering their warnings of coming disaster from block to block, from house to house.

By noon, huge segments of the Southern Rights population of Saint Louis were on the move. They were not gathering, as James Peckham put it, "for the purposes of resistance, but took off in headlong flight toward the country, over the river, down the river, up the river; anywhere to escape the fury of the Dutch." He continued:

"Every vehicle that could be obtained was engaged conveying passengers, baggage, furniture, and so forth to places of supposed security. Hackney coaches, furniture carts, transportation wagons, were not so numerous but all found engagement. Drivers of each, in the midst of a competing crowd of patrons, charged their own prices. Exorbitant as those prices were, in a large majority of instances they received them.

"Many of the half-and-half Union people caught the infection. The Memphis Packet Company placed its splendid boats at the service of the terror stricken, and landed them at different places along the river, at sufficient distances from the Dutch to permit the blood to return to their pallid cheeks, and the eye to assume its wonted cast.

"In their flight, many forgot to lock their houses; others neglected to take even a change of underclothing or to provide themselves with money. By 2 o'clock, 2,000 to 3,000 refugees must have left the city and the panic was raging with increasing excitement. . . . Those who did not flee barricaded themselves in their homes and awaited the coming of the enemy with loaded guns.

"The scene at the Planter's House that afternoon, at the time of the departure of the omnibuses with passengers for the trains, was especially ludicrous. Every bus and baggage wagon was loaded down to utmost capacity, and there were hundreds who could not obtain conveyance to reach the cars."

Suddenly the frenzied buzzings of the panic-stricken grew louder. It became known that General Harney had ordered four companies of regular Federal infantry and artillery from the Arsenal into the city. Why? To quell the rioting no one had actually seen? Or to restrain the vengeful Home Guards no one had really observed? No one knew, but everyone feared the worst. If the regulars were needed, things must be getting out of hand. Such was the general conclusion. Harney's act served only to pour oil on the flames.

When Harney's orders, to place Totten, Sweeny, Saxton, and Lothrop at the head of the out-bound troops reached the Arsenal, Lyon and Blair agreed that Harney's purpose could be to enforce his original project to disarm the Home Guards. The atmosphere of suspicion that prevailed is revealed by their promise that if they were ordered to move against the Home Guards, the four officers would co-operate with Lyon and Blair in placing Harney under arrest. However, as was presently shown, there were no such intentions in the general's mind. The troops were merely stationed and quartered near Harney's headquarters on Fourth near Market Street.

In midafternoon, Harney issued a proclamation which cleared the air and removed the misunderstanding created by his remark to the effect that he had "no control" over the Home Guards. This document follows, in part:

No one can more deeply regret the deplorable state of things existing here than myself. The past cannot be recalled. I can only deal with the present and the future. . . . I trust I may be spared the necessity of resorting to martial law, but the public peace must be preserved and the lives and property of the people protected. Upon a careful review of my instructions, I find I have no authority to change the location of the Home Guard.

To avoid all cause of irritation and excitement, if called upon to aid the local authorities in preserving the public peace, I shall in preference make use of the Regular Army.

When Mayor Taylor received his copy of the proclamation, he rushed to the center of the turmoil of the moment—the lines of train-ferry omnibuses in front of the Planter's House. Standing on the top of the hotel's wide flight of marble steps, he waved the procalamation to catch the attention of the crowd. Next, at the top of his voice, he shouted:

"There's no insubordination among the armed men known as the Home Guards. They are entirely under the command of their officers and there is no reason whatever to believe that there will be riots and bloodshed. There is no disturbance at the Arsenal and the Regulars are in the city only for the purpose of aiding the police, if necessary, in preserving peace and quietness and restoring confidence to our citizens."

After that, the Mayor read the contents of the proclamation and urged his audience to disband and go home. Most of them did. By sundown, Saint Louis had recovered some of her normal Sunday quiet.

Two events transpired on Monday morning that revealed

a drastic change of attitude in the city of Saint Louis. Heading Company C, Third Regiment, Home Guards, Captain Anthony Niederweiser marched up to a building on the southeast corner of Broadway and Pine Street, opposite the Minute Men's headquarters in the Berthold mansion. There, on the rooftop in plain sight of the controversial secessionist emblem, he hoisted the Stars and Stripes and left a detachment of 40 men to guard it. There was some scattered hooting, but no show of violence at all.

Hardly had the Union flag gone up, when the Confederate flag on the Berthold mansion went down. It was lowered, despite vociferous objections from the now large and excited crowd, by Police Captain Daniel R. Grace on orders of the Police Authority.

In the crowd that had watched the lowering of the secesh emblem was a short, square-set, black-bearded man. His dark-gray broadcloth garments had seen better days as had the hat on his head. When the crowd broke up, he threw the butt of a cold cigar into the gutter and boarded a horsecar that would take him to the Arsenal. He was about to pay his respects to Nathaniel Lyon, an old comrade in arms. The man was Ulysses S. Grant, a former Army infantry captain who would like to return to the service.

Next to Grant in the conveyance sat a young fire-eater from the deep South. He was shocked to the core by the flag incident and did not care who knew it. Turning to Grant he shouted:

"Things have come to a damned pretty pass when a free people can't choose their own flag. Where I come from, if a man dares to say a word in favor of the Union, we hang him to a limb of the first tree we come to."

The man, who in time was to accept General Lee's surrender, faced the youngster calmly. In his slow, even voice he replied:

"Oh, we are not so intolerant in Saint Louis as we might be. I have not seen a single rebel hung as yet, nor heard of one. But there are plenty of them who ought to be, however."

It seems that the interchange ended right then and there. The young man evidently had reached his destination. At any rate, he descended hurriedly from the horsecar.

Captain Grant had resigned from the Army under an undeserved cloud in the 1850's. Since then, he had dabbled in real estate, farming, and in his father's leather business in northern Illinois. There is a wide but unsubtantiated belief that Grant may have come to Lyon in the hope that Nathaniel might help him get a commission in the Missouri Volunteers. If that thought had occurred to Captain Lyon and if he had acted on it, how different the unfolding of the Civil War might have been. Two interesting but wholly imponderable *ifs*.

However, Grant's desire to make himself useful in the conflict—and concerning which he had deeply rooted pro-Union convictions—was to be realized a few weeks later when Governor Yates of Illinois placed him in command of that State's 21st Infantry with rank of colonel. In some respects, Ulysses Grant and Nathaniel Lyon were very much alike. As soldiers, they were men of dogged determination, great initiative, and endowed with the priceless military gift of tactical improvisation. They played, so to speak, the tunes of Mars by ear and had the courage to discard orthodox concepts when occasion required. Great generals may have been born with certain sparks of greatness, but they only rise to full stature through the tough trials of battle. In the spring of 1861, both Lyon and Grant had much to learn in the realm of making war. Grant survived and climbed to his country's highest positions of military and civil leadership. Numerous contemporaries of Lyon, after the end of the war, believed that had he lived he and not Ulysses Grant would have emerged as the Union's greatest Civil War commander. Idle speculation, to be sure, but none the less an often stated part of the record.

Chapter 4

The Conservatives Plot
to Oust Lyon

The Contest Shifts to the White House

Encouraged by the realization of whatever share they may
have had in the return of Brigadier General Harney to departmental command, and the downgrading of Lyon's position, a group of conservative citizens of Saint Louis met in
secret. Their object was not to stop at the restoration of Harney but to follow through with the complete elimination of
Captain Lyon from the Missouri scene. They were a lot of
strange bedfellows these conservatives—Conditional Union
Democrats and Unconditional Union Republicans. While
they had widely divergent political opinions, they were in
accord on one point: there would be no unity in Saint Louis
and no peace in Missouri until Lyon was out of the way.

The upshot of the meeting, which was held Sunday night,
May 13, behind closely drawn curtains in Mayor Taylor's
office, was that James Yeatman and Hamilton Gamble—two
Unconditional Republicans—volunteered to go to Washington.
There they were to call on Attorney General Bates and urge
his co-operation in laying the situation before President Lincoln. Gamble and Yeatman started east that very night.

Information about the meeting reached Franklin Dick Monday forenoon. After a hurried consultation with Frank Blair,
he rushed across the river to catch the next train with connec-

tions for Washington. Even as Gamble and Yeatman intended to use influence of Cabinet stature, so Dick planned to enlist the formidable aid of Postmaster General Montgomery Blair.

Being an astute politician, who knew the folly of leaving any stone unturned in order to gain victory, Blair cast about for other avenues of action.

Suddenly he recalled that Dr. Charles A. Bernays, editor of the German-language newspaper *Anzeiger des Westen,* was not only a close personal friend of Abraham Lincoln but also a warm admirer of Nathaniel Lyon. Bernays, he knew, not only would have ready access to the White House, but the President would be aware that Bernays had no political axes to grind. How to enlist the Herr Doctor's co-operation? The answer came in a flash. Lyon was the man to do it. He and the German editor were great friends.

To streamline this phase of the underground battle for control of Union forces in Saint Louis, Lyon consented readily to Blair's request that he call on Dr. Bernays. After some discussion, the latter agreed to undertake the mission. Lyon offered to pay Dr. Bernays' expenses. The latter objected. Lyon insisted. They compromised by Dr. Bernays accepting a round-trip Army railroad pass which Lyon had the power to issue.

Even as Dr. Bernays was rolling eastward, Yeatman and Gamble arrived in Washington with Franklin Dick hot on their heels. From the railroad station, Dick rushed to the office of the Postmaster General. There he damned the coalition against Lyon into the hottest corner of hell. He said that he wanted a chance, and right away, to tell the President that the real Union men of Missouri wanted freedom from interference with loyal officers such as Lyon.

Montgomery Blair needed no convincing. He led his caller to see Simon Cameron only to learn that the Secretary of War had gone to the White House. On being told there that the President was in conference with Attorney General Bates, Secretary of War Cameron, and the Secretary of the Interior,

Blair grinned. Chidingly, he told the White House aide who guarded the President's door that one more Cabinet member would only strengthen the President's hand. Pushing Dick ahead of himself, Blair entered the President's study where Bates was in the very act of explaining the horrible mess Captain Lyon had made of things in Saint Louis and urging his removal.

While Bates pushed his arguments toward their doleful conclusion, Mr. Lincoln sat as immobile as a statue. When the Attorney General had finished, the President invited Mr. Dick to air his views. Some of the atmosphere of that meeting is preserved in a confidential letter which Dick wrote to Major Farrar a few hours after the meeting's conclusion. Highly satisfied with the impact he made on the gathering in his arguments for Captain Lyon and against General Harney, Franklin Dick wrote:

I would at once have got all I wanted but for Judge Bates. He had seen Yeatman and Hamilton Gamble. They had told him their story and Bates asked Mr. Lincoln not to decide upon action until he had heard those two gentlemen. While I was talking, Judge Blair wrote out a memo for an order removing Harney and appointing Lyon a brigadier general. He presented it to the President for his signature. Lincoln would have signed it, but for the request of Bates.

Captain Lyon stands in high position with the administration for his great achievement. It is felt that he has brought honor upon the Government by it; and the howlings of the traitors is correctly evaluated here. The result is that the President and the Cabinet fully endorse his conduct and will appoint him a Brigadier General, and effectually remove Harney out of his way. Lyon must go ahead now and win new laurels.

A couple of days later, Montgomery Blair forwarded two top-secret communications to his brother Frank by way of Major Farrar. There were wide, and probably well-founded, suspicions that Colonel Blair's mail was frequently tampered

86

with. One document was a commission of Nathaniel Lyon as Brigadier General of Volunteers, effective as of May 17, 1861. The other was an order that granted General Harney leave of absence until further notice. This order was to be delivered to the general only when and if Colonel Blair believed it in the best interest of the service to do so. To this order, Montgomery Blair attached the following note for Farrar's attention:

I had great difficulty in accomplishing these results. The Secretary of War was against both. As to Lyon, the rule against granting leaves of absence to officers of the Army was the chief difficulty. As to Harney, his public course, viewed from this point, seems reasonable enough, and the leave of absence goes to Frank Blair to be delivered to Harney only if in his judgment it is deemed advisable to relieve him from command. I think it possible that— if Harney had about him some resolute, sensible men—he would be all right all the time. It is only because he falls into the hands of our opponents that he is dangerous; his intentions being good, but his judgment being weak.

Proof of the great heart of President Lincoln—who, in the midst of the pressures of war, matériel problems, and politics, could turn his thoughts toward sympathetic consideration of the plight of a single being—is found in a sort of second-thought letter to Frank Blair on Harney's removal. Dated May 18, 1861, it follows:

Dear Sir—We have a good deal of anxiety here about Saint Louis. I understand that an order has gone from the War Department to you to be delivered or withheld in your discretion, relieving General Harney of his command.

I was not quite satisfied with the order when it was made, though on the whole I thought it best to make it; but since then, I have become more doubtful of its propriety.

I do not write now to countermand it, but to say that I wish you would withhold it unless, in your judgment, the necessity to the contrary is very urgent.

There are several reasons for this. We had better have him a friend than an enemy. It will dissatisfy a good many who otherwise would be quiet. More than that, we first relieve him, then restore him; and now, if we relieve him again, the public will ask: "Why all this vacillation?" Still, if in your judgment, it is indispensable, let it be so. A. Lincoln.

From Captain to Brigadier General

It goes without saying that Colonel Blair took the President's message very much to heart. Like his older brother, Frank Blair felt that Harney's status of unreliability had been reached over the years through close and continuous association with slave-owning planters and other men of vested interests. Blair would proceed with great caution in reaching a decision and take his time in doing it. He did not relish serving this order on Harney, but he felt that events would compel him to perform that unpleasant duty.

With respect to placing Lyon's commission, as Brigadier General of Volunteers, in Nathaniel's hands—so as to make the promotion effective—Blair let no grass grow under his feet. With appropriate ceremonies on the Arsenal parade, Lyon was made aware of his elevation to one-star rank. It came to him as a great and heart-warming surprise. Equally surprising, but not at all heart-warming, was the news of the promotion to the members of the political coalition which had sought to oust the hated Missouri Yankee. This was the first direct implication they had of the failure of their ambassadors to eliminate the soldier who was such a thorn in their sides.

Dr. Bernays also had spoken to Mr. Lincoln on Captain Lyon's behalf. He returned to Saint Louis fully reassured that neither Lyon's Army career nor his Arsenal assignment were in jeopardy.

Always unpredictable, Brigadier General Harney took highly surprising steps during the week that followed the taking of Camp Jackson. First he told Lyon that he had sent a favorable endorsement of the action to General Scott. He topped that act of surprise with the issuance of a proclamation, on May 14, announcing that Missouri must share the destiny of the Union. He denounced the new military law as a secession ordinance, unconstitutional and in conflict with the laws of the United States. He promised to protect the "good and law-abiding people of the State" and to suppress "all unlawful combinations of men, be they formed under the pretext of military organizations or otherwise."

The red-hot secessionists, as well as the lukewarm Conditional Unionists, found no comfort in this stand on the part of a man whom they had come to regard as friendly and reliable. At first Brigadier General Lyon was encouraged. Wonder of wonders, would the Old Man actually take measures against Jackson and Price? Harney had gone out of his way to compliment Lyon—whom he had known since Nathaniel was a second lieutenant in the Mexican War—on having equipped and brought into being a military force of 10,000 men in the short time span from April 21 to May 11. But if he had hoped that Harney would use this army as a weapon of enforcement against the secession element in the State, Lyon suffered a swift deflation of such hopes. Harney made it clear that, with respect to any police power he might be called upon to exercise, he would use only the regular Federal troops at his disposal. Should he need more, he would not pit Missouri Volunteers and Home Guards against Missouri State Guards or mobs of rebels. He would ask for troops from other states. There just was no way of taking the initiative against the conspirators with Brigadier General Harney in command.

Encouraged by their own growing strength in numbers, State Guards, secessionists, and just plain lawless mobsters became daily more arrogant and destructive in disturbances aimed at Unionists in almost every part of the State. Some of the rowdyisms inflicted on Union men and their families were so unbearable that Lyon—Harney or no Harney—decided to take punitive action. The place chosen was Potosi, a rough, tough lead mining town some 70 miles southwest of Saint Louis. Aside from a profitable and illegal traffic in lead for

Confederate bullet molds, the ruffians specialized in hunting down Union men. When caught, the Unionists were brutally beaten and thrown into jail without cause or trial.

On the night of May 14, Captain Nelson Cole and a detachment of 150 men of the First Missouri Volunteers boarded a train from Saint Louis to Potosi in compliance with orders issued by Brigadier General Lyon. The soldiers arrived at their destination before dawn and surrounded the town. Later in the morning, the inhabitants found themselves surrounded by a tight cordon of soldiers with loaded guns and bayonets ready for use. Despite their mutters of complaint, the fire-eating Southerners gave oaths of allegiance to the United States meekly enough. Only nine gang leaders were placed under arrest and taken to Saint Louis for trial. At the lead manufacturing plant, almost 1,000 pigs of lead were confiscated and thus channeled away from Confederate guns.

While at Potosi, Captain Cole received word that big doings were slated to be staged that noon at nearby De Soto. A newly organized company of State Guard Mounted Riflemen was to give a tone of martial air to the raising of a Confederate flag on the town square. The mounted riflemen took to their horses' heels when the Federals were seen streaming out of the coaches of an incoming train. Nelson Cole let them go. Since a flag-raising was called for, he ordered the infantry's own Old Glory hoisted to the flagpole. But one mystery bothered him. What had happened to the Stars and Bars?

Assigning Surgeon Edward C. Franklin to head a search party to enter a suspected house, Cole went along to observe the thorough but unproductive quest. The woman of the house was evidently in what was called a "family way." Judging by her rather formidable bulk, the new arrival could come at almost any moment. This was particularly interesting to Dr. Franklin. She was, he noticed, rocking a baby who could not be more than six months old. The woman put on the show of an impending mother who was momentarily "expecting."

"You must be most uncomfortable, ma'am," said Dr. Frank-

90

lin, using his best and most sympathetic bedside manner. "I'm a doctor and if you'll stand up, I'll see what I can do to bring you relief."

The woman, not knowing what else to do, got slowly to her feet. Employing as much delicacy as the situation permitted, Dr. Franklin lifted the hem of the lady's dress and—what with a corner of it showing—successfully and with a masterful flourish, delivered the lady of a huge Confederate flag.

In Saint Louis, acting on information that weapons of war were hidden in the State Tobacco Warehouse on Washington Avenue and on the premises of the Central Metropolitan Police Station on Chestnut Street, U. S. Marshal Rawlings conducted a brace of fruitful raids. Although armed with warrants, Marshal Rawlings was strengthened by a couple of platoons of Federal regulars commanded by Captain Sweeny on orders approved by General Harney. This, thought Lyon, was more like it. He was even happier when the raid on the police station—headquarters of Basil Duke and the Governor's Police Authority—yielded two pieces of light artillery and some 200 up-to-date rifles. At the Tobacco Warehouse, more than 1,000 rifles, muskets, and cavalry pistols, all with USA markings, were brought to light as were numerous boxes of small-arms ammunition. From day to day, in several other less conspicuous places, lesser quantities of arms and ammunition were unearthed.

Then on May 21, Harney performed an act that literally rent the skies and made the world of Union men tremble. He entered into a compact with Governor Jackson and Major General Price. The treaty was designed to restore "peace and good order to the people of the State in subordination to the laws of the General State government." The Harney-Price agreement was, essentially, to this effect:

General Price having by commission full authority over the Militia of the State of Missouri undertakes, with the sanction of the Governor of the State, already declared, to direct the whole power of the State to maintain order within the State among the people thereof.

And, General Harney publicly declares this objective thus assured, he can have no occasion, as he has no wish, to make military movements which might otherwise create excitements and jealousies which he most earnestly desires to avoid.

And there it was, big as life and twice as ugly—the stark and naked fact that the United States had been placed in a secondary position to that of Governor Jackson's blatantly secessionist military dictatorship of Missouri.

Harney Gets His Walking Papers

Shouts of angry protests rose from Union men in every section of the State. The coalition of Conditional and Unconditional Union men, formed in Saint Louis to put that Yankee out of bounds, splintered into microcosms. Here lay a course which Unconditional Union men could not follow. In a letter dated May 26, to his cousin Captain Miner Knowlton, Lyon describes the aftermath of the signing of this agreement:

All our Union people are disgusted with this treaty, and General Harney gets roundly scolded; for it is regarded only a trick of the secession Governor, to gain time, get arms and prepare again for war.

General Harney arrived the evening after my Camp Jackson affair, and his authority over me of course arrested other persistent and persevering measures needed to head off the villainy of secessionism. It seems to be taking comfort and consolation now under shelter of his authority. The very Government—against which the secessionists have been so long, and are still, conspiring—is thus used to shield them from the just consequences of their own treachery. Indeed the Government seems unwilling to resist those who would cut its throat, for fear of exasperating them. Upon this pretext we have all along been betrayed. Our friends here all feel this and deep are their mutterings. . . .

Indisputable proof that Harney meant what he said when it came to his lack of dependence on troops (other than those

92

of Jackson's State Guard) came to the fore a few days after the publication of the general's "surrender manifesto." A group of patriotic Saint Louis Union men had organized a unit of American Zouaves (it afterward became the Eighth Regiment Missouri Volunteers). A delegation of officers, attired in their gaudily colorful Zouave uniforms, called on General Harney and requested authority to be mustered into Federal service.

The general received them peevishly and told his callers that they had better go home and attend to their regular vocations. Churlishly, he added that there was too much of the spirit of fight abroad and that the Federal Government had too many troops already. With bruised feelings, the officers then repaired to the Arsenal. When they told Lyon the story, he said:

"You are a fine-looking body of men and no doubt ought to be accepted. But General Harney has the power, I have not. Had I the mustering authority, I would take you and all others presenting themselves. I'd finish this business up at once by putting the traitors in such a position that they could not organize. You had better keep up your spirits and organization. The present state of affairs cannot last very long."

Tempted as he was by the chain of developments to put Harney out of business, Frank Blair bided his time. He hoped against hope that the aging soldier would discover the artificiality of his position; that he would learn, without too much damage to his pride, that the honor of a politician is not necessarily as brassbound as that of a soldier. All over Missouri, the true purposes of the State Guard became daily more synonymous with those of the Confederacy. Instead of slowing down, State Guard enrollments were speeded up; on the other hand, Union Home Guards were disbanded. Sweeping the State was a flurry of Southern Rights pamphlets. They urged Southern adherents to take with bullets the rights they could not win with ballots.

Even this message, sent him by the Adjutant General of the Army at the direct request of President Lincoln, failed to reorient Brigadier General Harney:

The President observes with concern that, notwithstanding the pledge of the State authorities to cooperate in preserving peace in Missouri, loyal citizens, in great numbers, continue to be driven from their homes.

It is immaterial whether these outrages continue through inability or indisposition on the part of the State authorities to prevent them. It is enough that they continue, to devolve on you the duty of putting a stop to them summarily by the force under your command, to be aided by such troops as you may require from Kansas, Iowa and Illinois.

The professions of loyalty to the Union by the State authorities of Missouri are not to be relied upon. They have already falsified their professions too often, and are too far committed to secession to be entitled to your confidence. You can only be sure of their desisting from their wicked purposes when it is out of their power to prosecute them.

You will, therefore, be unceasingly watchful of their movements and not permit the clamor of their partisans (and opponents of the wise measures already taken) to prevent you from checking every movement against the government, however disguised under the pretended State authority. The authority of the United States is paramount. Whenever it is apparent that a movement, whether by color of State authority or not, is hostile, you will not hesitate to put it down.

On the morning of May 30, General Harney found Colonel Blair waiting for him as he entered his office. To the general's gruff greeting, Blair made a soft reply. Then continued:

"I am deeply sorry, General, to come here this morning in an unpleasant but necessary capacity. You and I, and our families, have been friends and neighbors for many years. I cannot help but be mindful of that. At the same time, it is impossible, for men whose lives are at stake, to function under the command of one whose instincts seem to be openly against them. As I hand you these orders from Washington, I want to make it clear that they should not be constructed by you— or by others—to reflect upon your loyalty."

Blair handed the general a sheet of thrice-folded War Department stationery. Slowly, somewhat dazed as realization of what was taking place dawned on him, Harney took the sheet of paper. His hands shook a little and his fingers fumbled a bit as he opened it.

Special Order #135. Brigadier General William S. Harney is hereby relieved of command of the Department of the West and is granted leave of absence until further orders.

Harney stood rooted to the spot, the order dangling from his limp fingers, his eyes gazing vacantly into space. The years seemed to cascade over the gallant old man. They washed away the square set of his shoulders, his military bearing, and the proud tilt of his leonine head. The process of disintegration was almost instantaneous. One moment he had been the Old Man, a fine figure of a veteran soldier with a commanding presence. The next, he was just *an* old man, whose bent shoulders, rounded back, and down-tilted head revealed the burdens of his years. Irresolutely, Harney wondered what to do next. For the first time since he, a young lieutenant, had come to Saint Louis in the early 1820's, he was no longer subject to orders. From now on, his world would be like life on another planet. His active career was a thing of the past, like that morning's sunrise. He was only 61 years old, but at that hour he felt older than God.

If curtains of moisture had misted Colonel Blair's eyes as he turned his back on the pathetic figure presented by General Harney, chances are that they were granite-hard and dry again by the time Blair had finished his summary, in a letter to President Lincoln, of the circumstances that compelled him to execute *Special Order #135.* In fact, he expressed keen regret that he had not delivered it at an earlier date.

At times, he (General Harney) promised me that he would interpose, but afterward would say that there was no occasion for doing anything. I ascribe the conduct of General Harney to the influences by which he is constantly surrounded. His friends and advisers are bitter enemies of the General Government. Some of them pretend to be Unionmen, others are undisguised secessionists. Constantly surrounded by these enemies of the administration, and yielding to the advice and requests of such men, his conduct is such that, under him, the cause of the Union is rapidly sinking, and that of its enemies rapidly attaining power; and I feel, and know, that his removal has become absolutely necessary.

Blair folded and sealed the letter without a twinge of sorrow. Now, once again, the hard-driving and implacable Missouri Yankee—Lyon, whose only creed was human rights, whose only love was the Union created by the Constitution, and whose only aim was to keep Missouri in the ranks of loyal states—was firmly in the saddle. Coming without a hint of warning, Blair knew that Lyon's return to command would carry indescribable consternation into the ranks of the secessionists. They would know that the time for secret and subtle machinations was past. Up to now, under the mask of neutrality, they had worked with noiseless but desperate energy to gain time and to make thorough preparations for resistance to the Union. Only a few weeks more of delay were needed to set the stage for joining the rebellion. Now, with Lyon in command, they would be given neither time nor opportunity to make their plots and hatch them. The speed and determination shown by Lyon in recent encounters warned the rebels either to abandon their schemes, or stand ready to defend them at the risk of their lives.

Chapter 5

"Governor—This Means War!"

———◆———

Many Veterans Among Union Officers

Drill! Drill! Drill! Recruit the regiments to combat strength! And—drill, drill, drill.

Brigadier General Nathaniel Lyon, commanding officer of the First Brigade, Missouri Volunteers, took no outward pleasure—even as he gave no outward sign—in his promotion to one-star rank. He drove his subordinates as rigorously and vigorously as ever. And he showed his disdain for spit-'n'-polish soldiering by continuing to wear his threadbare old uniform coat. When he thought occasion demanded it, Lyon would fasten a brigadier general's gold-fringed epaulets on his shoulders instead of wearing a general's double-breasted coat. Thanks to the masterly job of mustering performed by Lieutenant Schofield, and the alertness of Chester Harding as acting adjutant general, the total strength of the volunteer regiments and those of the reserve corps totaled 10,730 men on June 1 when Lyon took charge of the Department of the West. The rosters of the organizations stood as follows after morning roll call on that date:

First Regiment Volunteers, Colonel F. P. Blair	1,220
Second Regiment Volunteers, Colonel H. Boernstein	1,128
Third Regiment Volunteers, Colonel F. Sigel	1,103
Fourth Regiment Volunteers, Colonel N. Schuettner	1,027
Fifth Regiment Volunteers, Colonel C. E. Salomon	926

(Continued on next page)

Battalion of Artillery, Major Bischoff	253
Company of Pioneers, Captain Voerster	120
First Regiment, U. S. Reserve Corps, Colonel H. Almstedt	1,195
Second Regiment, U. S. Reserve Corps, Colonel H. Kallman	736
Third Regiment, U. S. Reserve Corps, Colonel J. McNeil	839
Fourth Regiment, U. S. Reserve Corps, Colonel B. Gratz Brown	1,169
Fifth Regiment, U. S. Reserve Corps, Colonel C. Stifel	1,014
	10,730

In addition, Lyon had several companies of infantry regulars and recruits as well as Company F, Light Artillery, USA, commanded by Captain James Totten. To build up the quality of the officer corps in the volunteer regiments, Lyon had assigned officers of the regular infantry as captains of volunteer companies. The regulars, meanwhile, were commanded by hard-bitten veteran noncoms. Actually, this was against Army policy which opposed the attrition of career officers into volunteer units.

The problem of finding good officers—in the Federal as well as in the Confederate armies—was perpetual and troublesome. In the early months of the war, both sides were plagued by swarms of inexperienced and inept political hacks, social butterflies, and other self-servers in quest of commissions. Nathaniel Lyon actually struck it rich when he discovered strong traces of previous military and combat experience among his officers and men. Even his regimental commanders were no armchair soldiers. Frank Blair, out of a sense of modesty, had enlisted and served as a private in the Mexican War until he won a battlefield promotion. In the Civil War, he became a major general commanding an Army corps. Colonel Boernstein had had a military education in his native Austria and had seen active service in the 1848 revolution. Colonel Sigel, small and chipper as a sparrow, was an expert artillerist and had served as Commanding Officer of Baden in the '48 revolt. Now, at 37, he was principal of the German

Institute of Saint Louis. In 1862, Sigel was a victor at Pea Ridge. Before the war ended, he was a major general, outstanding at times.

Nicholas Schuettner, contractor and builder, not only had seen service in the 1848 uprising, but had also been the main spirit in organizing the military structure of the Saint Louis *Schwarze Jaeger Schuetzenverein*. Lastly, Colonel Salomon of the Fifth was also one of the fighting patriots who had fled to this country when the Prussians took over.

In organizing his personal staff, General Lyon promoted Lieutenant Schofield to a majority and made him Chief of Staff. It had not taken the keen-eyed Yankee long to see that in Schofield he had the services of a brilliant military mind. The latter was graduated from West Point in 1853 but, after a few years of active service, resigned because "there was no expectation of a captaincy within the lifetime of an ordinary man." In time, Schofield was to become a brigadier general, major general and, lastly, lieutenant general, commanding the Armies of the United States. In his book *Forty-Six Years in the Army,* Schofield marveled at Lyon's deep knowledge of the details of every job he undertook to handle. Wrote Schofield:

Lyon was a man of ability and scholarly attainments, an earnest student, keenly alive to the nature and magnitude of the struggle in which the country was about to engage and eager to take the initiative as soon as he had at his command sufficient force to give promise of success. . . . Subsequent events showed how elusive was the hope of averting hostilities in any of the Border States and how fortunate it was that active measures were adopted at once.

Other members of Lyon's staff were: Major Samuel Simmons, Ast. S/C; Major Horace A. Conant, secretary; Lieutenant Colonel Chester Harding, Jr., Acting Adjutant General; Major Chauncey P. Johnson, paymaster; and Major Bernard G. Farrar, aide-de-camp. With the exception of Schofield, none of these staff officers had previous military training. These ap-

pointments were thoroughly indicative of Lyon's way of thinking. He did not feel that he could afford to spare experienced
soldiers for mere staff work when they were so badly needed
on the drill ground.

While Lyon had over-all command over volunteers and
Home Guards, he passed command of the five Saint Louis
Home Guard Regiments to Captain Thomas L. Sweeny—the
breezy but go-getting Irishman of the regular infantry—with
the rank of brigadier general. Originally the commission had
the approval of General Harney who, it was discovered later,
had failed to forward it to Washington for final acceptance.
Sweeny, lusting for a fight, had come to America at the outbreak of the war with Mexico. He served as captain of a company of New York Irish volunteers. At the end of that war,
he entered the Regular Army. Not being a West Pointer,
Sweeny's promotion had been more than usually slow. The
recognition extended him by Lyon lit fires of enthusiasm in
Sweeny's loyal heart. Had he had two arms, the gigantic Irishman would have given the diminutive Yankee a rib-cracking
squeeze. But since he had lost his right arm, from the elbow
down, in Mexico, Sweeny merely saluted with his stump and
expressed his appreciation with a glint of savage joy in his
gray-green eyes.

Lyon knew that Major General Price would have much
greater training problems than his own by virtue of the raw-
ness of his recruits. On the other hand, he realized that Price
could count on a formidable number of sure-shot marksmen.
Largely pioneers who grew up dependent on their sharpshoot-
ing skills, they were completely familiar with the use of firearms for fight or survival. They might know no more than
Sioux about small-arms drill or military formations, but they
were of the breed that would fight with cold and telling feroc-
ity when bugle calls for combat sounded. In an effort to even
the odds, Volunteers and Home Guards were taught to make
lesser targets of themselves by stretching flat on the ground
and instructed in how to load and fire from a prone position.

This, a time-honored practice among Indian fighters, took some learning on the part of awkward and bored recruits who became weary unto death of the ceaseless commands:

"Load! Aim! (Aim for their knees! Then you're sure to hit them in their bellies!) Fire! (Damn it all! Don't yank those triggers off. Squeeze them, damn you! Squeeze them!)"

Drill! Drill! Drill!

"Forward h-u-u-u-P!"

Four abreast, the men—sweating under the merciless June sun—would move forward in full field gear: a gun that weighed nine pounds; 40 rounds of ammunition and 50 percussion caps in their respective boxes—four pounds or more; belt, bayonet, and scabbard—two pounds; one day's rations and haversack—three and a half pounds. Blanket roll—three pounds. Add it all up and a soldier—besides the clothes he stood in and the fears and wonders that weighed on his mind—lugged a total of at least 22½ pounds. Not for an hour or two. But all day, day after day.

Drill! Drill! Drill!

"Trail arms on the double—h-u-u-u-P!"

(Mind your steps, soldier. That double-quick is tricky and the men around you could trip over the dragging butt of your rifle.)

"Watch out, you clodhopper. Twenty-eight inches to the step. Count 'em, damn you! Exactly 165 steps to the minute. Not one more. Not one less."

Powder, cartridge paper, and shot being scarce, there was very little target practice. Just enough to give the men a superficial knowledge of their guns. But not enough to build up easy familiarity. The cartridges were cylinders of thick gray paper that contained charges of coarse black gunpowder and one 1-ounce Minié bullet or buck and ball (one largish ball and several buckshot). The trick for the novice to learn was how to rip the bottom of the cartridge open with his teeth as part of a fluid movement from the cartridge box to the muzzle of his gun.

"Don't take all day chewing that cartridge! What d'you think it is—terbaccy? Bite that paper off. And don't spit it out, rookie! No time for that. Swaller it, damn you, swaller it!"

By order of Lyon, heavy punishments were not dealt out to the volunteers unless they were guilty of grave misconduct. In those days, the Regular Army handed out swift and brutal penalties for the smallest infractions of rules. Most common among these were the lash or a 12-pounder iron ball fastened to a leg by a chain so short that a man, to carry it, would have to bend double in order to walk. Other men were hog-tied and left for hours on the ground; still others had their hands chained to their sides and sugar syrup smeared into their hair; unable to drive flies and other insects off, they suffered the tortures of the damned as, at bayonet points, they were marched up and down the parade.

Whenever Captain Totten was putting Company F, Light Artillery, through its paces—and every section was an expert drill team—there was always an audience. Captain Totten not only was one of Uncle Sam's best artillery men, but his manner of handling his guns by the battery, by the section, or by the piece was inspiring as well as entertaining.

From his stiffly held position in the expensive saddle on his magnificent horse, Captain Totten—his breath rich with old brandy, his voice bland and yet robust with the tone of command—would issue his orders to Lieutenant Immels:

"Take that limber to the rear, God damn you, sir!"

"Bring that piece to bear, God damn you, sir!"

"Limber and get to hell out here, God damn you, sir!"

As the battery limbered up and the horses leaned into their harness at the urgings of their respective mounted cannoneers, elegantly lean Captain Totten would sound off with a deep cough. With an air of great deliberation, he would unscrew the cap of his canteen, lift it to his lips, and take an exploratory sip. Finding the stuff to his liking, the captain would take a generous swallow, recap the container, and set off after his battery with an air of complete satisfaction. And why not?

His was the best battery in the Army and his canteen held the best brandy in the world. Totten served with distinction as a brigadier general during the Civil War and received no less than four brevets. But brandy became such an overriding urge with him that General Grant, of all people, had to dismiss him from the service in 1870.

The organization headed by General Lyon had no cavalry which admittedly was a handicap. One could take it for granted that most of Price's State Guard would be made up of mounted riflemen. This was because the average resident of rural Missouri—and he would, by far, provide the majority of Price's men—felt naked and helpless without his horse. The only mounted men in Lyon's outfit were the Company A Cavalry of 20 men in the First Regiment, U. S. Reserve Corps. They wore pearl-gray uniforms and huge white hats. To a man, they were blond, beef-complexioned, barrel-chested German brewers who sat their heavy mounts proudly in Fourth of July parades, political campaign spectacles, and other events that called for public displays and the oompah-oompah of bands. Company A served Lyon as a mounted guard, couriers, and orderlies. Lyon's personal orderly, Albert Lehman, was a lance-corporal in the outfit.

In order to accommodate his expanding command—some of which were housed at Jackson Barracks, ten miles south of Saint Louis, and in buildings near the Arsenal—the larger structures in the Arsenal were turned into barracks for volunteer regiments. Quarters for officers were built on unoccupied ground within the Arsenal enclosure. Companies of the Home Guard, sworn into the U. S. Reserve Corps, remained at their own homes and left their muskets in gunracks at their respective headquarters where detachments were always on duty. They had daily roll calls with occasional dress parades. These latter did not appear too impressive as individual Home Guard members provided their own uniforms—blue jeans and dark-blue woolen shirts. On Sundays, their officers, instead of engaging in Bible reading, studied Hardee's Tactics and Scott's little brown Field Manual prior to attending Arsenal drill schools for officers and noncoms. Many of the companies were so completely German that officers and noncoms, at the start anyway, had to learn how to issue their orders in both languages. Others had accents so thick that they could be sliced with a bread knife. Yet some of these officers showed such military aptitude that they went on to become generals in the Union Army. As the lessons took hold, the Home Guard gradually was transformed into a highly presentable military organization. Guardsmen received neither pay nor subsistence allowances and very little credit.

During June, the Federal Government sent 10,000 rifles and muskets, with sets of accouterments, for distribution among the loyal inhabitants of Missouri. After General Harney stepped aside, more than 200 companies, with a total enlistment of 17,000 Home Guards, were formed in all sections of the State. They took firm root and played important roles in suppressing bushwackers, guerrilla bands, and other marauders. This influx of antisecession weapons compelled Major General Price to issue a proclamation to his subordinate brigadier generals in which he expressed the opinion that Brigadier General Lyon should feel himself honor bound to respect the so-called Harney-Price agreement.

Meanwhile, military activities to the south of Missouri began to assume shape and purpose. Toward the end of May, Brigadier General Ben McCulloch—famous Texas Ranger and one-time California lawman—established himself at Fort Smith, Arkansas, with a Confederate Army made up of regiments from Louisiana, Arkansas, and Texas. His orders had been to "guard" Indian territory against Federal "invasion." However, the Indians did not want his protection and instructed him to get off the reservation. In northern Arkansas, the secessionist Army of Arkansas—some 2,200 men strong under Brigadier General Nicholas B. Pearce (West Point, 1850)—marked time to repel invasion from the north by Lyon. Pearce and

McCulloch were under explicit orders not to take the offensive into Missouri.

Naturally, the spring air of Missouri was thick as fog with all sorts of conflicting rumors. It was reported that Governor Jackson had taken $50,000 out of his treasury to enlist the aid of 15,000 armed Indians. Simultaneously there was talk that the Lincoln Administration would release an avalanche of Negro troops on Missouri. Lurid pictures of what such an invasion would mean to the unprotected white population were drawn by slavery proponents who, beneath their blusterings, were no little afraid of the shackled giant they had created. One did not know what to believe, but virtually everyone wanted to believe something. And strangely enough, the wilder and more preposterous the rumors were, the more credence they were given. At that particular period, there was a decided undersupply of skepticism in the Show-Me State.

Driven by common fears, the peace-at-any-price Conditional Union Democrats and Unconditional Union Republicans had joined causes again, although they at no time had been very far apart. They had lost out on Harney, to be sure. But with a little luck and delay, they might be able to continue the status quo long enough to send Lyon packing. Up in Jefferson City, the Governor and his general knew that almost any day now young Captain Colton Greene, of the defunct Missouri National Guard, should arrive in Fort Smith, Arkansas, to plead with Ben McCulloch to march north with his Confederate Army and invade Missouri. Greene's orders were to proceed from Fort Smith to Little Rock and make similar requests of the State's secessionist Governor with respect to the well-equipped Arkansas State Militia.

With Colton Greene's mission in mind and feeling certain of its success, Jackson and Price were eager for any kind of delay until McCulloch and Pearce came marching north. Therefore, with Judge William A. Hall and T. T. Gantt acting

105

as intermediaries, the duo made overtures early in June for a conference with Lyon. The meeting was to be held in Saint Louis. The State's side would be represented by Governor Jackson, Major General Price, and Colonel Thomas L. Snead, now acting adjutant general of the Missouri State Guard. On June 8, Lyon accepted. Although no order of arrest had been issued against any of the three, Lyon's state of mind as regards their "neutral" position was plainly shown by an order that accompanied his letter. It guaranteed the trio from arrest "on their journey to and from the city and during their sojourn here up and to midnight on June 12th, 1861." The Unionists would be represented at the conference by Brigadier General Lyon, Colonel Blair, and Major Conant.

A Smoke-Filled Room in the Planter's House

On the morning of June 11, aboard a "palace car" drawn by a locomotive, the Jackson Mission reached Saint Louis. The three States' Rights spokesmen were met by a large but undemonstrative delegation. They were escorted to the Planter's House and ensconced in this splendid hotel's most luxurious suite. Word was sent to Brigadier General Lyon at the Arsenal of their arrival. The New Englander immediately dispatched a courteous note. It informed the Governor that the writer would send a carriage to the hotel to take them to the Arsenal for the meeting. None too cordially, the Governor exploded that he would be damned if he would be pulled about like a bull with a ring through its nose. He had come all the way from Jefferson City to see the general. And now, by the toe of the Prophet, Lyon could journey the rest of the way to the Planter's House and meet him.

In order to give the Governor and his party time to enjoy their breakfast, Lyon, Blair, and Conant did not appear at the hotel until about 11 o'clock. By then, the news of the conference had become known far and wide throughout Saint Louis. A great crowd had gathered on Fourth Street in front of the hotel. Even the surrounding side streets were thronged.

(*Left*) Brigadier General Nathaniel Lyon, U.S.A.

(*Right*) Major General Francis Preston Blair, U.S.A., Late in Life

(*Left*) Claiborne Fox Jackson, Secession-Minded Governor of Missouri

(*Right*) Major General Sterling Price, C.S.A., Commander of the (Secessionist) Missouri State Guard

(*Photos courtesy State Historical Society of Missouri*)

OPPONENTS IN MISSOURI, 1861

Major General John C. Frémont, U.S.A.
"The Great Pathfinder"

Lieutenant-General John M. Schofield, U.S.A.,
as a Major General

Major General Francis (Franz) Sigel, U.S.A.

Brigadier General Nicholas Pearce, C.S.A., commanding the
Army of Arkansas, Who Fought at Wilson's Creek

BATTLE OF WILSONS CREEK

Artist's concept of Wilson's Creek, which, although mistaken in many details, does show at close quarters the fighting of the Artillery

DEATH OF GENERAL LYON.

at the head of his troops while successfully charging the rebel forces, at the Battle of Wilsons Creek, Missouri, Aug. 10th 1861.

Currier and Ives at their worst. Incredibly inaccurate version of General Lyon's death

An unknown artist depicts Schofield holding Lyon's body, unfortunately not true. Lyon's orderly, Lehman, leans on his musket, but was a cavalryman, and had none

But, unlike the mobs that had screamed curses on those very spots only a few weeks earlier, the men who gathered there that day stood, for the most part, silently waiting. The volatile elements that had driven Saint Louisans to such frenzied fury in the days of the taking of Camp Jackson evidently had taken a back seat and did no driving.

On this occasion, Lyon had pushed personal preferences aside and put on the double-breasted uniform coat of a brigadier general with its twin rows of gilded buttons divided into groups of two. The garment's high and close-fitting collar was topped by a rim of stiffly starched linen. Gold-trimmed and gold-fringed epaulets rode on his shoulders, each with the single gold star of his rank. While he wore a yellow silk sash around his waist and a dress belt, the sword that hung on his left side was the same old dragoon blade encased in a worn and dented metal scabbard. For the occasion, his trousers were free from wrinkles and his usually scuffed boots had been made to shine by Al Lehman. For once, in all the years that had passed since Lyon first set out on the one long warpath that was to be his entire life, he did not dress with the real or pretended indifference to military protocol of the veteran Indian fighter.

Blair, who was both a member of Congress and the colonel of a regiment in Federal service, was dressed in his usual garb of compromise. His civilian and political status was revealed from his neck down by a handsomely fitted black broadcloth coat, dark-gray trousers, gaily embroidered vest, frilly shirt and a wide, black silk bow tie, the badge of any member of the halls of Congress. His only military identification was a garrison cap with its U. S. infantry insignia embroidered in gold. At this time of his life, Frank Blair did not wear a beard. But he sported full and sweeping mustaches that would have brought a flush of pride to the cheeks of any cavalry colonel. His brownish hair was neatly trimmed, except in front; it swept in a heavy flow across his forehead and stopped just short of his right eye. Blair was a man of intense views. He

107

possessed an impulsive, often violent, energy in promoting them. He was pleasantly passive when in repose, but a hawk-like, predatory look blazed into his eye when he crashed into an argument. As his brother, "Judge" Montgomery, so often said with a quiet smile: "When Frank goes in for a fight, he generally goes in for a funeral." And, in his mind, the fight Frank Blair had lined up against Frost, Jackson, and Price was truly tantamount to a funeral. To him, Frost was already among the living dead. Soon, so swore Blair, Jackson and Price would see black corteges strung out behind their political coffins.

Jackson and Snead were in civilian clothes. The former, to suit the mood of the occasion, wore the mournful look of a Hamlet about to burst into his soliloquy. Colonel Snead, a cadaverous-looking man of uncertain years, had been a reporter, editor, and pamphleteer. He was to become a member of the Confederate Congress and a Civil War historian whose contributions were masterpieces of completely objective writing. One might say that Truth was Snead's only real hero. In his three books about the War Between the States, Thomas L. Snead wrote without malice, bias, or favor although he was wholeheartedly with the South.

General Price, an accomplished gentleman of the old school, with dignity of bearing, speech, and manners, was attired in his cavalry general's uniform of Mexican War vintage—cocked and plumed hat, curved sword, and tall boots that shone like jet mirrors. To be sure, Major General Price had a brand-new State Guard uniform which by some peculiar coincidence was Confederate gray. However, in view of the loudly proclaimed "neutrality" of the Jackson administration, General Price deemed this garment inappropriate for the occasion. And yet, so far as Lyon and his two companions were concerned, the visitors from Jefferson City might as well have worn Confederate uniforms. They knew, for a certainty, that the three of them had Confederate points of view and that the meeting was held to hoodwink Lyon into consenting to a delaying action that would benefit the secessionists.

The Planter's House conference settled down to its task around a large oval mahogany table in the overstuffed, overdraped, and overly opulent parlor of the suite. Through the open windows, the rising and falling murmur of many voices came and went like the sound of a distant surf. As time went on, despite the wide-flung balcony windows, the room became thick with the smoke of many cigars and opaque with the smog of heated arguments.

At the outset, General Lyon said that he was present as an observer and that Colonel Blair would do the talking for the Federal side. But, as the argument rolled on from a low opening to a gradually higher and higher throttle setting, the argumentative and highly partisan Yankee could not hold his tongue in check. He entered into the discussion with such fervor that, in time, he had both Blair and Conant relegated to the positions of listeners.

The combatants squared off after Governor Jackson had set the premises for the discussion with a rather comprehensive, yet very much to the point, opening statement. As released much later to the press, this is a summary of his remarks:

I said that I would disband the State Guard, and break up its organization; that I would disarm all the companies which had been armed by the State; that I would pledge myself not to attempt to organize the militia under the Military Bill; that no arms or munitions of war should be brought into the State; that I would protect all citizens equally in all their rights, regardless of their political opinions; that I would suppress all insurrectionary movements within the State.

I said that I would repel all attempts to invade the State from whatever quarter, and by whom so ever made; and that I would thus maintain a strict neutrality in the present unhappy contest and preserve the peace of the State.

109

I further proposed that I would, if necessary, invoke the assistance of United States troops to carry out these pledges. All this I proposed to do upon condition that the Federal Government would undertake to disarm the Home Guards which it has illegally organized and armed throughout the State and pledge itself not to occupy with its troops any localities in the State not occupied by them at this time.

Major General Price added that this was in perfect harmony with the concepts held by Brigadier General Harney and himself in the execution of their agreement; he saw no reason why this understanding, if it were acceptable to Harney, should not be acceptable to Lyon.

Up to this point, Colonel Blair had been running but slight interference with the Governor's remarks and hardly any with those presented by General Price.

Then Lyon burst forth with the penetrating sharpness of a rocket's flare on a starless night.

How, he wanted to know, would the Governor be able to protect the rights of citizens without a State Guard when he could not even protect them with a State Guard?

By what miracle, he asked, could the Governor suppress insurrectionary movements within the State when the woods were full of bushwackers and the State was doing its utmost to obtain arms and munitions from the South to replace the war stores stolen at Baton Rouge but confiscated at Camp Jackson?

How could the Governor prove, once the Home Guards had been disarmed, that he would insure the protection of loyal citizens by calling in the limited contingents of Federal troops stationed in Saint Louis, troops that would have no power to move anywhere in the State without his absolute direction and consent?

To sum it up, asked the flat-voiced little Yankee, how could Jackson expect to maintain peace in the State through the unique procedure of disarming and disbanding all military forces and in that manner repress disorder, punish violence, and repel invasion?

It was a head-on clash that narrowed down to the irreducible arguments of States' rights as opposed to Federal supremacy. Hours dragged by without the discovery of the smallest point of arbitration between the opposing parties. Lyon stoutly maintained that, with the fate of loyal citizens in the balance, the Federal Government would be neither able nor willing to shrink from its duties nor abdicate its rights. It was free-soil and slave-soil all over again. As the arguments rolled back and forth, Lyon recalled that Jackson was the man who had led thousands of gun-toting, ballot-stuffing Border Ruffians from Missouri into Kansas and who started the flow of blood in 1854. The same Jackson, who in 1861, had conspired with Frost to seize the Arsenal and snare Missouri out of the Union. He determined not to yield an inch to this man whom he considered one of the arch-enemies of human rights and his determination made him eloquent.

In an interview given to a reporter of a Cincinnati newspaper in 1877, Thomas Snead made several revealing observations. Among other things, it showed how he—a rabid pro-slavery secessionist—had been swayed and impressed by Nathaniel Lyon during that Planter's House meeting. In part, he said:

Lyon was the greatest man I ever saw. That has been my statement everywhere. I felt it and said it the day we held that memorable interview with him at the Planter's House in Saint Louis.

He was Jefferson Davis all over again, but not as narrow and prejudiced as Davis. He was like Davis, however, in his intensity and tenacity and about of the stature and leanness of Davis. We were to hold that interview in order to see if war could be prevented. I am the only survivor of it. Claiborne Jackson and Sterling Price were the ablest politicians of Missouri; Price had become the head of the State's Democratic Party after the death of Senator Benton.

Lyon came there with Frank Blair and Major Conant. Price was

111

a successful military officer and Major General in the War with Mexico. Lyon was nothing but a little captain of the infantry but such was his clearness, force and real genius, that he met those old politicians on every point, conceding nothing but never discourteous —his reason and his will equal.

The whole party felt him to be the master mind, and Federal historians do not err when they put him down as the greatest man the North produced—greater than any produced on both sides— west of the Mississippi River.

Lyon advanced into that room, a small, red-bearded, red-haired, precise, positive, plain man. He sat down and crossed one leg over the other stiffly, and his face was serious and stern. He spoke each word separate from the other, pronouncing the little words as *my* and *to* with as much emphasis as the longer words. Occasionally, he raised his right hand automatically as the conversation proceeded, and brought it down with a jerk, with forefinger extended, yet never speaking in higher or lower tones than at first. We felt the sense of war and government in all his bearing.

The meeting ran its predestined course the way an hour-glass comes to a stop when its upper half runs out of sand and there is no hand to turn it. When spoken words began to drag on faltering tongues, Governor Jackson sought to gain more time. He proposed to continue the discussion through correspondence. To this General Lyon replied that their views were too far apart and that correspondence would lead them nowhere. He proposed that each one should then and there put down his view and that they should be given to the press. Jackson would not accept that arrangement.

With every possible argument swept from the table and compromise of any sort beyond reach, Lyon pulled slowly on his cigar. Next, he watched intently as the fire burned the brown leaf into ashes. Then, with an air of finality, he placed the cigar on a tray that stood before him, leaned toward Jackson and said:

"Governor, no man in the State of Missouri has been more ardent in his desire to preserve peace than myself. Let me

112

say this: Heretofore, Missouri has only felt the fostering care of the Federal Government, which has raised her from the condition of a feeble French colony to that of an Empire State. Now, however, from the failure on the part of the Chief Executive to comply with constitutional requirements, I fear she will be made to feel its power."

He spoke deliberately, almost painfully, slowly. He spoke with the air of one who was eager to imprint the weight of what he was saying on the minds of his listeners. He rose with a light feline motion. Following a brief pause, he continued:

"Rather than concede to the State of Missouri the right to demand that my Government shall not enlist troops within her limits, or bring troops into the State whenever it pleases, or move its troops at its own will into, out of, or through the State; rather than concede to the State of Missouri for one single instant the right to dictate to my Government in any matter however unimportant, I would,"—he stood straight with squared shoulders, and looked unexpectedly tall as he said this. Pointing, in turn, to everyone in the room, he concluded —"see *you,* and *you,* and *you,* and *you,* and *you,* and every man, woman and child in the State dead and buried."

To this man who had no creed above that of human rights, no love greater than his love of country, it was inconceivable to compromise with those who would destroy those rights and the Union who was their sword and buckler. To save the nation from such a calamity was worth the greatest sacrifices.

Then, so that each word fell separately like leaden pellets in a shot tower, he spoke four words:

"Governor, this means war!"

Lyon took out his watch stiffly. As he glanced at it, his facial muscles turned into hard knots; his eyes were steely with determination. However, his voice was almost conversationally even as he said:

"It is now 3 o'clock, gentlemen. You shall have safe conduct out of my lines for one hour. Meanwhile, you can get your dinner. I trust you'll enjoy it and regret that I can no longer break bread with you."

With that, and without farewells, he about-faced and closed the door softly behind him. The five men left in the room had been in opposing political camps over the years, but never personal enemies. Now Blair and Conant rose as Jackson, Price, and Snead came to their feet. The former shook hands with the latter as they parted.

Thus, General Lyon—whose single, undeviating aim was to keep the State in the Union whatever the cost—brought the Civil War to Missouri.

Chapter 6

War Comes to Missouri

Lyon Plans a Pincer Movement

On his return to the Arsenal, Brigadier General Lyon called a high-echelon staff meeting which included all regimental commanders of volunteers. His strategic plan—conceived with the aid of Colonel Blair and Major Schofield, plus the invaluable assistance of Congressman John S. Phelps of Springfield, a hard-rock Unconditional Unionman—already had been drawn. Now, all that remained was its tactical execution.

This plan fell into two major movements. Provided, of course, that all went as expected. If the enemy reacted as was hoped, the two movements would develop into the arms of a pair of sharply pronged pincers.

One of the movements would be the sending of troops into the southwestern section of the State to block ingress and egress between western Missouri and Arkansas. Thus the chances of Confederate troops marching into Missouri—or of shipments of arms and ammunition into the State from Arkansas—would be minimized. At the same time, avenues would be blocked for groups of Missouri rebels to effect a junction with Southern troops below the Arkansas–Missouri border. For easy identification, this arm of the pincer could be called the Southwestern Column.

The second movement was based on the belief that the Missouri State Guard would not be able to hold Jefferson City and might not even attempt to defend it. Moving along

115

the Missouri River toward Kansas, Lyon's Army of the West (as it came to be called) would have a twofold purpose:

First, to sweep rebel troops from Jefferson City to the westward until the enemy broke for the south. There might be resistance on the south bank of the Osage River near Warsaw or Osceola, en route to a rendezvous with Confederates in or below the southwestern corner of the State.

Second, to control all traffic on the Missouri River by waterborne and shore patrols. This would make it impossible for the strongly secessionist counties of northern Missouri to send their quickly swelling ranks of State Guard companies across the river to join their hard-pressed comrades to the south. Below the Osage, the pincers would close when Lyon's Army of the West and the Southwestern Column met and held the State forces between them.

Before the conference started, Lyon sent a telegram to the War Department. He reported the outbreak of war in Missouri, asked for permission to recruit an unnamed number of troops, and requested 5,000 additional rifles and muskets with proportionate amounts of other war supplies. Finally, he sought power to draw upon the Governors of Illinois, Kansas, and Iowa for troops to protect the highly essential and very vulnerable railroad systems in northern Missouri. The requests were granted by return wire. Among Illinois regiments that were to take up service in northern Missouri was Grant's 21st Volunteers.

Lyon's Southwestern Column would include both Volunteers and Home Guards and was to be commanded by Brigadier General Thomas W. Sweeny. This handy arrangement insured a seasoned regular at the head of the entire organization. That very afternoon (June 11, 1861), the first contingent —the Right Battalion of Sigel's Third Regiment Volunteers— entrained under the command of Lieutenant Colonel Francis A. Hassendeubel.

While Hassendeubel's slow accommodation train poked its way toward Rolla, Governor Jackson's special "palace car" arrived at Jefferson City way past midnight on June 12, due to operational delays despite right-of-way clearances. But even so, time sped quickly aboard the special. Plans were discussed and adopted. And each of the trio was assigned his task.

The Governor was to go directly to the Executive Chamber and write a proclamation that called upon 50,000 true Missourians to enlist under the colors of the State.

Colonel Snead was to locate the various State officials, inform them that Missouri was at war and that they were to pack at once all valuable State papers and public records so that they might be shipped to Boonville. Also, they were to be ready to leave Jefferson City with the Governor for that destination at the break of day.

Lastly, Major General Price had three missions. First, he was to send the redoubtable Captain Kelly with a well-supplied detachment of men by locomotive down the railroad tracks to destroy, with torch and gunpowder, the Gasconade and Osage bridges. Also, the telegraph wires to Saint Louis were to be cut at liberal intervals.

Orders went to Brigadier General Monroe M. Parsons at Tipton, to the west of Jefferson City, to march north to bolster the defense of Boonville. Lastly, all rolling stock in the Jefferson City railroad yards was to be moved to the western end of rail at Sedalia. All bridges were to be burned and telegraph wires cut by a platoon of State Guards aboard the last westbound train.

John S. Marmaduke, now colonel of the First Regiment of State Guard Rifles, was strongly opposed to making a stand at Boonville. His trained military mind saw, as Nathaniel Lyon's had seen, that the logical place for the State Guard to make a stand would be somewhere between Warsaw and Osceola on the Osage River. This great waterway comes into being in eastern Kansas and wriggles east-northeast in a snakelike pattern through Missouri until it enters the Missouri River some distance east of Jefferson City. Sensing disaster ahead, the one-time West Pointer laid the matter before his uncle, the Governor. The latter explained that the reason for making a stand at Boonville was his firm belief that an army could be concentrated, under its protecting shield, at Lexington from the highly populous and strongly pro-Southern counties of western and northern Missouri. He further reminded his nephew that Brigadier General Parsons would even now be making ready to march to Boonville and that Brigadier General John B. Clark already had reached the town with some 1,500 men from northern Missouri. To this, Marmaduke drily replied that, from what he heard, they were mostly youngsters and poorly armed. Many with no arms at all. All of them wholly untrained for front-line duty. The young man ended by saying that if he got out of Boonville alive and kicking, he would offer his services to the Confederate Army. In parenthesis, it may be noted that this is what he did. Marmaduke emerged from the Civil War a major general with an outstanding record for military acumen and soldierly courage.

However, there was a measure of good sense in Jackson's attitude as regards Boonville. If Lyon were given full possession of the Missouri River's south bank, he could choke off the flow of volunteers who could be counted on from the northern tier of counties. Missouri, even then, was a large state. Its 1860 census showed about 236,000 men of military age. If only 25 per cent responded, they would more than fill the 50,000 quota to be asked for. Jackson figured that in the big slaveholding northern counties (they held about 50 per cent of the State's slave population) there would be enough hot-blooded country lads who would seek to quell their thirst for adventure in the rigors of camp life and the grim demands of battle. He also had a hunch that, because disloyalty had gone unpunished for months on end, these youths had developed a contempt for the fighting capacity of Union men. ("Shucks, one secesh could lick five Dutchmen with one hand tied behind his back!") Lastly, the sights and sounds of spreading violence could have served to whet their youthful appetites for the even greater excitement of war. To Jackson, it was the rekindling on a larger scale of the fires and furies of the Border Ruffian days. He knew that the counties along the Missouri–Kansas border had suffered from the incursions of Jayhawkers and other abolitionist raiders. Hate and the urge for revenge were eloquent recruiting factors. On the subject of 236,000 men of military age in 1860, it is interesting to recall that before the Civil War ended about 110,000 Missourians had volunteered for service in the Union Army and some 40,000 for the Confederacy.

Jackson's proclamation—calling upon 50,000 brave-hearted Missourians to rise and drive out the "invaders"—was off the press on the morning of June 12. When it had been placed into channels of circulation, the Governor joined his fellow State officials, Major General Price and Colonel Marmaduke's First Regiment of Rifles aboard the steamer *White Cloud*. They reached Boonville the next morning after an all-night layover. Price, ill with dysentery, continued westward to his Chariton County home.

Union Forces Launch an "Invasion"

Just about the time the *White Cloud* made fast at Boonville, on the morning of June 13, four steamboats were making ready for departure; the *Iatan,* the *J. C. Swon,* now a Union ship, the *Louisiana,* and the *McDowell.* During the two days that had passed since the Planter's House conference, Lyon had equipped and organized his expeditionary forces. Aware that the railroad bridges had been destroyed, he had been compelled to place dependence on the slower river craft. He also knew that they were highly vulnerable. It was easy for shore-placed marksmen to take potshots at vessels moving upcurrent at slow speeds in dangerous waters. As a measure of protection for pilots, Lyon had ordered boiler plate to be installed shoulder-high around the wheelhouses of the ships.

119

The *Iatan* left at 11 o'clock that morning with part of the First Regiment Missouri Volunteers, commanded by Lieutenant Colonel George L. Andrews, one company of regulars, and a two-gun section of Totten's battery.

The *J. C. Swon* sailed at 2 o'clock in the afternoon with General Lyon and his staff, Colonel Blair and the remainder of the First Regiment Missouri Volunteers, two companies of regular recruits, also commanded by sergeants, and one two-gun section of Company F, Light Artillery, under Captain Totten.

The *McDowell* carried Colonel Boernstein and his Second Regiment of Missouri Volunteers, plus a third two-gun section of Totten's Battery and Captain Voerster's Company of Pioneers (Engineers). This vessel also served as an escort to the *Louisiana* which was slowed by a cargo of supplies that loaded her almost to the swamping point. All in all, Lyon's forces comprised about 2,000 men.

As crowds cheered from the levee and the United States flag whipped in the breeze from housetops, windows, and the masts of moored river vessels—whose whistles hooted their strident farewells—the ships of the Army of the West pushed northward on the Mississippi to the point where the muddy waters of the Missouri run into the yellow current of the Mississippi.

The Southwestern Column to Springfield

A few hours after the departure of the four steamers, the Left Battalion of the Third Regiment Volunteers, band playing and flags held high, marched out of the Saint Louis Arsenal under the command of Colonel Sigel. On the heels of the snappily swinging infantry came the rumbling guns and caissons of Major Bischoff's six-gun light artillery and closed with two Volunteer Rifle companies commanded by Captain A. Albert and Captain Joseph Conrad, respectively. They were bound for Rolla by rail, thence Springfield by road.

On the 15th, the last contingent of the Southwestern Column entrained from Saint Louis under the leadership of Colonel Salomon. They included Salomon's Fifth Regiment Volunteers, Colonel Gratz Brown's Fourth Regiment Home Guard and Colonel McNeil's Third Regiment Home Guard. The Home Guards were mainly to patrol railroads and maintain the safety of the Rolla-Springfield road against guerrilla attack. When watchful and jittery peace-at-any-price conservatives in Saint Louis learned that Home Guards were sent away on military duty after Brigadier General Harney had been informed that he had no power to send them out of town, many tore at their hair and whiskers. They had been hoodwinked, they howled. Harney had been bilked. But their bayings subsided when they learned that all five Home Guard regiments had voted unanimously to serve wherever they might be needed.

For the first time in months, the Arsenal no longer boiled and bubbled with masses of marching, countermarching, and skirmishing men. The shouts of command had faded into comparative silence. All the work and planning crammed into a few weeks, in order that the Federal Government might keep Missouri in the Union, had been done. Soon the labors of Lyon, Blair, and countless others were to be submitted to the acid test of action.

Left in the Arsenal—besides the few remaining troops and the organizing Seventh Regiment Volunteers under Colonel John D. Stevenson—were Brigadier General Thomas Sweeny of the Home Guard and Lieutenant Colonel Chester Harding. In the hands of the latter, as acting adjutant general, had been entrusted the complicated liaison duties that in a few weeks were to become an almost paralyzing burden of frustrating responsibilities. Harding was an energetic and resourceful young lawyer. He knew nothing of high-echelon army work, but he was an apt student.

As for Thomas Sweeny, who had command of the entire Southwestern Column, he did not head for Springfield until well toward the end of June. Tremendous logistic problems had to be solved in Saint Louis to insure a steady flow of matériel, supplies, provisions, and other stores from Saint Louis to Springfield. The travel by rail from Saint Louis to Rolla was easy enough once the mountain ranges of goods were gathered, and mountains they were. Lyon, when he left the Missouri and headed south along the State's western border, on the heels of the secessionists, would have to travel too light and too fast to be burdened with more than he needed.

For those reasons, long-range wants would have to be provided for in Springfield. And the 120-mile stretch between the end of rail at Rolla and the thriving city of Springfield was not worthy of being called a road. It was, rather, a worn, rutty, and rocky trail where horses had to lean hard into their collars to make the wagons roll; where teamsters, time and again, had to lighten loads in order to raise their wheels out of hub-deep depressions.

But, backbreaking as this distance was, no army could travel it unless it brought along its own transport wagons, mules, oxen, or heavy draft horses, and teamsters. There were not enough wheels or hoofs to be requisitioned in either Rolla or Springfield to haul a single infantry company's requirements for one week. This had been the firm and excellent warning voiced by Congressman Phelps. Therefore, Sweeny, first with the aid of Sigel, then Salomon, had had to explore every possible source in and around Saint Louis to round up supplies, drivers, animals, and wagons. He succeeded because he knew he had to succeed. This was the stuff of which Lyon's only lifeline was made. The slow work of expediting the teams to Rolla was started before Sweeny left to take command. But hardly had his train pulled out of the station, when Quartermaster McKinstry, out of sheer malice toward Lyon, discharged the remaining teamsters with all their dray animals and wagons. At the same time, the irate major canceled all future arrangements made by Brigadier General Sweeny for supplies and similar services. The trouble was that Sweeny, under the pressures of urgent necessity, had been compelled to bypass the quartermaster in purchasing supplies. Narrow-minded McKinstry, who lived by the book of regulations, decided that the arrangements had been made without proper authority since they had not been made through him. And because at the time there was no authority in Saint Louis above him, McKinstry got away with it. Lyon and his Army of the West were to wait anxiously and frustratingly for weapons, ammunition, clothing, and food that never reached Springfield. In 1863, the Army ordered McKinstry to put his uniform into mothballs. But by then it was much too late to make amends to Nathaniel Lyon and the Union men in the Battle of Wilson's Creek who had to retreat for lack of ammunition, as well as food and clothing.

Capital and Boonville Taken

Returning to Lyon's transport flotilla, the four ships laid-to during the night of June 13 a few miles west of Saint Charles. From here on, until he reached his ultimate destination, Lyon expected trouble. He was certain of that. At least Lyon knew that had he been in Jackson's shoes, he would have had sharpshooters, perhaps even artillerists, at hand to hinder the vessels' progress.

As the steamers plied westward, rifle experts were stationed as lookouts at every vantage point aboard. The fieldpieces on three of the ships were placed where they could command the widest fields of fire and manned for instant action. At any rate, Lyon was not to be caught napping. Once past the mouth of the Gasconade, the dangers doubled because Calloway County, which here runs along the northern bank, was strongly pro-Southern. West of the Osage, the dangers trebled because the counties along both shores were peopled by hemp-producing slaveholders. Lyon knew that the State Guard had the four brass cannon, taken from the Liberty Arsenal. Using that knowledge as a departure point, it was easy for him to imagine how simple it would be to hide a battery somewhere along the riverbanks. A few well-directed shots, could easily put the transport vessels out of business. Throughout the long run to Jefferson City, Lyon was on tenterhooks. But nothing happened. Not a shot was fired as the steamers puffed and picked their way up the treacherous channels of the Missouri River.

When the ships reached the capital early in the afternoon of the 15th, the tension slacked off. There had been no reason to point all six of Totten's guns, loaded with canister and ready to roar, on the streets opening on the landing; nor to line infantrymen, with loaded rifles, along the rails. With Jackson and his cohorts gone, the capital was a friendly city that made a great display of loyalty to the Union. Even so, the troops disembarked on the double and took immediate possession of all high and commanding positions such as the capitol, State penitentiary, and other sites.

Before he stepped ashore, Lyon received information from a Boonville Unionist, who had stolen down the river in a rowboat. He was told that armed rebels were throwing up fortifications at Boonville; that reinforcements were expected hourly from Tipton and from across the Missouri.

That afternoon, as he stood before one of the windows in the Governor's office, Lyon looked thoughtfully out over the smiling springtime countryside with unsmiling eyes set in a face as hard, wrinkled, and brown as the surface of a Connecticut nutmeg. He had attained his second objective toward insuring Missouri's position in the Union. Her capital was empty of all State rule and the Jackson administration had been reduced to a government which, if not actually in exile, was at least on the run and, therefore, deprived of its power to function.

The next objective was Boonville. It might, or might not, be a tough nut to crack. But once he had laid Boonville by the heels, the Union would have control of the Missouri River. By putting a stop to cross-river ferry traffic and closing river navigation to all vessels except those authorized by the United States, he could actually isolate northern Missouri and put an end to secessionists from that part of the State joining up with the forces of General Price south of the river. Later, General Price informed Jefferson Davis that Lyon's swift tactics and clear strategic thinking had deprived him of from 5,000 to 10,000 potential State Guard troops from northern and western Missouri.

As thoughts of conquest ran through his mind, Brigadier General Lyon presented a most unmilitary figure. In deference to comfort, he had shelved his old captain's uniform coat. In its place he wore a long, light-gray linen duster, and on his head was a coarsely woven wide-brimmed straw hat à la Zachary Taylor. His glance turned toward the river, and he wondered briefly what might be awaiting him in the line of resistance before Boonville. Reports placed from 2,000 to 3,000 rebels in well-defended positions, with guns dominating the river. Well, nothing like finding out. He made up his mind and issued orders to proceed against Boonville the following day, Sunday, June 16. As a safety factor, he left Colonel Boernstein in occupation with three companies of his Second Regiment Volunteers and a platoon of Pioneers. The remaining six companies of the Second Regiment went on to Boonville under the command of Major Peter J. Osterhaus. He was a brilliant and courageous officer who eventually attained general's stars. Now the Army of the West had been reduced to less than 1,800 men.

Lyon took his time covering the 50 miles of water between the two cities. He was extremely watchful because potential dangers rested on either hand. On both sides was slave country, as black as the cotton lands of the Deep South. But the Sunday peace remained undisturbed, and the only sounds were those of the chugging engines, the slap-slap of the paddle wheels, and the quick rush of fast water down the sides of the vessels.

The Federal steamers passed the night just west of the town of Rockport some 15 miles short of Lyon's objective. At Rockport, he learned that the enemy had thrown up breastworks quite a distance east of Boonville. As they neared that city, a large island was observed in the middle of the channel. The contour of the river was such that the island hid Boonville, some eight miles off, completely from view. The flotilla came to a halt.

Sheltered by the island, Lyon, Blair, and Schofield were taken ashore to study the terrain. They found themselves on a broad meadow of bottom lands that ran, about one and a half miles wide, between the river and a tall, steep bluff that swept in both directions. Along the bluff, the river road ran in a fairly straight line. However, as it went westward, the road was pushed closer and closer toward the river by the steadily encroaching heights. Finally, as the bluff almost reached the river, its wall fell off in a series of wide terraces. They rose gently enough for the road to climb them.

Scouts brought word that the enemy, in force, had placed himself on one of the terraces along a lane that crossed the river road. At the inland end of this terrace stood a grove of trees; and at the river end of the lane was a brick house. The trees and the house could be sheltering artillery. In other words, the forces of Colonel Marmaduke had been well placed. They faced not only the river road, as it climbed from the bottom lands, but could subject it to enfilading fire from the grove and from the house on opposite ends of the terrace.

At Lyon's orders, all units disembarked and deployed into line of battle on both sides of the road. With Lyon in the lead, and Totten's Battery in the center, the forward march began. Presently, State Guard lead began to fly. Totten wheeled his pieces into position and subjected the grove and the brick house to a thorough drenching of shot and shell. At the same time, the skirmish lines of the infantry advanced. When the State Guards delivered hot musket volleys, the Federals flung themselves flat on the ground and maintained a steady response from prone positions.

The enemy fire had been particularly annoying from the house and from the grove. Now Totten dropped shells and canister into the building and the woods. The house swayed as if in an earthquake; the trees shook as if in the grip of a hurricane. Men who had been stationed there ran for dear life. The troops who held the lane, infected by the debacle, quickly followed suit. On the summit of the bluff, they bravely formed again under a steady rain of fire. But, before they could make a heroic stand, Lyon, at the head of his men, his heavy saber flashing in the sunlight, came over the last crest of the bluff in a headlong rush. The long and threatening rows of gleaming bayonets—a sight that can make even veterans quail—were too much for the young recruits to take. They streaked toward town. A vigorous pursuit was impossible because of the lack of cavalry as well as Lyon's decision not to subject Boonville to artillery fire. Presently, the Mayor, and citizens who had pro-Union leanings, came out under flags of surrender.

Only a few of the escaping recruits were taken prisoner. All were paroled and instructed to return to their homes. One country lad said disgruntledly, as if complaining of unfair play:

"This yeah business of a-firin' an' a-loadin' while a-layin' on the ground—that's what whupped us!"

Acting on previously made arrangements, Governor Jackson and General Clark had made off toward Tipton 20 miles to the south and from which point Parsons had failed to bring reinforcement.

From a military standpoint, Boonville was not even a minor victory. It was scornfully called the "Boonville Races" by both sides. But Lyon had the great satisfaction of knowing that his men could be handled under fire in companies, battalions, and regiments without mix-ups. Orders had been executed with machine-like precision. No disorder. No confusion. Federal casualties were two killed and nine wounded. The State Guard, ten killed and an unknown number of wounded.

Brigadier General Lyon's first step in orienting his new

position was to get word to Chester Harding to expedite the sailing to Boonville of Colonel John D. Stevenson and his Seventh Regiment Volunteers. No time must be lost in establishing a strong and vigilant watch along the Missouri and the restriction of all traffic. From that hour on, the Missouri was a Union river, a position that would strengthen Federal hold on other waterways such as the Ohio, the Illinois, and the Mississippi as far south as Cairo.

The following day, General Lyon issued a proclamation in which he exposed the "plottings" of Governor Jackson and summarized the action taken by himself. The document closed with the following appeal:

Having learned that those plotting against the Government have falsely represented that the Government troops intended a forcible and violent invasion of Missouri, for the purposes of military despotism and tyranny, I hereby give notice to the people of this State that I shall scrupulously avoid all interference with the business, rights and property of every description, recognized by the laws of this State, and belonging to law abiding citizens; but that it is equally my duty to maintain the paramount authority of the United States with such force as I have at my command, which will be retained only so long as opposition shall make it necessary, and that it is my wish, and shall be my purpose to devolve any unavoidable rigor arising in this issue, upon those only who provoke it.

All persons who, under the misapprehensions above mentioned, have taken up arms, or who are now preparing to do so, are invited to return to their homes and relinquish their hostile attitude to the General Government, and are assured that they may do so without being molested for past occurrences.

Importance of Results Attained

Meanwhile Lyon's staff busied itself with the task of preparing for the next step. First came moves to entrap the State Guard brigades recruiting at Lexington. This encampment was under the over-all command of Major General Price and the direct supervision of Brigadier General James S. Rains and Brigadier William Y. Slack. When word of Governor Jackson's further retreat toward Warsaw reached him, Price at once left Rains in command at Lexington with orders to retreat to Lamar in Barton County. There Jackson, Clark, and Parsons would meet up with them. With his staff, and a small escort, Price rode with the greatest possible speed toward Arkansas to obtain assistance from the Governor or McCulloch.

Due to his quick follow-up, Lyon had disrupted whatever thoughts Price may have had for making a stand along the Osage, such as Marmaduke proposed. He issued orders for the First Iowa Volunteers, then in northern Missouri, to join his forces with all possible speed at Boonville. At the same time, Major Samuel D. Sturgis, USA, at Fort Leavenworth was directed to march southward with his then available force. This turned out to be the First and Second Regiments, Kansas Volunteers; four companies of regular infantry, four companies of cavalry, two companies of dragoons, one company of Kansas Mounted Rangers, one four-gun battery of artillery, and one company of regular recruits. This force, which comprised some of the toughest professional fighting men in the Army, totaled about 2,300 men. In the Kansas regiments were hundreds of men who had been dry-nursing scores to settle with Missourians since the dark days that began in 1854. In fact, Colonel George W. Deitzler, of the First Kansas, was the very same Deitzler who risked his neck by running Sharps' rifles, donated by Yankee abolitionists and boxed as bibles, through the Missouri blockade so that free-soilers would have guns to fight back with. Since then, the Kansans had learned how to handle "Beecher's Bibles" (as the guns were called) and other firearms. Now they were just itching to show the Missourians the high grade of their marksmanship.

These grudge-fighters and their comrades were to march

on the Osage in the hope that they would arrive there in time to check the southward march of Slack and Rains or Clark and Parsons.

Naturally, Lyon's progress up the Missouri to Jefferson City and on to Boonville had become Page One news for the nation's press. In the North, the campaign was lauded to the skies and Lyon's fame became a bright and encouraging star in Northern skies. The entire country speculated on the nature of a soldier who, out of nothing and with little help from the War Department, had forged his own victorious Army of the West. The encouragement he gave the Northern cause was a timely shot in the arm. The do-nothingness of the Washington Administration and Mr. Lincoln's reluctant generals was a painful, but nonetheless constant, topic of conversation.

And, to do him justice, Lyon had done the best he could with what he had. In his book, *The Fight for Missouri*, Colonel Snead made the following significant observation on the importance of Lyon's campaign and its fruits:

Insignificant as was this engagement [Boonville], in a military aspect, it was in fact a stunning blow to the Southern Rights people of the State and one which did incalculable and unending injury to the Confederates.

It was, indeed, the consummation of Blair's and Lyon's statesmanlike scheme to make it impossible for Missouri to secede or, out of her great resources, to contribute abundantly of men and materials to the Southern cause as she would surely have done had her people been left free to do as they pleased.

It was also the crowning achievement of their well conceived military campaign.

The capture of Camp Jackson had disarmed the State, and compelled the loyalty of Saint Louis and all the adjacent counties.

The advance upon Jefferson City had put the State government to flight, and taken away from it that prestige which gives force to established authority.

The dispersion of the volunteers who had rushed to Boonville to fight under Price for Missouri and the South, extended Lyon's conquest over all the country lying between the Missouri River and the State of Iowa; closed all the avenues by which Southern men of that part of Missouri could make their way to Price's encampment at Lexington.

It made the Missouri River an unobstructed Federal highway from its source to its mouth; and rendered it impossible for Price to hold the rich, populous and friendly counties in the vicinity of Lexington.

Price had, indeed, no alternative but to retreat in all haste to the Southwestern corner of the State, there to organize his army under the protection of the forces which the Confederate Government was mustering in northwestern Arkansas under Brigadier General Ben McCulloch, for the protection of that State and the Indian Territory.

As the first week of Lyon's occupation of Boonville drew to a close, he had high hopes that his plans, to gather and organize a supply train, would be realized on an early date. He was anxious to begin his pursuit of Jackson, Price, and all on or about June 26.

Chapter 7

Patterns Take Shape

———◆———

Jackson and His Generals Move South

Paul Revere never rode faster nor shouted his tidings of alarm louder, than did portly "Pap" Price on his long ride from Boonville to Cowskin Prairie. The latter was a stretch of grassland in the extreme southwestern corner of Missouri. Maysville, Arkansas, was some score miles to the south. The nearest city, thriving Neosho, was Newton County's seat. Many a man, who counted less than half of Sterling Price's years, could have been proud of the horsemanship and endurance shown by the major general of the "Butternut Boys." This nickname was given to the State Guards because their only uniform consisted of everyday homespun that had been dyed a rather tired-looking brown with the aid of butternut juice. Incidentally, since many Union Home Guard companies in the hinterlands of Missouri wore identical garments, it was, at times, extremely difficult to figure out who was friend and who was enemy. As a means of identification, some State Guards eventually took to wearing large clay-colored headpieces made of felt. They were known as horse thieves' hats. Home Guards, on the other hand, adopted black felt campaign hats similar to those worn by some Federal infantry.

Price left Lexington with a small escort. By some magic means, seemingly by prairie wireless, the countryside ahead of Price's line of travel heard about his coming. By the pair, by the dozen, by the company—by the hundreds—mounted

men joined his informal cavalcade. They included rich planters, well-to-do farmers, and log-cabin cornhuskers. Some
small-town folks were among them. But most of those in
Price's party were from the rural regions. All of them were
expert horsemen. Quite a few brought along firearms. The
greater part of these were either shotguns, revolvers, light
hunting pieces, old-time muskets, and even a few buffalo guns.
However, many of these willing patriots were unarmed. By
the time Price reached Cowskin Prairie, his force amounted
to about 1,200 horsemen. The hundreds of eager but horseless
men along his route who wanted to fight under the colors of
Missouri were informed that Governor Jackson and his generals would soon come marching along. They were warmly
invited to join the infantry and to spread the word as far as
they could.

It was effective recruiting, but the total who took up arms
that 1861 summer under Major General Price fell short by
more than 40,000 of the number asked for by Jackson in his
proclamation.

As soon as Price's contingent was established on Cowskin
Prairie, he rode down to Maysville where Brigadier General
N. B. Pearce had his Army of Arkansas encamped. Here Price
succeeded in borrowing 600 one-time Federal muskets and
also sent word to McCulloch. In a few days, the famous Texan
paid a call on Price. As an escort, he had the neatly uniformed,
finely mounted Second Arkansas Mounted Rifles (Confederate
Army) commanded by Colonel James McQueen McIntosh.
This colorful former U. S. Army captain had the ineradicable
West Point seat aboard a saddle, as well as the dash and daring of the true cavalryman. McCulloch, who put no faith in
anyone who could not master a horse, set great store by
McIntosh, who could ride a fire-breathing dragon. In fact,
McIntosh was his Chief of Staff and unofficial second-in-com-
mand.

The meeting on Cowskin Prairie must have been something
of a letdown for McCulloch who was a bit of a snob as far

as appearances were concerned. Personally, he was not only expensively attired in elegantly tailored garments—he disliked uniforms—but also something of a showman. A high-crowned, snowy five-gallon hat sat on his massive head. His footgear were masterpieces of the bootmaker's art. His velvet coat, gray with yellow cuffs and lapels, fit his well-knit figure to perfection. McCulloch's staff officers, and the 400 cavalrymen banked behind him, sat their mounts like professional soldiers and as immaculate as though they were mounted for parade in piping days of peace.

Set against his own backdrop of martial elegance and military perfection, McCulloch looked down his nose on the dusty, dirty, and motley crowd of Missourians who had not been able to wrap their patriotic sacrifices in sartorial splendor. Unshaven and unwashed, their eyes were dull with fatigue, their cheeks hollow from hunger, and their bodies weary unto death from ceaseless days in the saddle. They had a few scattered tents and a handful of wagons. Their horses munched on whatever grass they could find. The men themselves had subsisted on the slim pickings of the countryside. Mostly, it had been cornmeal mush morning, noon, and night with, now and then, a piece of side meat thrown in for good measure. Anyway, food made no difference since they had no cooking utensils, and, besides, they had not joined "Pap" Price just to eat.

Officers and noncoms were distinguished by pieces of colored cloth stitched on their shoulders or 'kerchiefs tied around their arms. Then and there, McCulloch made the great mistake of allowing himself to plant a seed of distrust in his attitude toward these men. He concluded that this ragamuffin mob would never become an army and fight like soldiers. After a brief visit, McCulloch returned to Maysville. His orders were to stay out of Missouri and he was more than willing, at that moment, to take them literally.

Moving at a slower rate than Price—toward their common rendezvous at Lamar, some 50 miles south of the Osage River

—Jackson and Rains marched south in two separate columns. As they progressed, their ranks increased. In the neighborhood of Cole Camp, Jackson was joined by Lieutenant Colonel Walter S. O'Kane with 350 State Guards. O'Kane had several hundred extra rifles. They had been collected from some 500 Home Guards whom they had struck down in a night surprise attack, killing 206 and wounding almost as many. This cheering news put fresh vigor into lagging State Guard steps.

Another encouraging event occurred when diminutive Joe Shelby—who, despite his small size, was to gain great military stature—joined up at the head of a troop of handsomely mounted and well-armed horsemen. One of the richest men in the state, Shelby owned an immense ropewalk manned by slave labor. He had a large stake in the continuance of Negro thralldom and was perfectly willing to fight for his property rights.

A smaller surprise package, but one which in its way was to be just as important as the coming of O'Kane and his men, reached Jackson just after he had crossed the Osage. Here he was met by Lieutenants Henry Guibor and William P. Barlow who had been in charge of General Frost's militia artillery until the surrender of Camp Jackson. Both had been paroled, but both claimed that they gave their oath under duress. South of the Osage, Jackson also met Captain Colton Greene, ready to report on his mission to Arkansas. The news was unfavorable. When McCulloch had applied by express messenger to the Confederate War Department in Montgomery, Alabama, for permission to help Governor Jackson, the reply was a firm: No!

Greene produced a copy of the reply sent to McCulloch by the Secretary of War of the Confederacy. It read in part:

The position of Missouri as a Southern State in the Union requires much prudence and circumspection. It should only be when necessity and propriety unite that active and direct assistance should be afforded by crossing the boundary and entering the State.

Jackson was furious and Greene's comments added fuel to his rage. Greene had seen McCulloch's well-equipped Confederate Army. It consisted of two regiments of infantry and three regiments of mounted rifles—2,700 men. He also had been within view of Brigadier General Pearce's Arkansas troops—infantry, cavalry, artillery—2,200 men. All of them marking time and doing nothing just because the politicians at the helm in Montgomery could not shake off their lethargy. In that respect, the South, in the summer of 1861, was not too different from the North. Greene also reported on the safe arrival at Cowskin Prairie of Major General Price with no less than 1,200 men. Well, anyway, thought Jackson, good old "Pap" Price could be expected to plunge into a hole on the prairie and pop up with a brood of prairie chickens.

On July 3, Jackson and his four generals—Rains, Parsons, Clark, and Slack—reached their mutual camping grounds about three miles north of the village of Lamar and 20 miles north of Carthage. It had been a grueling march, beset by shortages of every sort: from food to clothing for the men and fodder for mules and horses. In addition to that, they had been slowed down, now and then to a standstill, by high waters in rivers and streams, heavy rains, and impassable road conditions.

Parsons in particular had encountered a difficult transportation problem. His wagons carried the State Guard's only supply of gunpowder. Since most of his vehicles had been obtained from farms and plantations, Parsons had no end of trouble keeping his powder dry. One might ask, what about the missiles to go with that powder? As luck would have it, the answer to that question was fairly simple. There was lead galore in the Granby mines in the strongly pro-Southern Neosho region in southwestern Missouri.

At roll call that afternoon, it was shown that Rains had 1,200 infantry and 600 cavalry, also Bledsoe's three-gun battery; Parsons had 400 infantry and 250 cavalry, and Guibor's four-gun battery; Clark had 360 infantry, 273 cavalry; and

Slack 700 infantry and 284 cavalry. In addition, there were about 2,000 unarmed and unequipped horsemen in camp.

Thus, as the sun set on July 3, to rise again on Independence Day, Jackson's command had a total complement of about 4,000 effectives. But, he wondered, where was Lyon? And would he be able to catch up with the State Guards before they established a junction with the forces of Major General Price? Lastly, would an actual threat from Lyon be sufficient for McCulloch and Pearce to regard their assistance as both "necessary and appropriate"?

Problems Beset Lyon in Boonville

There was no need for Jackson to entertain fears that the Army of the West was on his heels. Had he but known it, Lyon, because of one delay after another, did not march south from Boonville until 3:30 on the morning of July 3—the very day Jackson's State Guards made their rendezvous at Lamar.

The matter of assembling a transport train proved much more difficult than Lyon and his senior officers had contemplated. To begin with, the State Guards had taken the best wagons and draft animals in the immediate region of Boonville. Notices were distributed far and wide that the Federals were in the market for sound animals and strong wagons. To insure fair price levels, a commission of two officers and two civilians was established with Quartermaster Captain Alexis Mudd at its head. The response was wonderful—a wonderful headache. It seemed every owner of decrepit animals and rickety vehicles wished to offer his possessions for sale and expected fancy prices. It took a lot of verbal threshing to winnow the worthwhile from the sway-backed crowbait that tottered on spavined legs. Although Lyon allowed only one two-horse wagon for each company, he faced almost unsurmountable obstacles in filling his needs. He hated to set this limitation because beneath company wagons are the wheels that enable an army to march on its stomach. In Lyon's

137

army, one small wagon had to carry all company property, the company desk, tents, cooking utensils, rations for three days, the sick, the exhausted and—early in the morning or late in the afternoon—venture forth on forage parties. Lyon could not depend on finding enough food to live on the country as he marched along. It took no less than seven large wagonloads a day to feed the 2,300 men who formed his command.

Foraging from Boonville for more than 2,000 men and a steadily expanding herd of animals was no picnic either. However, this assignment was hugely enjoyed by the men selected, for to them it was a rather pleasant duty. For one thing, they usually could count on generous farm wives to ladle out some welcome homemade meals. Then, too, high-proof 40-Rod whiskey could be bought for anywhere from a dime a quart to two bits per gallon at the still. In those days, there were neither excise taxes nor revenue agents in Missouri. The average small-area farmer was his own distiller. He grew corn for three purposes—fodder, meal, and likker.

Almost every day, one or two steamers reached Boonville with supplies. Now they usually wore the marks of snipers' bullets. On June 23, no less than 11 vessels were unloading at Boonville's limited wharf facilities. But, by that time, Lyon had little hope of being able to start on June 26 as he had contemplated. His prospects of catching up with Jackson and the State Guard were getting slimmer every day. All he could do was to pin his faith on the hope that Major Sturgis' expedition from Fort Leavenworth would reach the Grand River in time to prevent Jackson from crossing. Having had no word from Sturgis as to his whereabouts, Lyon was completely in the dark.

On June 27, Colonel John D. Stevenson, with four companies of his Seventh Regiment Volunteers, and Colonel Charles A. Stifel, heading his Fifth Regiment Home Guard, reached Boonville. Under the command of Colonel Stevenson, with headquarters in Boonville, they established posts at ferry crossings and other vital river points. Gradually, as they came to hand, they confiscated small, fast vessels, armed them with 24-pound howitzers, and turned them into patrol boats. Lyon had hoped to add Colonel Schuettner's Fourth Missouri Volunteers to the Southwestern Column. However, in order to reinforce his control over the Mississippi—as it flowed between Union-held Missouri and Illinois—the *Schwarze Jaegers* were divided between Cairo (at the mouth of the Ohio) and Birds Point, just opposite, on the Missouri side of the Mississippi.

Having been thwarted in joining the State Guard, the secesh element in northern Missouri did not take its defeat lying down. Guerrilla bands that formed and dissolved like drifting fog, many mere rabble, raided and burned the homes of Unionists, committed foul murders and acts of ruthless violence. The hit-and-run tactics of bushwhackers made pursuit difficult for the Illinois, Iowa, and Kansas regiments sent into the area to keep order and maintain the operation of railroads. Also, the depredations of the gangs kept so many Federal troops occupied that they could not be spared for essential front-line duty. Hence, patriots-out-of-uniform—and many fine young men did take to the bush—or just plain outlaws posing as patriots, the bushwhackers performed a distinct service for the South.

Meanwhile the troops in Boonville were not kept idle. Improvised corrals held increasingly large numbers of draft animals; horses and mules that had never been broken to harness and had to be trained. To get a green mule bridle-wise takes quite a little doing, as many a blue-bottomed soldier discovered with pain and anguish. Then there were wagons to be fixed. Some were virtually rebuilt. Hoops had to be secured in their sides so that canvas could be spread tightly across their tops.

And there were drills. And more drills. And still more drills. From platoons to regiments in full marching outfit—including filled canteens. And skirmishing formations. Five to six hours without stop. Whenever he could, Lyon would find time to watch the various evolutions. There was something about these masses of men marching smartly over the drill field, their arms and legs moving in rhythm as they wheeled according to orders, that strummed on the strings of his heart in a strange and inspiring manner. He could not find words of his own for it, but it reminded Lyon of the phrase spoken by Joseph Choate in 1855 when he urged the nation to:

"Keep step with The Music of the Union!"

That is what it was, that rhythm of many booted feet—the purposeful, steady, and indomitable beat of The Music of the Union.

In watching the drills, Lyon was particularly fascinated by the snappy bearing and spruce appearance of the First Iowa Volunteers. This regiment, commanded by Colonel J. N. Bates, was uniformed in the tradition of Algerian Zouaves. Organized before the outbreak of the Civil War, it was actually an organization of spectacularly skilled drill teams. Their evolutions, with or without verbal orders, were impressive. They could march in a multitude of different steps. Moreover, they could march for hours. And, as they marched, they sang. Unlike the usually morosely indifferent regulars and the stolidly capable Germans, the Iowans were full of spirit, brimful of good nature and highly competitive. Having made up their collective minds that their regiment was going to be the best damn regiment in the Army of the West, the First Iowa set out to capture that feather for their caps with a will.

To look at them in their colorful uniforms, they appeared, indeed, like the cocks of the walk. Their jackets were of azure-gray cloth (this color to be important later), with red flannel cuffs and facings. Their trousers had the color and texture of buckskin. Their gray felt hunting hats wore brilliant red ribbon cockades. They were young. They were eager. And they were as full of fizz as bottles of unchilled champagne.

Drills. Drills. Drills.

Even quartermasters drilled. Teams were hitched up, wagons loaded and driven around like regular covered wagon

140

trains. Then they were unloaded and the job started all over again in a race against time. It was quite a sight to see those big Army trucks that had come downriver from Fort Leavenworth. They were drawn by three span of mules—the lead, the swing, and the wheel. The driver sat astride the nigh wheel mule and drove the team with the aid of a jerk-line attached to the bridle of the nigh lead mule. The driver drove with a jerk-line, a bull-whip, and a ready tongue. A man who knew how could talk a mule into doing most anything. But it required sulphurous curses as well as plaintive sweetness.

In order to relieve Brigadier General Lyon of as much of the organizational burden as possible, Colonel Blair had taken over the handling of most of the paper work with the assistance of Major Schofield. He also interviewed many of the refugees who poured into Boonville from the southwestern sections of the State. From them, he collected a fairly comprehensive picture of the local struggles between loyal and secessionist citizens. As in Saint Louis, Blair and Lyon were a finely adjusted team. On subjects of policy, matters of procedure, and evaluation of political situations, Blair was to Lyon like a lighthouse to a mariner in the night.

Then lightning struck suddenly out of a cloudless sky, and the guiding beam of the lighthouse was lost.

This came about when word arrived from Montgomery Blair in Washington that the anti-Lyon faction of Unionists in Saint Louis had executed a coup that could prove fatal to the mission of keeping Missouri in the Union. On the advice of Lieutenant General Scott, or through the secret solicitation of Attorney General Edward Bates, Missouri had been removed from the command of the Department of the West and made the responsibility of the Department of the Ohio with headquarters in Cincinnati. At the time, that department was headed by Major General George B. McClellan. This meant that Lyon was no longer his own boss.

To say that Blair hit the ceiling when he learned about this bit of skulduggery would be putting it mildly. Lyon was grimly desperate. He did not see how his organization could function when his plans were subject to the scrutiny and approval of McClellan some 800 miles from Lyon's area of operations. To put him in the right light, Major General McClellan was far from pleased with this additional responsibility. He was about to take the field into western Virginia and remarked that all he could do was to let Lyon follow his own ideas. Lyon dutifully reported his plans to McClellan and added that he lacked troops, provisions, ammunition, uniforms, shoes, transportation, and money to pay his troops. None of these items was forthcoming.

Realizing that the future of Missouri was suspended by the thinnest sort of a thread, Blair resolved that he had to be in Washington if disaster was to be averted by the continuation of this arrangement. Before he left, it was learned that Colonel John C. Frémont had returned to the United States from an extensive absence in Europe. There, thought Blair, would be the solution if it proved impossible to restore command over the Department of the West to Nathaniel Lyon. The latter agreed wholeheartedly. He had no particular ambition for command. All he wanted was freedom to pursue the Jackson-Price combination to its destruction. To be sure, Frémont was quite unpopular in the Army. He had been court-martialed out of the service—but permitted to resign—when, as a lieutenant colonel, he had tangled with Brigadier General Kearney in California in 1848. However, he had great prestige in Union circles in Saint Louis and Missouri generally, having been the first Presidential candidate ever put up by the Republican Party. Also, being the son-in-law of Missouri's famous Senator Benton, a power in the U. S. Senate for 30 years, Frémont was virtually regarded as a native son. The selection, thought Lyon, would be good for the Union and good for Missouri. Still, until the McClellan matter was settled, the Army of the West would be operating at a distinct disadvantage.

At this point in his career, when his temple of purpose

seemed to be collapsing all about him, a letter came to Brigadier General Lyon from one of his Knowlton cousins in New York. The latter wrote that newspaper editors and reporters, as well as other writers, almost continually besieged him for information about Lyon's career. Could Cousin Nat take time out to write a memo on the most conspicuous events of his life in the Army? Answering this, Lyon wrote in part:

Boonville, June 28, 1861—Dear Cousin, I have your two notes asking for points of my military service. I have not answered, because I have no time, and do not think the subject of the least importance. This great and most wicked rebellion absorbs my whole being to the exclusion of any consideration of fame or self-advancement. In this issue, if I have, or shall have, a conspicuous part I would share it and the honors of it equally with everyone who contributes to sustain the great cause of our country which I have so much at heart. . . .

With the departure of Frank Blair had come the arrival of heavy rains. The skies turned black as mourning on the afternoon of June 26 and launched downpours that lasted for several days. On the heels of that, July opened with strong winds and more rains. Being wise to prairie country and its behavior, Lyon knew that all waterways, creeks, and rivers would be running white, deep, and swollen. There would be no fords to wade or wheel across. Ferry equipment would be needed. Knowing the temper of the inhabitants of the western counties, Lyon was aware that he would have to bring his own ferry equipment since neither boats nor bridges would be at his disposal if the natives knew of his coming.

From various ships' supply places, Lyon obtained coils of two-inch rope and cable, lengths of heaving line, bales of hemp, kegs of pitch, crosscut saws, carpenter's tools, nails, and similar stores. Under the supervision of Captain Voerster and his Pioneers, the stuff was loaded into a six-mule wagon. By means of these supplies, Lyon hoped that Voerster could direct the construction of the rope ferries and rafts that might be required to make the crossing of such potential major obstacles as the Grand and the Osage rivers.

Even the earliest cocks had not dreamed of crowing when rolling drums and bleating bugles roused the men of the Army of the West to the new day. The dawn when they were to take their first steps toward a battle that was to lead hundreds of them down the Glory Road into the unknown beyond.

"Forward . . . March . . ."

At the head of the long column of marching men, artillery, and wagon train, Nathaniel Lyon turned his handsome and high-spirited charger down the main wagon road that ran from Boonville toward Georgetown, Greenridge, and Clinton about 100 miles to the southwest.

The hour was 3:30.

The day was July 3, 1861.

"Where in Hell Did Those Federals Come From?"

The Fourth of July had passed without oratory or fanfare among the State Guard units in encampment at Lamar. Even Old Sacramento, the massive and ancient 12-pounder in Hiram Bledsoe's three-gun battery, did not clear its brassy throat. Men and animals were tired. Those who were not needed for forage parties were allowed to lounge about as they pleased. Information from the north was that a strong force from Fort Leavenworth was marking time at the Grand River, evidently waiting for Lyon's Army of the West. Of the latter, there were no up-to-date tidings.

Feeling that they had nothing to worry about, Jackson and his commanders concerned themselves mostly by making plans for the future organization of the State Guard. As matters stood, they had about 2,000 unassigned recruits, nearly all horsemen. And, not a baker's dozen among these had any kind of a firearm. The training problems ahead demanded serious attention, as well as those of supply.

That particular Independence Day was clear, dry, and as

hot as the inside of a bake oven. So, not until after the sun was past its zenith, was a large forage party sent toward Carthage. This was a full score miles to the south over open and rolling prairie. Carthage, an important market town and trading center even in 1861, stands in Jasper County. Like the other eight Missouri counties that border on Kansas, below the Missouri River, Jasper was strongly pro-Southern. It was not that the countrymen or townspeople in those counties were extensive slaveowners—most of them were too thrifty and their holdings too small for such luxury—but they hated free-soil Kansas so thoroughly that the boys of the region imbibed enmity toward nigger-lovin' Yankees with their mothers' milk.

Carthage was no exception. Therefore, when Colonel Monroe, Quartermaster of Brigadier General Parsons division, entered the town with several wagons in quest of supplies, he and his men were given hearty welcomes. During the early hours of the evening, reports came to the colonel that seemed unbelievable. A patrol of Federal troops was approaching the town from the south. After checking on this disturbing bit of news—"Where in hell did those Federals come from?" he wanted to know—the colonel found the amazing report to be correct. Being first of all a Quartermaster General, and a good one, Monroe stepped up the loading of his wagons and then headed them toward Lamar with orders to the teamsters not to spare the animals. Then he took a position on the northern edge of town, just to watch developments. First of all, naturally, Monroe had sent a rider posthaste to Parsons, reporting that he was in contact with Federal forces of unknown strength.

Brigadier General Parsons—whose hide still stung over what he considered wholly unjustified criticism of his failure to come to the rescue of Boonville—decided to act without delay. Consulting no one, he issued orders for his Sixth Division, State Guard, to be ready to march toward Carthage at 10 o'clock that night. This was just after sunset. Then he reported his information and action to Governor Jackson. At first, neither Jackson, Rains, Slack, nor Clark believed the news. Where in the world would Union troops come from if they marched up from the South? That was where Price, Pearce, and McCulloch were. Or were they? Uncertainties hammered heavily on Jackson's thinking. Then rotund, brilliant Lieutenant Governor Thomas C. Reynolds came up with the correct answer: from Springfield by way of Rolla!

During this conference, another messenger arrived with information that the enemy was advancing on Carthage in force with artillery as well as infantry. Jackson canceled Parsons' order. In taking over-all command, he announced that the entire contingent would march on Carthage at sunrise on the following morning. Captain Shelby's well-mounted and well-armed company of mounted rifles would lead the advance. He would be followed by Rains' Eighth Division, Parsons' Sixth Division, Slack's Fourth Division, and Clark's First Division. At dawn, they marched as planned.

Shelby's Mounted Rifles served as the advance guard. After them, the two leading companies of Weightman's Infantry of Rains' Division flanked the head of the column as skirmishers. Lamar was about five miles to the rear, when Colonel Monroe, his horse a-lather, bore down on Governor Jackson and brought his animal to a rearing and plunging halt.

"Governor," he bellowed, "it's that little whipper-snapper Sigel. Him and Charley Salomon! They and their Dutchmen marched through Carthage this morning in the hope of finding you napping in camp at Lamar."

Jackson's usually mournful features broke into a rather becoming grin. He chuckled as he shot a quick glance at the officers who had reined close to hear what news Monroe might bring.

"Somebody should have told them," he replied, "that we were only cat-napping!"

The State Guard column moved along until Jackson brought it to a halt on the crest of a prairie ridge that fell off in a gentle southerly slope toward Coon Creek. This little waterway is a tributary to the Spring River. At this point, it runs about nine miles north of Carthage. There were about two miles of open prairie between the crest of the ridge and the creek. The latter was thickly bordered on both banks by solid growths of timber and jungle-thick bush.

On the southern side of the creek, toward Carthage, the prairie lifted again in a long, lazy rise that ended with a well-rounded ridge. The distance between the two heights was, roughly speaking, about four miles.

Jackson and his generals hardly had stopped to scan the country ahead of them, when figures—made tiny by the distance—were silhouetted against the southern horizon. Slowly and deliberately, like a thick, dark liquid, the Federal column trickled down the opposite slope. Now bayonets and rifle barrels reflected the light of the sun. There was no cavalry, but six pieces of artillery. Judging from the breaks in the column between companies, State Guard observers estimated that the Federal force of two infantry regiments totaled about 1,000 men.

Deciding that it would be better tactics to tempt the enemy to storm his uphill position, Jackson ordered his forces deployed into line of battle and to remain in position on the ridge.

Moving toward the left from the extreme right, this was the line-up of the State Guard: Rains' cavalry: Cawthorne's Brigade, 600; Rains' infantry: Weightman's Brigade, 1,200; Bledsoe's three-gun battery; Slack's infantry: Thornton's and Hughes' regiments, 700; Guibor's four-gun battery; Parsons' infantry: Kelly's Regiment, 400; Clark's infantry: Burbrige's Regiment, 360; and, on the extreme left, three regiments of mounted riflemen. They were: Brown, 225; Major, 273; and Rives, 284. The 2,000 unarmed cavalrymen were ordered to the rear with the wagon train.

Thus, as the morning sun swung high over the mountain ranges to the east, Jackson and his men stood in silent but confident ranks. They watched stolidly as the Federal column reached the bottom of the southern slope and was lost to view behind the screen of trees and thickets along Coon Creek.

Sigel Seeks Trouble—and Finds It!

Brigadier General Sweeny, commander of the Southwestern Column, found that his command had taken to the field when he arrived in Springfield on July 1 from Saint Louis by way of Rolla. He learned that Salomon, with his Fifth Volunteers, had joined Sigel and his Third Volunteers at Neosho. This town, a veritable hotbed of secessionism, is about 20 miles due south of Carthage and some 60 miles west-southwest of Springfield. By virtue of his greater military experience, Sigel was senior in command of the expedition which also included Bischoff's six-gun battery of light artillery.

Sigel, first to arrive in Springfield (on June 23), had organized as rapidly as he could and headed toward Neosho. This was the point, previously designed by Lyon, where the Southwestern Column would wait for Jackson with the Army of the West closely on his heels. However, while Jackson was actually southbound, Lyon was, on July 1, still waiting out stormy weather at Boonville. Salomon reached Springfield on June 27 with only eight companies of his regiment. He had left one at Lebanon, halfway between Rolla and Springfield, to guard road traffic and the telegraph wire against bushwackers. Without waiting for Brigadier General Sweeny, whose contingent included the Third and Fourth Regiments, U. S. Reserve Corps (Home Guard), Salomon pushed west to Neosho where he joined forces with Sigel. The latter told him that he had missed Major General Price and his cavalcade by several days. They could wait in Neosho or push northward to help Lyon close the pincers on Jackson's army wherever the opportunity might offer. The latter course was decided on. To guard against enemy attack from the rear, Captain Joseph Conrad was left in Neosho with two companies of infantry.

Sigel believed, and wisely, that the farther north of Cowskin Prairie Jackson was caught in the trap, the less chance he would have of getting help from Price, McCulloch, and Pearce. Therefore, Sigel pulled out of Neosho on July 3. Toward evening of July 4, the Southwestern Column went into camp behind the Spring River near Carthage. That day Sigel's troops had marched a rough, hot 20 miles. But there was not to be much rest that night for the foot-weary soldiers. Tents were just going up, and company cooking fires lit, when scouts reported contact with foraging State Guards in Carthage. Following a brief conference, Sigel and Salomon decided to strike tents, pack all wagons as soon as the men had had a chance to eat, and move forward to take possession of Carthage. This was done. Both hoped that if they moved early enough the next morning they might catch Jackson off guard. That night, the men slept on their arms. They were roused by the imperative long roll of the drums before sunrise and fell into ranks without breakfast, to be ready for any contingency. Soon Sigel learned that Jackson's troops, 4,000 strong, were marching south from Lamar. There was no chance of surprising him. Nor any tendency on the part of Sigel to pull back in the face of odds of four against one. As day spread its light, the 1,000 men in the Southwestern Column marched forward. After covering a distance of about nine miles, they observed Shelby's Mounted Riflemen, together with Weightman's skirmishing infantry, swarming over the great plateau north of Coon Creek. The rest of Jackson's forces stood on the top of a distant ridge in battle formation.

Just why Sigel and Salomon undertook to charge up a hill against Jackson and such overwhelming numerical odds has never been explained. They were inferior in gunpower as well as rifle fire and they lacked the highly essential element of cavalry. It could, of course, be that, like McCulloch, they made the grave error of underestimating the natural fighting instinct of Missourians. Their own soldiers may have been better trained, but the weight of numbers—rolling down hill

—gave Jackson a clear-cut advantage and he made the most of it.

Both sides held their fire as the Missourians silently watched the Saint Louis regiments, and their six cannon, follow the prairie trail across its ford at Coon Creek. Then the infantry vanished as it deployed to right and left into the sheltering woods. The right wing was formed by Salomon's Sixth tipped by a 6-pounder piece. Sigel's Third was on the left. Its extreme end also had a protecting 6-pounder. In the center were the remaining four guns of Bischoff's battery.

As the infantry emerged from the brush, on both sides of the forward moving artillery, it formed into line of battle at a distance of about 1,200 yards from the enemy. Slowly up the slope came the puffy-eyed and sweating Germans. Even this early in the morning, the day was hot for an uphill climb under full combat pack.

Suddenly, at 900 yards, there were shouted commands. Bischoff's cannon were swung into line, the Federal infantry slung itself prone on the ground. Then the silence of the morning and the small sounds of the prairie were shattered and drowned out by the short, harsh bark of artillery. The Federals began the firing. The State Guard gave ready answer.

For the better part of an hour, the guns kept hammering as the infantry watched. Sigel used round shot, shell, and canister. Guibor and Bledsoe replied, but only with solid shot and a few shells. They had no canister. Afterward, Sigel's forces claimed that they had silenced Bledsoe's 12-pounder and some of Guibor's guns. Also that the infantry in the center was badly shaken. On the other hand, the secessionists asserted that the artillery barrage was quite ineffectual. So far as the impact of State Guard artillery on the Federals was concerned, no mention was ever made of it.

However, the very fact that 2,000 unarmed State Guard horsemen were sent to shelter in the woods to the right of the rebel line-up would indicate that the Union cannon caused Jackson and his generals some degree of discomfort. From his post of observation, Sigel saw the great horde of horsemen vanish into the woods. He had no way of knowing that they were unarmed, nor had he any way of knowing what they were up to. But, being a cagey tactician, he suspected the start of an encircling movement. Such a large unit of cavalry could swarm on him like hornets. This suspicion was heightened when Rains' and Parsons' cavalry swiftly fanned out on both wings. Deciding that he might become subject to attacks on his flanks, baggage train, and line of retreat, Sigel decided to pull out while the pulling was good.

He acted at once and staged a well-ordered, splendidly executed retreat in the face of a hard-pressing and superior enemy force.

A two-gun section of artillery, under Lieutenant Essig, was whipped back across Coon Creek, followed by five companies of infantry on the run. The remaining pieces maintained a rapid canister fire as Essig's guns were hauled at full speed about a quarter of the way up the slope, unlimbered, and swung into position so that they commanded the ford.

Now the retreat began. Sigel's men were well across the ford when Jackson's forces left the ridge and rolled down the hill toward Coon Creek in determined pursuit. But they were brought up short, about 400 yards from the ford, by Essig's steady downpour of canister and basket shells. These artillerists held the Coon Creek crossing with unfaltering fire until the rest of Sigel's outfit had a good start. Then, one by one, Essig moved his two cannon—in a sort of leapfrog movement—on the heels of the retreating troops. One piece would fire. The other was rushed toward a new position further up the slope and swung into place. Thus it went for quite a spell. Lieutenant Essig was undoubtedly the outstanding hero of the Battle of Carthage. The casualties were: Federals, 13 killed, 31 wounded. State Guard, 10 killed, 64 wounded.

The retreat continued in good order, followed at a distance by skirmishers. When they buzzed too close in too large numbers, Sigel would employ his expert use of artillery to

151

brush them off. Eventually, he crossed a fork of Spring River without interference. After a brief halt at Carthage to rest the horses, Sigel sent his baggage train eastward to Mount Vernon by way of Sarcoxie. At the same time, he placed his men under cover of the houses and fences of Carthage and held them there for several hours until the baggage train was well under way. After dark, the Federals stole off. They caught up with the train at Sarcoxie at 4 o'clock the next morning. By then Sigel's troops had marched 34 miles around the clock without food and tangled with the State Guard at Coon Creek to boot. From Sarcoxie, Sigel marched on to Mount Vernon and, after a breather, back to Springfield.

Captain Conrad came to grief in Neosho. Agents for Major General Price sped word of his presence to Cowskin Prairie and about the northward march of Sigel. Price hastened to McCulloch, explained the situation, and pleaded for help. This time McCulloch threw the Montgomery red tape to the winds. With two companies of Confederate cavalry, headed by Colonel McIntosh, he accompanied Price to Neosho. There Conrad gave up without a struggle. Learning that Jackson was heading their way after a victory at Carthage, they waited until a junction was established. It was a happy hour when "Claib" Jackson and "Pap" Price joined forces. The victory at Carthage removed much of the bitter aftertaste following the rout at Boonville. The date was July 7.

Lyon Learns of Sigel's Defeat

About the time Price, Jackson, and their generals celebrated their reunion with whatever the occasion afforded, Brigadier General Lyon's Army of the West established contact with Major Samuel Sturgis and his Kansas contingent. It was during the midday halt, on July 7, when Lyon's scouts reported sighting the Sturgis encampment just north of the brimful banks of the Grand River to the west of Clinton.

Before the men fell into ranks, word was sent to all commanders of the impending meeting with the Sturgis column.

Orders directed every company captain to have his men appear as saucy and snappy as if they were parading up Chouteau Avenue past cheering throngs. Musicians were to take their instruments from the wagons; flags were to have appropriate color guards. Here, on the hostile prairies of Missouri, Nathaniel Lyon was to exhibit the military machine that he had wrought to the critical eyes of the hundreds of professional soldiers—officers, noncoms, and enlisted men—in Major Sturgis' command.

Color-bearers held their standards high. Musicians played their instruments with a will. Soldiers bore their heads high, chins up, chests out, bellies in, and muskets at the proper angle as they marched upon and past the Sturgis encampment. Twenty-two hundred Kansans rushed out of tents and company streets or dropped whatever duties they were performing. They spread with the speed of prairie fire along the line of march and cheered as if with one throat.

First came Lyon on his gray-dappled stallion, followed by his staff and 10 mounted bodyguards in steel-gray uniforms and in lines of five. A company of regulars and recruits, armed with rifled muskets, preceded Voerster's Pioneers. The latter had Sharps' rifles slung across their backs, hunting hats on their heads, and axes, shovels, and picks on their shoulders. Next came Totten's Battery, each section drawn by heavy and well-matched horses, and accompanied by veteran artillerists.

Now came the real show-stopper. The First Iowa Regiment in azure-gray jackets, feathered hats, and marching with such precision that it seemed but the single footstep of a giant. Less spectacular, but equally impressive in soldierly appearance, was Blair's First Missouri led by Lieutenant Colonel George L. Andrews in the absence of Colonel Blair whose Congressional duties kept him in Washington. Both regiments were singing "The Girl I Left Behind Me."

A wagon train, that appeared more utilitarian than impressive, snaked its way over a stretch of two miles to the rear.

A drove of cattle and Osterhaus' Battalion of the Second Missouri brought up the rear.

This may be the place to underscore the fact that, at this stage of the war, the dark-blue uniform that was to distinguish Union troops from Confederates in gray had not gone into general distribution. Most of the regular artillery and infantry still wore various shades of blue-gray. As for cavalry and dragoons, their uniforms had still much of the dash and color that characterized mounted soldiers during the Mexican War.

Thus it was that, when Lyon's men marched past Sturgis' encampment that afternoon, they actually were not Boys in Blue. The regulars wore their old-time, gray-toned uniforms, and the volunteers were garbed in whatever colors their regimental spirits dictated. The same applies to the units commanded by Major Sturgis.

As for the South, Confederate gray was by no means standard in rebel regiments as early as the summer of 1861 on the Western border. In the forthcoming battle at Wilson's Creek, the Third Louisiana's uniform of blue-gray was almost identical with that of the First Iowa, a situation that led to double-edged confusion. Similarly, other Southern troops at Wilson's Creek displayed uniforms of nearly the same shade of steel-gray that was worn by Sigel's Third Regiment Volunteers.

Some of the turns of the tide of that battle swung on this element of confusion. It is therefore vital to bear in mind that, in the summer of 1861, the Boys in Blue were often gray and the Boys in Gray were often blue.

While the Army of the West broke ranks to set up camp, Lyon and his top commanders went into conference with Major Sturgis and the latter's second-in-command, Captain Gordon Granger. Major Sturgis was a harsh-faced, bow-legged horseman who had spent his entire military life in the cavalry or the dragoons. A brilliant cavalry officer, he knew his limitations when it came to commanding foot soldiers and artillery. He had, therefore, come to lean on Captain Granger who, in the infantry and mounted rifles, had acquired a more

154

practical general knowledge than that possessed by Sturgis. Mutual love of horses had drawn the two together while they attended West Point in the early 1840's. Sturgis was to become a brigadier general, while Granger reached the rank of major general.

The march from Boonville to the Grand River by and large had not been an easy one for men or beasts. Also, there had been occasional false alarms. Having no cavalry, Lyon had to rely more or less on the good will and sharp eyes of local mounted Union men who rode on the flanks as voluntary scouts. There were frequent reports that big groups of rebels were forming ahead, on the flanks, or to the rear. They never proved true. But Lyon dared not disregard the rumors because he was marching through a country that was inhabited mainly by pro-Southern plantation owners and farmers.

In the early stages, they marched through well-settled country. Then they reached the open prairie where the trail ran through deep grass and was cut by many small streams. The country was wet from past rains and the road somewhat muddy. Still, the Army of the West kept sloshing along. On the second day out, a heavy storm spread thunder, lightning, and wind-driven rain on their entire route. The soft prairie soil became tenacious mud. Horses and mules were unable to pull the wagons. Ropes and cables were dug out from Voerster's supply wagon, attached to the vehicles, and, with dozens of men to each rope, enabled the train to keep moving through the clinging mire.

And yet, the Iowa boys sang. Every hour, on the hour, for 15 minutes, they would burst forth with such popular songs as "The Belle of the Mohawk Vale," "The Happy Land of Canaan," "Jordan Am a Hard Road to Travel," plus the everlastingly popular "Girl I Left Behind Me."

Lyon was not accustomed to the ebullience of volunteer soldiers. He was used to the regular infantry way of hoarding strength on long marches, and it was beyond his understanding why young men could be so noisy. Whatever reserves he

155

once may have had in matters of personal gaiety, good humor, and easy ways had been consumed during the past few months by demanding duties and oppressive anxieties.

Now, in July, with problems and pressures surrounding him at every turn, the ready smile had died on his lips and the merry glint had left his deep-blue eyes. His expression was stern, almost forbidding; his manner brisk and impatient; his voice had a biting edge of poorly concealed irritation. To be absolutely candid, he was generally unpopular in the eyes of his volunteers. They did not understand him any more than he understood them. His officers, especially the West Pointers, would follow him through hell and beyond. Not because of affection, but due to their full reliance on his capacity to lead.

Although there is no record that he expressed himself on the subject, it is quite probable that Lyon angrily wondered why Sturgis had not taken steps to insure their passage across the Grand River—or even why he had not tried to save time by crossing it. But Sturgis was a soldier who went by the book, and there were no orders in his book other than to wait for Lyon as he had done. It would be wrong to hold this lack of initiative against Major Sturgis. In the old Army, following the book was almost an occupational failing because of the pitfalls that awaited officers who acted without orders.

Soon after his arrival, Lyon inspected the river. It had a tumultuously brawling current and flowed far beyond its banks. Being an old hand at overcoming unfavorable river crossings, Lyon soon issued orders that set thousands of hands to work. First, foot soldiers, protected by cavalry and dragoons, were sent east and west along the river to find and return with whatever usable river craft they might find. Volunteers were asked to swim three heaving lines to the opposite bank and make them fast so that they could be used in hauling ferry ropes and cables across the river. As soon as the ferry ropes were secured, additional volunteers swung hand over hand to the other side. It was getting dark. Men had to collect wood for huge bonfires—more than a dozen of them—to light up the scene. Discovering that the approach to the river was too muddy to carry traffic, sweating and straining men chopped, sawed, and carried trees to build a corduroy road from solid soil to the water's edge.

Great rafts, large enough to float wagons, caissons, guns, and limbers, were built by the Pioneers. The rafts were nearing completion when searchers appeared from upriver and downriver with one large and one smallish flat-bottomed boat, plus several canoes and skiffs. The large boat was assigned to the lower ferry cable, the smaller to the upper, and the rafts to the center cable. Now the actual ferry work began in earnest. Straining, cursing, slithering men loaded the heavy and stupidly resisting equipment on the rafts. Others ferried them across, hand over hand, pulling and hanging on for dear life as their clumsy overladened craft breasted the brute force of the current.

Midnight came and went. Still, there seemed to be hardly a dent in the pile of stuff to be shipped across. During this time, there had been a slow but steady trickle of men moving across the river in the flatboats. At 3 o'clock, the rain started to come down in torrents. Yet, nobody gave much of a damn. It seemed to most of the men that nothing on this side of hell could add one whit to their cold and wet discomforts and weary misery.

The sun rose, faint behind a thick cloud cover. But there was neither breakfast nor rest. And that man Lyon was everywhere. Seeing everything. There was no soldiering on this job. Once on the south bank, there was neither peace nor pause. The land rose steeply from the river and a road had to be built to the top of the rise. A planked wagon road, if you please, so that the wheels would not stick in the mud and to give the horses a foothold.

Even before that road was hewn through the riverbank, one company of cavalry and two of infantry had scrambled

157

up the steep and slippery grade to make a forced march to the Osage River. The purpose of the mission was to secure the crossing and hold the ferries on the Osage, 25 miles to the south of the Grand.

By noon, cavalry, artillery, dragoon, and wagon animals had been swum by their halters across the river. Soon the last ton of supplies had been ferried to the other side. As for the drove of cattle Lyon had collected, he let it drift. He had no hope of swimming cattle across that torrent without their landing too far down the river to justify the effort.

The Army of the West reached the banks of the Osage on the afternoon of July 9 in the heart of a dense forest some dozen miles above Osceola. Soon after Lyon's arrival, while he was planning his crossing, Major Schofield brought a man with a beaten-out look before Lyon.

"Sir, he's a messenger from General Sweeny," explained Schofield, "and he had orders to report to you verbally and personally."

"What is your message?" asked Lyon tartly.

The man, a sergeant, saluted, gave his name and rank, and reported to this effect:

General Sweeny had word at Springfield that the Southwestern Column, under Colonel Sigel, was badly beaten on July 5 by a secessionist army at Carthage. At the time the news was received, Colonel Sigel was escaping toward Mount Vernon. General Sweeny at once went to the aid of Colonel Sigel at Mount Vernon with the Saint Louis and Springfield Home Guards at his command.

When he had heard the stiffly formal report, Lyon began to draw the messenger out. It seemed that he had quite a bit of additional information, obtained, probably, from the messenger Sigel sent to Sweeny. Among other things, he intimated that one of the reasons for Sigel's failure to stop Jackson had been the low number of casualties inflicted on the latter's forces. Very few rebels had been seen dead or disabled on the prairie.

Directing that the messenger be given food and rest, Lyon took out pad and pencil. For a moment, he chewed the point of the pencil between his teeth. Then he wrote:

Sweeny—I have heard of Sigel's affair at Carthage and how his men behaved. They fired too high and did but little execution. I am marching at the rate of forty miles a day to get to you. I am afraid that I will run out of provision.

He handed the message to Schofield with instructions to have one of the mounted bodyguards take it to Sweeny at once.

News of the engagement at Carthage swept the entire organization and magnified Sigel's predicament way out of proportion to actual fact. Regimental and battalion commanders pleaded for the privilege of being the first to cross the river and rush to the rescue of the "imperiled" column.

Eighty miles to go!

Colonel Bates said that he and his Iowa boys could do it in a breeze in 36 hours.

But Lyon refused to be pushed off balance. The Army of the West would cross the Osage in regular order and approach Mount Vernon by forced marches. At the Osage, fortunately, the cavalry had arrived in time to secure the ferry. There also had been time to collect several fairly large river boats. Hearing rumors that a heavy rebel force was approaching from the south, Lyon threw up breastworks and gun positions on the south bank of the river to protect the crossing operation.

The sun was barely over the horizon on July 11 when the Army started from the south bank of the Osage. The entire night had been occupied in transporting the men, guns, horses, and company wagons, together with a few baggage (ambulances) vehicles, across the stream. This was done as companies of infantry and sections of artillery stood vigilant guard against surprise attack on the improvised fortification on the top of the riverbank. The task of ferrying an army across a river, on little more than rafts and firm resolve, is a back-breaker. But the prospect of soon meeting the enemy—almost any hour now—seemed to immunize the young soldiers against fatigue. All were eager for battle. Among themselves they boasted what they would do to Johnny Reb. The Kansans recalled the old scores they had to settle with Missourians and their trigger fingers started to burn with a pleasant itch. The Germans remembered the taunts, jeers, and physical assaults they had suffered as the hated *God Damn Dutch* from Missouri's strongly intrenched element of Know-Nothings.

To travel fast and light, the men carried only their muskets, bayonets, 40 rounds of ammunition, and canteens. All other stuff was stored in company wagons, to each of which, in addition, was distributed 3,000 rounds of extra ammunition. The march began at dawn. As the day grew older and hotter —unbearably hotter—men dropped from sheer fatigue. They were placed along the sides of the trail to be picked up by the baggage wagons that followed in the rear. The company wagons, with their precious extra ammunition, had to follow their respective companies and were not permitted to stop for anything short of dead or disabled horses.

The army halted for dinner 27 miles south of its Osage crossing at 3 o'clock in the afternoon. Dinner was cold corn mush and insipid coffee. Just before sundown, the march was resumed. By dark, the road entered a heavy forest wherein the solid panoply of overhanging branches shut out the feeble light of the waning moon. Without any light to guide them, the men had to grope their way through almost total darkness. Above their groans and curses vibrated the irritating sylvan symphony of katydids, whippoorwills, tree frogs, and crickets.

The trail, it really was not a road, was little traveled and almost overgrown by tall weeds and thorny brush. This was no longer rolling prairie country but one of steep hills, deep gorges, swift streams, and miry sloughs. On the right flank, the Sac River ran its serpentine course. Gullies had been

160

washed out by the rains. Rocks, scattered about everywhere, were stumbling blocks on which the marching men hurt their feet and cut their shoes. Stumps of dead trees and toppled trunks that had fallen across the path were frequent obstacles. It drained the energy of men to have to wrestle them out of the way in the Stygian darkness. Many were the bruised legs, broken artillery or wagon wheels, and bogged down company or baggage wagons. For 36 hours, the men had been almost constantly on the go. During this forced night march, insurmountable drowsiness overcame almost all of them. Now and then, when the line came to a halt, whole companies would fall asleep in their tracks. Arousing as the column began to move, men would prod their comrades awake. Mile by weary mile, the army struggled on until 3 o'clock in the morning, when Lyon ordered a halt. Now the Osage was about 50 miles to the rear.

Scarcely had the order to fall out sped down the ranks before all but the sentries were deep in slumber. Few took the trouble to dig out blankets or seek sheltered spots under the trees. Wherever they stood, they dropped on the ground—officers and enlisted men alike—with the earth for their bed and the sky for their covering. Cavalrymen and mounted artillerists fell from their drooping horses like sacks of meal. As for the train of commissary and supply wagons, it was left so far behind at Osage that it was not even across the river until several days later. Anyway, the fatigue of the men was far beyond the point of hunger. As things stood, no rations were on hand, anyhow. There were not enough crumbs in any company wagon to feed a family of field mice.

The tough little leader of the Army of the West was well satisfied with his men. They marched and behaved like veterans. Throughout the long hours, he had continually ridden up and down the winding column. Unfortunately, he was not the type of military leader who inspired his men with enthusiasm by fiery or inspiring speeches. In fact, he did not open his mouth except to give orders to keep the column on the move whenever it ground to a stop. In the dark, Lyon was virtually invisible. But his men knew he was there, because his dappled-gray stallion was the only light-colored horse in Lyon's army. And this apparently tireless steed seemed to be everywhere at once.

The 50-mile halt gave the army a breathing spell until the false dawn sent the first thin shafts of light into the woods. In obedience to orders, the string began to move. About six hours and 12 miles later, the tottering men and faltering animals staggered into the town of Stockton. Here, Lyon learned that his forced march had been an unnecessary effort. Sigel and Sweeny were safe in Springfield and there was no threat whatever of any imminent enemy attack.

Lyon drew a breath of relief but took time out to damn the slowness of communications in the wilderness of western Missouri. Still, Stockton was a good place to stop. A strong pro-Union town, its citizens went out of their way to make the worn-to-a-frazzle army comfortable. There was food galore for empty stomachs and pretty girls to see that every man received his share of the town's hospitality. But any hope held by the men that they might remain in Stockton overnight was blasted when fall-in commands were shouted. Again the army picked up its sore and weary feet, now to march toward Springfield. That night, Lyon went into camp a dozen miles from his objective.

Chapter 8

The Army Is United
in Springfield

---◆---

Days of Uneasy Waiting Begin

Springfield, a bustling boomtown of 2,000 souls, barely had started to rouse itself from a night of oppressive heat when a solitary horseman rode into the city over the Dadeville Road. Horse and rider made an odd contrast. The former was a magnificent, full-blooded beast, a handsome-coated, gray-dappled stallion. At the moment, however, it was all lathered up with the thick suds of sweat. The rider was a small, somewhat scrawny man whose heavily lined, leathery features were almost hidden by a scraggy frame of reddish whiskers that fringed his face. He slumped in the saddle and his head was bent forward with fatigue.

Even one who knew him well would have had some difficulty in recognizing Nathaniel Lyon that sunup as, all alone, he arrived in Springfield several hours before his troops would reach the town. On his back was the same old captain's coat he had worn on the February day he arrived in Saint Louis. Only now it was more faded, more threadbare by travel and use than ever. There were no stars on his shoulders to indicate his rank. His black felt campaign hat carried no service insignia. In fact, the only signs that identified him as a soldier and as an officer were the military correctness of his

163

saddle and trappings, a dragoon sword, and two Army Colts in heavy holsters.

When Lyon reached the town square, he rode around it and gazed up and down the side streets in the hope of finding some sign of a military headquarters. He was almost immediately rewarded with the sight of sentries on duty before a building. Within minutes, he was shaking Brigadier General Sweeny's welcoming left hand. Brushing off casual remarks and small talk—even time out for breakfast—Lyon got down to the matter of business at once. Sweeny, who was deeply fond of his cyclonic commander (a feeling that was mutual), was shocked at the physical change in the man since their last meeting in Saint Louis. Lyon had lost a great deal of weight he could ill afford to spare. His face was haggard and his blue eyes were deeply set, like mountain lakes in twin craters.

First on the agenda was placed a general meeting of all officers to take place at noon. Could a church be had for such a gathering? Sweeny assured him that it could and sent an aide scurrying to make arrangements. Before the meeting, at 11 o'clock, Lyon also wanted a conference with his brigade commanders and their seconds-in-command at his own headquarters. He presumed that Sweeny had made the necessary arrangements for headquarters. Smiling proudly, the Irishman assured Lyon that indeed he had. Lyon's general headquarters were on nearby College Street, just a house or two west of Main. It was an unrented building that belonged to Congressman John S. Phelps.

Later that morning, Lyon had a brief but important meeting with Congressman Phelps. The latter, a square-set, full-bearded man in his late forties, was one of the pillars of Unionism in Springfield and surrounding country. He was closely associated, politically as well as personally, with the Blair brothers. In letters from Frank, in Washington, he had learned that placing Missouri in the new Western Department had not been easy; the appointment of John C. Frémont had been even more difficult. The Blairs had gone to President Lincoln to urge the commissioning of Lyon as a major general in command of the Western Department. But the President had been restrained from doing so by the vigorous opposition of conservative Saint Louisans led by Attorney General Bates and supported by Lieutenant General Winfield Scott. McClellan, with greater ambitions than to hold down the Department of the Ohio, had no appetite for the Missouri command. The Bates and Scott faction advocated the appointment of Brigadier General David Hunter, an aging but supposedly reliable conservative. Hunter would never do, argued the Blairs. They had to yield. Frémont, as a compromise candidate, was selected over the vigorous objection of General Scott, who detested Frémont, both as a man and a soldier. Frémont, who had arrived in New York City from Europe toward the end of June, was willing to take the assignment.

But from the very moment he had been assured of the command, Frémont—so said Blair's advices to Phelps—had been playing hard to get. The new Western Department was created on July 3. But Frémont, instead of jumping aboard his new job and making the dust fly, did not accept until July 9. As of the current date, July 13, Mr. Phelps had no knowledge of the whereabouts of Major General Frémont. The telegraph wire between Saint Louis and Springfield was still open occasionally. And no word had come from Adjutant General Chester Harding with respect to plans on Frémont's part. In fact, poor Lieutenant Colonel Harding was almost at the end of his rope as a liaison between an absentee army and absentee commander. First Lyon. Then McClellan. Now Frémont.

The first of the many messages and letters Harding was to receive from Lyon in the course of the next four weeks did not detract from the former's burden of concern. It did not take Lyon long to discover that the mountain of supplies he had expected to find in Springfield was not there. Some had reached Rolla by rail. But, owing to lack of transportation facilities, very little of it had been transported by wagon to

165

Springfield. The herds of draft animals and trains of wagons arranged for at Rolla by Sigel, Salomon, and Sweeny had not come down from Saint Louis. This, despite an order in Lyon's mail issued by Colonel Meigs, Quartermaster General of the Army, dated July 6. Instigated by Frank Blair, it instructed Quartermaster McKinstry at Jefferson Barracks (Saint Louis) to fill all of Lyon's needs. But, as we know, that worthy officer not only discharged and canceled all transportation hired for the Army of the West but also even withdrew wagons and animals that had reached Rolla from Saint Louis.

In the course of his conference with his brigade commanders and their seconds-in-command—Sweeny, McNeil, Sigel, Salomon, Sturgis, and Granger—Lyon ascertained that his entire command, not including Home Guards, stood at about 6,000 potential effectives. As for Home Guards, Sweeny had approximately 2,000 from Saint Louis on various kinds of sentry and patrol duty. In Springfield and vicinity, local Home Guards, numbering about 1,200, were being organized and armed.

With respect to the enemy, reports were that Price's ranks were swelling so rapidly that they totaled about 30,000. Further, it was said that Governor Jackson had left for Tennessee to seek the co-operation of Brigadier General Leonidas Polk for an early invasion of Missouri. McCulloch in Arkansas, so the rumors ran, was being reinforced from Texas.

All in all, the situation was none too encouraging even if the estimate of Price's cohorts was cut to 20,000. But time was the governing factor. The time to strike was before the rebels could put a large, trained, and equipped army into the field. While Lyon at the moment might have adequate manpower to risk the staging of a surprise attack on Price, he did not have the wherewithal to launch it. He needed clothing, particularly shoes, for virtually all of the men who had made the march from Boonville and Leavenworth to Springfield. Provisions were low. Ammunition, too, was required, but not to the same extent. Lyon had included a good supply of gunpowder in the early shipments that escaped McKinstry's interference. Also, Arsenal equipment for the casting of missiles had been transferred to Springfield in time for safe arrival. The nearby Granby mines could provide an ample supply of lead.

But time played against Lyon in Springfield, even as it had in Boonville. There he had vainly raced against a June 26 departure deadline. Here in Springfield he was to crash into a head-on collision with Washington's timid and shortsighted arrangement that all the Volunteers and Home Guards—who joined the colors in response to the President's April proclamation—enlisted for 90 days only. The larger portion of Lyon's Volunteers joined up during the latter part of April, his Home Guards during the early days of May. In another week or two, time would begin to trigger their releases. There was one small ray of light in this dark aspect. Before Blair's First Regiment Volunteers left Saint Louis, it had re-enlisted for the duration of the war. Also, the service terms of the Kansas regiments exceeded 90 days. However, the First Iowa was in the same boat as the Saint Louis regiments. The brisk Zouaves would return to civilian status early in August. It was within the power of the Army to accept volunteers who sought to re-enter the service at their own free will. But no man could be held in the service against his wishes after his three months were up. By the end of July, unless a mustering miracle came to pass, Lyon would be down to three regiments of Volunteer infantry and artillery, plus about 1,000 infantry, cavalry, and artillery of regulars.

At the meeting that noon, all company officers were urged to familiarize themselves with the attitudes of the men within their respective companies as regards further service and to urge them to re-enlist. When asked to state their views, the great majority of captains and lieutenants who spoke up declared that the men could take hunger and hardship in their stride. But waves of disappointment had swept over the organizations when they found that neither clothing replacements, provisions, nor pay awaited them in Springfield. None of them had seen the color of Uncle Sam's money since the very day they put on uniforms.

Sick reports revealed that, while many men were under the weather, they suffered nothing that sleep, food, and a bit of leisure would not cure. Quartermaster Alexis Mudd reported that baggage wagons and other vehicles of the transport train would be slow in coming into camp. He observed that most of the animals would be pretty well exhausted. Some would not have survived the journey. Others would be so spent that they would have to be destroyed. Unimpressed, Lyon tersely ordered Mudd to co-ordinate with regimental quartermasters in selecting animals, wagons, and teamsters to form a wagon train, take it to Rolla, and return at the earliest possible date with as heavy loads of supplies as the animals could haul.

With steadfast pushing, the round trip betweeen Springfield and Rolla could be made by a wagon train in a couple of weeks. In going and coming, Major Mudd could take his choice between two so-called highways. One, called the High Road, ran over the ridges of the mountainous 120 miles of country between the two points. It had few ravines and no major river crossings. On the other hand, it was longer than the Low Road, had fewer camping places, and was less traveled. This road ran through an inconceivably rough and rocky, barren and dreary country. Extensive growths of "black jack" (scrub oak) and other stunted forest trees, bore gloomy testimony to the poverty of the soil. The lands along the Low Road were more populous, especially where rivers and streams crossed the highway. The latter was a part of the old Wire Road that carried the telegraph line from Saint Louis to Fort Smith. Among villages and towns along that road were Lebanon and Waynesville.

Mudd was warned that the Low Road was dangerous because of the frequent raids on Unionists by bushwackers and other marauders. Although longer and gloomier, the High

168

Road was safer although difficult to travel. While the wagon train would have an armed escort, it was more important to get the supplies through from Rolla than to invite trouble along the way.

That afternoon, Nathaniel Lyon had Major Schofield send the following message to Colonel Harding:

All idea of any further movement, or even maintaining our present position, must soon be abandoned unless the Government furnishes us promptly with large reinforcements and supplies.

Our troops are badly clothed, poorly fed and imperfectly supplied with tents. None of them have as yet been paid and three months volunteers have become disheartened to such an extent that very few of them are willing to renew their enlistments.

Before he retired for the night, Lyon had weighed the situation. His only chance, he decided, was that the reinforcements he requested would come before the end of the month. That being the case, he could plan on attacking Price at Cowskin Prairie during the last week of July, before the attrition of his volunteers became too great.

Little did he know, as he closed his eyes in a valiant effort to stem his racing thoughts, that worse things were to come with the arrival of another day.

News that galvanized Lyon into speechless fury against Winfield Scott and the War Department came in the form of orders directing that nearly all of the regular infantry and cavalry in the Western Department should proceed to Washington at once. They even specified that five companies of the Second U. S. Infantry should be returned under the command of one-armed Tom Sweeny. As for the cavalry, if five companies of the First U. S. Cavalry and Dragoons had not been on the march with Lyon at the time the order was received, they would not be with him now. In itself, the order for the transfer of the troops does not amount to much. However, as a sign of the Potomac jitters that then held Washington in their grip and the lack of understanding in the War Department of the needs and importance of the Mississippi-Missouri theater, it stands as a monument.

Lyon's mood on receiving the order—which, fortunately, he had canceled—is reflected in the following portion of a complaint he sent to Colonel Townsend, Adjutant General of the Army, in Washington:

If all these troops leave me, I can do nothing and must retire. In fact, I am badly enough off at the best, and must utterly fail if all my regulars go. At Washington, troops from all northern, middle and eastern states are available for the support of the Army in Virginia. More are understood to be already there than are wanted. It seems strange, that so many troops must go on from the West and strip us of the means of defense; but if it is the intention to give up the West, let it be so.

I can only be the victim of imbecility or malice. Scott will cripple us if he can. Can't you stir up this matter and secure us relief? See Frémont if he has arrived. The want of supplies has crippled me so that I cannot move and I do not know when I can. Everything seems to combine against me at this point. Stir up Blair.

Among the factors that worried Congressman Phelps, as well as other Union men throughout Missouri, was that Jackson would succeed in getting help from the Confederacy to launch offensive plans drawn up by Price. They were particularly fearful that such a campaign would be mounted on or before July 22. On that day, the pro-Union State Convention would reconvene in Jefferson City to declare all State offices and all legislative seats vacant, as well as to repeal the Military Law, and other acts that made Governor Jackson a virtual dictator. Lyon, of course, was heartily in favor of being ready to defeat any secesh movement that would interfere with the proceedings of the convention.

On July 19, Lyon requested Harding to send him the Fourth and Fifth Iowa Volunteers if they were not needed elsewhere. They never arrived. The following day, Harding obtained authority from the War Department to "receive as many new Missouri volunteer regiments as shall offer their services."

On the same day, July 20, and naturally before Lyon's July 19 letter could reach him, Harding wired Frémont in New York City:

Nothing late from Lyon but I have obtained authority to accept regiments as soon as offered. Can soon reinforce him. Will begin next week. When will you start?

The encouraging news about early reinforcements reached Lyon soon after the time he, on July 22, had come to the conclusion that if Jackson-Price had not acted by now to disrupt the State Convention, they would not have time to act at all. Therefore, in a very few days, Jackson would be the head of a government that had no status and Price would lead an army no longer entitled to the use of Missouri's State flag.

Then, on July 26, came the paralyzing news of the overwhelming Confederate victory in the Battle of Bull Run. In pro-Southern states, jubilation ran high and served as a builder of confidence. Southwestern Missouri, with its growing rural population, was held together by strong Southern ties. The rural counties shook with surges of rambunctious and vociferous enthusiasm. Men and boys, who until now had been uncertain about joining up, flocked to Cowskin Prairie to get into the fray, join the Dutch hunt, and kill themselves a few Yankees while the going was good. Everybody knew that this was going to be a short war. Price became more audacious. Heavily armed foraging parties would come within a few miles of Springfield, raid Unionist farms, burn homes, barns, and smokehouses.

There would be rumors of impending hit-and-run attacks near various outlying areas in which the Army of the West was encamped. Sudden scares, frequently justified, would flare up in the Federal camps. Jittery sentries would discharge their weapons. Weary men would be called to arms by the commanding long roll of the drums. Cavalry dashed in and out of the lines in pursuit of will-o'-the-wisp phantoms of the Confederacy. Picket posts were formed by whole companies instead of mere squads. Approaches to Springfield were guarded by infantry and artillery day and night. To make sure that spies could not report the accurate positions of these defenses, the cannon and men were moved to new posts nightly after dark.

Thus things were at sixes and sevens when the stunning defeat of First Bull Run hit the Army of the West. On the very same day, about 2,000 Volunteers and Home Guards, whose terms had expired, or were about to, left for Saint Louis under the command of Lieutenant Colonel C. L. Wolff. They included the Home Guard regiments headed by Tom Sweeny.

Sadly, the tall, angular Irishman removed the single star of the brigadier general from his shoulder straps and replaced each with the twin bars of a captain. With the troops who elected him their general no longer in the Army, Sweeny was a brigadier without a brigade. Now he reverted to his regular rank and would serve Lyon in whatever capacity he could. Had Tom Sweeny been able to peek below the horizon, he would have seen that the twin stars of a major general were not too remote in the future.

On that July 26—when the hopes and expectations of Union men in southwestern Missouri struck bottom, as their pro-Southern neighbors took on new courage and women saw their menfolk ride off to Cowskin Prairie—Major General John Charles Frémont arrived in Saint Louis to take command of the new Western Department. This now covered all the states and territories west of the Mississippi River and east of the Rocky Mountains, including New Mexico.

Frémont's "Hundred Days" Start

Major General Frémont took, what seemed to many, an uncommonly long time in assuming his many and demanding duties in Saint Louis following his July 9 appointment. After

172

remaining for a few days in Washington to obtain a clear-cut directive from the High Command on a plan of campaign down the Mississippi to the Gulf—which he did not get—Frémont went on to New York. There he stayed until July 23, the day following the Battle of Bull Run. His reason for remaining in New York was that he had been informed that the Western Department had neither munitions nor weapons and that the best place to get these essentials was in the East. His critics, and among these the Blairs were soon included, claimed that he was frittering away valuable time. Some of his detractors even went as far as to conclude that the amount of publicity given Lyon's campaign in Missouri stuck in Frémont's craw. There could be something to the argument that here was Frémont—a flashing, somewhat theatrical but none the less heroic figure—playing second fiddle to a daredevil Yankee who was taking Missouri by storm.

Throughout the East, Lyon's campaign was receiving a veritable blizzard of newspaper attention. A corps of reporters, representing newspapers from New England to California, was with Lyon at Springfield. And the four leading New York newspapers, *The World*, *Times*, *Herald*, and *Tribune*, carried almost daily stories about the "Whirlwind in Pantaloons" who had swept through Missouri with cyclonic speed. His army was affectionately described as "Lyon's Flying Dutchmen." For one who loved the limelight of attention as much as Frémont did, this Lyon worship could have been bitter tea indeed.

Frémont was cutting a swath in New York social circles when President Lincoln began to wonder when his newest Major General would get down to brass tacks. Holding the Blairs responsible for the appointment, the President actually seems to have hounded his Postmaster General on that score. Anyway, at the risk of taking time too much by the forelock, here are a few words by Montgomery Blair on the subject. They were part of testimony given by him later before a Congressional Committee on the Conduct of the War:

As soon as he, Frémont, was appointed, I urged him to go to his Department. I did so both on my own judgment and because the President expressed to me, every day he delayed, a growing solicitude for Lyon's command. Frémont, however, after his appointment, went to the City of New York and remained for some time; I forget how long. It seems to me a very long and most unaccountable delay.

The President questioned me every day about his movements. I told him so often that Frémont was off or that he was going next day, according to my information, that I felt mortified when reference was made to it; finally, on receipt of a dispatch from Lyon by my brother, describing the condition of his command, I felt justified in telegraphing General Frémont that he must go at once. But he remained until after Bull Run and, even then, when he should have known the inspiration that that would give the rebels, he travelled leisurely to Saint Louis. He stopped, as I learned, for the night on the mountains [Appalachian] and passed the day at Columbus [Ohio].

In truth, Blair actually had to light a fire under Frémont to get him out of New York and on to Saint Louis. It was done through an appeal by him to the Cabinet, on July 23, to instruct Scott to send Frémont a telegraphic order directing him to proceed then and there to his command.

In a speech delivered at a later date, Colonel Blair informed members of the House that Frémont knew all about Lyon's situation while he was in the East. Said he:

I received a dispatch from General Lyon while I was in Washington, during the extra session of Congress, on or about the 18th of July, stating that Price was advancing upon him with a force of thirty thousand men, and that he would be overwhelmed unless re-enforced. My brother, Montgomery Blair, transmitted that message to General Frémont in New York, urging him at the same time to proceed to the West.

Evidence in support of that assertion is that Frémont, on that same July 18, passed the buck to the War Department in the following laconic wire:

General Lyon calls for reinforcements.

On his arrival in Saint Louis, Frémont was greeted as a home-coming hero. He was accompanied by his wife, Jessie, daughter of Senator Benton, the late Missouri Democratic stalwart. In addition, the new Department Commander headed a colorful but bewildering retinue of staff officers, aides, and orderlies. Most of the officers were revolutionary veterans from Germany, Italy, Hungary, and other European countries. Some were out-and-out adventurers. At their head, as Chief of Staff, was General Alexander Asboth, who had served in the Hungarian 1848 revolution under Lajos Kossuth.

One may wonder why Frémont turned to refugees from revolutions and wars in Europe to meet his needs for staff officers. The plain truth is that he did not have much of a choice due to the lack of Army officers. There was the definite War Department policy against separating career officers from regular troops for service with nonregular commands. The loss of officers to the Confederacy had left the Army's officer corps of 1861 so small that it could not have met the complement requirements of one 1961 division. (According to the Army Register, January, 1861, the Army totaled 13,024 officers and men. The complement of a 1961 Infantry Division is 14,648 officers and men.) Every effort was made to keep this tiny group of professionals intact. Long established State Militia units had fairly efficient officers, but volunteer regiments had to find their officers where they could, and frequently the findings were pretty poor. One reason for this policy was the delusion in the War Department that the nation had a reservoir of trained military talent in former European officers who had come to this country in great numbers. In these men, wishful thinkers and poor planners in Washington vested the caliber of Lafayette, Steuben, and Pulaski. Experience was to show that while there were a number of competent military minds in the reservoir, the majority were small fry indeed. And they infuriated the still strong "Know-Nothing" breed of native American.

Frémont's first act was to set himself up in an establishment worthy of his rank. He rented, at $6,000 per month, the palatial

Chouteau Avenue Brant residence. Sentries were set to patrol approaching streets, the high walls that surrounded the estate, the gates that led through the walls, the portals that led into the house, and the doors that opened upon the various rooms. All in all, Frémont's personal bodyguard totaled some 300 men or a fairly complete battalion. Officers or civilians, who sought to see Frémont on important business, found it virtually impossible to penetrate this solid phalanx of interference. He worked strenuously for long hours. But he did not have the capacity to delegate major responsibilities. On top of this, he was so plagued by uncertainties, with respect to his own decisions, that he frequently countermanded his own orders, reinstating them only to countermand them once again. Competent testimony on that score is presented by Lieutenant General Schofield in his autobiography. He recalls, for instance, that orders for cannon assigned to him from the Saint Louis Arsenal by Frémont were twice issued and twice countermanded by the general.

It has been said of Frémont that—whatever greatness he may have had, and he had much—the Great Pathfinder was neither a good executive nor a competent soldier. Maybe that fits the bill. At any rate, he showed no aptitude toward dealing with the problems of war that confronted him. The new major general admittedly had been badly used by Kearney. Now he had a great opportunity to show the Army how wrong it had been in underestimating his value, but he made the least of that opportunity.

When he took command in Saint Louis, Frémont's situation was, as John C. Abbott put it in his *History of the Civil War in America:*

The position of General Frémont, as he assumed the command of the vast Western Department, was far more difficult than that of any officer in the Army. It was not only expected of him that he should keep his Department free from rebel control, but he was to raise and organize, and equip and train, the armies with which

176

this was to be accomplished. He was also expected to pierce and divide the Southern Confederacy by descending the Mississippi from the lakes to the Gulf; no plan for the campaign was afforded him; nor special instructions given; the accomplishment of the object desired, was entrusted wholly into his hands.

But his hands, it soon developed, could be as fumbling as those of Harney had been a few weeks earlier. His entire structure of vainglorious ego, kowtowing satellites in brilliant European regimentals, elaborate schemes and impractical plans were to tumble into the dust of dismissal one hundred days after he first took command.

When Frémont took stock of the situation facing him that July 26, he was first of all made aware of two priority problems. They were placed before him by Lieutenant Colonel Harding.

One was Lyon's perilous position in Springfield. His need of everything from soldiers to supplies. His danger of being attacked by the united forces of Price and McCulloch.

The other was the situation that confronted Brigadier General Benjamin Prentiss downriver at Cairo and Birds Point. Prentiss had sent several appeals to Harding for assistance. One, dated July 23, read:

Have but eight regiments here, six of them are three months' men. Their time expires this week. Are reorganizing now. I have neither tents nor wagons, and must hold Cairo and Birds Point.

Since Cairo and Birds Point were keystones in his projected conquest down the Mississippi, Frémont decided that these important strategic points had first priority. There were rumors that Braxton Bragg and Leonidas Polk were planning massive sorties from Tennessee into southeastern Missouri and against Cairo. The plan was to invade and capture Missouri.

Prentiss had to be reinforced. That was no mistake. But the error Frémont made was to devote himself and his facilities so thoroughly to this objective that he completely ignored

177

Lyon and the equally critical situation in southwestern Missouri. If that part of the State was left unprotected, western Missouri would become a pro-Southern corridor that led straight to the control of the Missouri River.

Because of the slowness of communication facilities, and because he knew that reports delivered by word of mouth capture more attention than written messages, Lyon sent a veritable stream of "ambassadors" to Saint Louis in order to give Frémont a clear picture of his situation and his requirements.

Again sticking to his belief, that victory comes to him who gets his blow in first, Lyon had no less than six messengers in or on their way to Saint Louis from Springfield at the time Frémont set up shop at Brant's house. They were, in the order of their arrival, Captain John S. Cavender, Congressman John S. Phelps, Dr. F. G. Porter, Major Bernard G. Farrar, Captain Marble, and Colonel Hammer.

First on the ground was Captain Cavender. Through his close friendship with Assistant Adjutant General Kelton, Cavender actually obtained an interview with the general.

After listening to Cavender's presentation of Lyon's case, Frémont said that he would take the matter under consideration and instructed the captain to report to him again that evening at 9 o'clock.

About 15 minutes before the appointed hour, Cavender made his way to the Brant mansion. A clearance card took him past the sentries on the street. However, when he came to the main gate, the headquarters were closed. Not a light showed from any window that faced the street. The massive iron gate was locked and the sergeant of the guard would not let him in. Circling the house and jumping the wall, the captain saw a lighted ground-floor window in the kitchen wing and realized that it was in Kelton's office. He entered and mentioned his 9 o'clock appointment with the general.

Kelton replied that Frémont could not be disturbed.

"But, damn it all," ejaculated Cavender, "he was to give me

an answer for General Lyon and I'm returning to Rolla on the morning train! A fine kettle of fish! Now, what'll I do?"

"Oh—as to that," chuckled Kelton, "have no worry. It's all right. I know from my own knowledge that a paymaster was ordered to go on the cars to Rolla tomorrow morning. Also, General Frémont has arranged to send reinforcements at once. At least 5,000 will go forward as soon as orders can reach them."

It was a happy Cavender who boarded the train for Rolla the next morning with the welcome burden of good news. True, a search through the train failed to locate a paymaster. Still, his cashbox may not have been ready on time. However, the promised paymaster never showed up; nor were the promised troops ever sent forward. After Lyon received Cavender's report, he waited anxiously from day to day. When he finally gave up hope, the hour was almost too late.

Next to gain General Frémont's ear on Lyon's behalf was Congressman Phelps. Again Frémont listened, but less patiently, as Mr. Phelps gave a graphic summary of Lyon's needs. When Phelps completed his monologue, General Frémont reportedly told the Congressman that:

Lyon was not in very desperate straits since McCulloch and Price could have nothing but an inconsiderable force because the country in that region was too poor to support a force in any formidable strength. Moreover, in Frémont's opinion, Lyon could take care of himself. And, finally, he had no troops to spare him anyhow. To this Frémont is said to have added that, according to word received by him from Governor Morton of Indiana, a large Confederate force and flotilla of gunboats under command of General Pillow planned to attack Cairo and Birds Point and that Frémont needed every available man to guard those points.

That was what Phelps got for Lyon.

The third caller to see Frémont on behalf of Lyon was Dr. Frank Porter. His message was that if Frémont could send Lyon the Thirteenth Illinois, recently arrived for guard duty at Rolla, and Stevenson's Seventh Missouri from Boonville, Lyon would be confident of success in any encounter with the secessionists. But, regardless of reinforcements or lack of them, Lyon intended to fight the enemy at Springfield. To this Frémont, according to Dr. Porter, replied:

"If General Lyon makes a stand at Springfield, he must do it on his own responsibility. General Lyon has his orders to fall back!"

In all the annals of the War of the Rebellion, '61–'65, there is no record to prove that any such order had been issued to Nathaniel Lyon.

By now, the end of July, enough Volunteers and Home Guards had returned from Springfield to Saint Louis to give the entire town a comprehensive idea of the southwestern situation. The men, many of whom changed their minds and re-enlisted by companies, had no confidence in General Scott and subjected him to more or less good-natured ridicule. But when it came to Frémont, they openly held him—and with much bitterness—responsible for the predicament of the Army of the West.

Meanwhile, Frémont bent all his energies on gathering forces to send relief to Prentiss. There was nothing wrong with that. The error was that in doing so he attacked the project to the exclusion of virtually everything else.

Frémont's greatest mistake—dictated by his own sense of drama—was that he decided to head the relief expedition in person. It was to sail, about 3,800 strong, from Saint Louis down the Mississippi aboard a flotilla of steamers headed by the *City of Alton* as the flagship of the major general in command. For about a week, Frémont played a role that was little more than that of a tour conductor. Meanwhile, pressing problems that affected the welfare of the entire State of Missouri, and his whole department as well, remained unattended. Lyon's Army of the West shrank in numbers while Price's State Guard Divisions on Cowskin Prairie gained new recruits with each passing day.

Chapter 9

Overture to Conflict

------◆◆------

An Army Grows on Cowskin Prairie

From the time Governor Jackson's generals joined forces with Major General Price at Cowskin Prairie, the latter had been diligently at work forging the material of raw but resolute manpower into an operational military machine. His first step was to gather from among the older men those who had combat experience in the Mexican War or who had acquired some sort of quasi-military discipline riding with the Border Ruffians into Kansas. Most of these were named noncoms; some, however, were given commissions. For the major part, the latter were issued to young men of good families whose education and aptitude made them acceptable officer material. Mainly, they were made company officers. Higher commissions were given to the comparatively few who had been State Militia officers.

For the task of turning his own, only partly armed cavalcade from a rabble into a regiment, Price selected Alexander E. Steen as drill master and brigadier general. Steen had been a lieutenant colonel in the Missouri Militia. A hard driver and a good judge of men, Steen first of all picked out from among the volunteer horsemen those who were well mounted, well armed, and fit for rigorous service. Steen divided his awkward and inexperienced organization into squads. For each squad he selected a drillmaster—almost any tyro who knew his right hand from his left.

Living conditions would, except for men fired by patriotic purpose, have been utterly unacceptable. There were few tents and little shelter. Men slept in wagons, or under them, or under the open sky; some with blankets, some without. But since the great majority of them were very young—hardly more than beardless boys—they had their red-hot hatred of the enemy to keep them warm. Provisions were a major problem for about 7,000 ever-hungry men. There was no commissary and no money to buy anything with. Incidentally, there was no cash on hand to pay members of the State Guard. Still, that was not a handicap; none of them expected any pay. Their main diet was faith, hope, and courage, plus whatever could be gathered around the countryside by foraging. When Frémont told Congressman Phelps that the soil of southwestern Missouri was too poor to sustain an army, he came close to speaking the truth. Only he did not know how far mere corn and water could go in keeping the hate fires burning.

The citizens' army not only had dawn-to-dusk drill schedules, but also other important chores, such as making ammunition. The State Guard had plenty of gunpowder, but it was low on missiles for guns and cannon. Cartridges had to be fashioned out of paper and filled by the tens of thousands. Bullets had to be molded. There was no dearth of lead from the Granby mines, but what about casting it into missiles? Fortunately, Major Thomas H. Price, who had been placed in charge of ammunition, had a gift for improvising. From green hardwood cut in nearby groves, he made crude but workable molds for turning out buckshot by the barrel and balls by the ton. It so happened that, while Bledsoe's and Guibor's batteries were fairly well supplied with solid shot and a low measure of shell, they had no canister—a deadly device shaped like a large tin can. On being fired from a cannon, it sprayed some fourscore one-ounce missiles at high velocity on the target.

That type of anti-personnel ammunition was especially

182

wanted for the kind of warfare ahead. Major Price put his brains into high gear to find a solution, and did. In friendly Neosho, he located the owner of a tin shop who would turn out case shot containers to exact size. Next, he arranged with a blacksmith to cut iron rods into one-inch slugs. Now Price had the cans and the missiles. Next objective was to fashion the gunpowder bags. He bought some bolts of flannel and set men to sewing the bags who had experience in harness making or repairing. It took a little doing. The first products looked like gargantuan mushrooms. But, after a bit of determined trying, the problem was licked and case shots were on the production line. Virtually all ammunition for smoothbore muskets—and there were but few rifles—was of the buck-and-ball variety. At short range, and hardly any of those guns were effective beyond 50 yards, they could inflict effective doses of slaughter. All hands were instructed by their gunnery officer, Colonel John Q. Burbridge, head of the brigade that bore his name, "to aim at their breeches buttons." This warning had a double purpose. First, it tended to overcome the natural tendency to aim too high; secondly, shotgun wounds in the stomach usually carry deadly results. A buck-and-ball cartridge contained one bullet and from three to six smaller slugs of lead, making hideous wounds.

Although Price had borrowed 600 muskets from Brigadier General Pearce of the Army of Arkansas, there were not enough weapons to go around. All in all, about 2,000 of the 7,000 men in the encampment—horsemen and footsloggers—were unarmed. The commander detailed these men to a somewhat gruesome but nonetheless practical duty. Like a peculiar breed of combat scavengers, they were to follow their comrades into action and arm themselves with the weapons and cartridges of the dead and the wounded. Friend or foe, it made no difference. The unarmed men were formed into groups to follow on the heels of preselected regiments as an instantly available reserve to fill the places of those who had fallen.

While these training activities went on, Governor Jackson

had gone to Memphis in the hope of persuading Polk to launch an offensive against Missouri. Jackson was particularly hopeful that he might stage it before the State Convention convened. But Polk was slow in acting. However, news of the victory at Bull Run generated Polk into action. Announcing a preposterous program of conquest, he sent Brigadier General Pillow across the Mississippi to New Madrid with 6,000 men on July 28—a move that set Frémont all a-dither in Saint Louis. However, no offensive action was staged by Brigadier General Pillow, and the projected offensive died on the vine.

It is possible that one reason for this was that crusty Confederate Brigadier General William H. Hardee, whose brigade was being organized at Pocahontas, Arkansas, refused to play ball. An indication of his attitude comes to light in his refusal to co-operate with Ben McCulloch against Lyon. The Texan, on July 19, asked for such co-operation. To this Hardee replied that he had only 2,300 men of the 5,000 he expected. Until he had his full force, well armed and with a full complement of artillery, he would "with every desire to aid and co-operate with the West, be compelled at this time to forego that gratification."

Toward the end of July, "Pap" Price felt that his State Guard was as ready for combat as it ever would be. Cowskin Prairie had served its purpose. There was not a man who did not shout for joy when the news got around on July 24 that they would strike camp the following day. It had been a grueling training experience—hard work under particularly galling weather conditions. In fact, the weather had never been right. When the sun shone, it was too hot and the men marched ankle-deep in dust that rose in suffocating clouds. When it rained, they were almost knee-deep in mud that splashed over and bespattered them as they executed their evolutions. But a great change had been wrought. The milling mobs that reached the encampment early in the month were no longer disorganized. They had learned the rudiments of soldiering; they knew how to take orders and how to use their equipment.

By previous arrangement with McCulloch and Pearce, Major General Price set out for Cassville on July 25, arriving there three days later. At Cassville, he was joined by Brigadier General James H. McBride with two infantry regiments of State Guards (Wingo and Foster) and Campbell's Company of Mounted Riflemen, a total of about 650.

On Monday, July 29, McCulloch reached Cassville with his well-armed Confederate brigade of 2,700 men. The following day, Pearce arrived with his brigade of 2,300 Arkansas troops, including Woodruff's and Reid's four-gun light artillery batteries.

The cast for the drama to be enacted on the stage of Springfield, about 50 miles away, had been assembled. There were three armies with a total strength (not including 2,000 unarmed Missourians) of at least 12,000 men. Also, there were three commanding generals. Unfortunately, each general was a king in his own right over his own command. Although Price was a major general, his extra star gave him no authority over McCulloch and Pearce.

Having formed their plans for attack, the commanders agreed to begin their march toward Springfield and Nathaniel Lyon on Thursday, August 1. There were to be three divisions: McCulloch's Confederate, First Division; Pearce's Arkansas, Second Division (with part of Price's infantry) and the Missouri State Guard—no longer in legal standing in the State—forming the Third Division. The First and Second Divisions left on August 1, with six companies of mounted Missourians (about 400) as an advance guard. The latter were commanded by Brigadier General James S. Rains.

That night, Rains and his advance guard went into camp on the Springfield Road about five miles beyond Crane Creek. McCulloch encamped on the borders of Crane Creek with Colonel McIntosh and his Second Arkansas Mounted Riflemen somewhat to the north of the main camp. Pearce's

Second Division encamped some 12 miles northwest of Cassville. Price was with this brigade because of the presence in it of much of his infantry. His own Third Division left Cassville on the morning of August 2, led by Brigadier General Steen.

Lyon Starts for the Enemy

In Springfield, Lyon had been tearing his whiskers and yanking his hair in mounting frustration over his inability to move. He was getting neither men nor messages from Frémont. The wagon train that had rumbled toward Rolla under Major Mudd's supervision about the middle of July was as slow in returning as cold molasses.

Frémont's bland and continuing indifference toward the perils that confronted southwestern Missouri prodded Lyon with such sharp torment that he would often flare into temper at the mere mention of the major general's name. This was a new Lyon to those who knew him well. While harshly self-confident and decisive, he always had held his anger under firm control.

Once during a conference, he leaped from his chair, paced up and down the room, banged the table with his sword hilt, and shouted:

"God damn Frémont! He is a worse enemy to me, and the cause of the Union, than Price and McCulloch and the whole damn tribe of rebels in this part of the State!"

Since the time of his arrival in Springfield, Lyon's commissary supplies had become nearly exhausted. They were without sugar or coffee and had little left of what the Army calls small rations, such as rice, beans, and similar staples. They had fresh beef, salt beef, and limited amounts of bread. The only reason the men had bread was because Lyon, foreseeing a potential shortage, had posted guards at the mills for some dozen miles around and obtained flour that way. Flour was scarce. The heavy rains had prevented farmers from thrashing their wheat, so little grist had come to the mills.

Day by day, Lyon's position grew more precarious. The exodus of 90-day men was a grave attrition. Moreover, because of inadequate food, many of his troops were wasting from privation. They needed clothes. Large numbers of them were entirely without shoes. On the other hand, as Lyon well knew, the Missouri State Guard was gaining strength and numbers on Cowskin Prairie. Lyon's spies, local men and women devoted to the Union cause, had kept him well informed. The day after Price broke camp and headed for Cassville, Lyon had the information. Putting two and two together, he concluded that an attack was in the wind. His concern multiplied when he learned that McCulloch and Pearce had also broken camp and were marching northward for a junction with Price. To Lyon, that could mean just one thing: a unified frontal attack on Springfield. The Federals had not built fortifications because the situation of the town was such that it could not be defended. Also, the Confederate-Arkansas-Missouri force had a strong contingent of mounted troops. Their high degree of mobility could interfere not only with a defense but also with a retreat. Lyon had reason to be concerned.

Evaluating the situation, it appeared to Lyon and his officers that the enemy might approach Springfield from three directions. If the enemy generals split their forces—so that one unit would come up from Cassville by way of Harrisonville, another by way of Greenfield, and the third and main force over the old Springfield-Fayetteville Road—then the Army of the West would have enough punch behind it to give the enemy's watered-down main force a sizable wallop. It could be accomplished with the resources at hand, provided the assault was timed so that the Federals would engage the foe when he was within two days' march of Springfield. Beyond that particular time limit, the operation was risky. Because, by scraping the bottoms of the provision barrels, the Army could muster field rations only for three days. It was decided to try the gamble. On the night of August 1, the Army of the

West was encamped on Terrell Creek where it empties into Wilson's Creek, some 12 miles below Springfield.

The Skirmish at Dug Springs

On Friday morning, August 2, McCulloch sent a messenger from his camp on Crane Creek down to the Pearce-Price encampment a dozen miles northwest of Cassville. He had information, McCulloch reported, that Union troops were in force on the road from Springfield. He added that he would remain on Crane Creek until the picture of what lay ahead was clearer. He suggested that the Second and Third Divisions come up. Pearce consequently moved forward to Crane Creek. Steen brought the State Guards into camp about three miles below it. Meanwhile, acting on the information, McCulloch had alerted Brigadier General Rains and his advance guard five miles to the north of Crane Creek.

Not long after the warning had been delivered, Rains' pickets were driven in by Lyon's advance guard. Taking the lead, Rains galloped up the road in the direction of Wilson's Creek followed by his 400 mounted riflemen. After a while, slowing his pace and sending out scouts, Rains found that he was in contact with the enemy advance guard at a place called Dug Springs. It lies about halfway between Cassville and Springfield. Determining, and quite correctly, that the enemy was in force, Rains sent word of warning to General McCulloch. The latter, rather rudely, replied by sending Colonel McIntosh forward with a party of 150 Second Arkansas Mounted Riflemen to make a personal reconnaissance. Accompanied by Rains, McIntosh made a survey of the situation that was more officious than thorough. Telling Rains that he outnumbered the enemy about three to one—and warning him not to bring on an engagement—McIntosh and his men returned to Crane Creek and left Rains in possession at Dug Springs.

If McIntosh had been less contemptuous of Rains, he might have found out that the Federal advance guard, which he estimated at 150 men, was really a massive spearhead of infantry, artillery, and cavalry. A severe skirmish ensued. In this Rains held his ground nobly, dismounting half his men to act as infantry. In fact, he did not retreat until Totten's guns subjected his unit to a lively peppering of canister and shell. As the retreating advance guard bore down on the camp of McIntosh, the latter spread his troops across the road to act as a barrier in breaking the Missourians' headlong pace. One of the least attractive messages written in the Civil War was penned that night by McIntosh and forwarded to McCulloch. It reflects the unfortunate ill-feeling and arrogance that existed at that time among the self-styled Confederate regulars toward unprofessional soldiers like "Pap" Price, his officers, and men. McIntosh wrote:

Three miles from your camp, the command of General Rains, as I expected, came down upon us in full flight and in the greatest confusion. I drew up my men across the road and rallied the greater portion of them and sent them back in regular order. General Rains had engaged the enemy unadvisedly and sent for my small command to reinforce him, which I respectfully declined, having no disposition to sacrifice it in such company. J. McIntosh.

Evidently some of the scorn McCulloch entertained toward Missouri's inexperienced and rather informal army, had rubbed off on his Chief of Staff. The Texan is on record as having defined Price's men as "splendid roasting-ear foragers but poor soldiers." This attitude on McCulloch's part was a God-given gift to the Army of the West. It was to save it from a complete catastrophe which otherwise could have engulfed it.

The following morning, August 3, Lyon continued his southward probings. A small enemy force was discovered at Curran Post Office, three miles below Dug Springs. A few salvos of artillery fire blasted the outpost out of the way. Lyon's main column went into camp that night at Curran Post Office. Colonel Mitchell and his Second Kansas Volunteers pushed Lyon's left flank to McCulla's Corner, two miles to the south. Now,

Lyon was fairly certain his opponents were encamped at Crane Creek. But, by then, it was too late in the day to mount an attack. Hence his troops bivouacked at Curran Post Office for the night.

There had been watchful waiting in Price's and Pearce's camps while McCulloch, so to speak, sulked in his tent. He resented what he called Rains' violation of orders and the apparent softness of his troops. Actually, he was speculating on the wisdom of turning about and withdrawing his support from an attack on Springfield. During the night, Colonel Greer arrived with his regiment of 800 South Kansas–Texas Mounted Riflemen. His wagon train was coming up way behind him. Although Kansas was predominantly Northern, many slave-soil die-hards fled into Texas from southern Kansas at the outbreak of war. Some of these joined Colonel Greer's command.

That Saturday evening, as the two armies lay facing each other, General Price begged McCulloch to attack. But McCulloch had now made up his mind not to co-operate with the Missourians unless Price would give him command of the combined armies. He refused to advance another yard and used the excuse that the Confederate Government opposed his entry into Missouri except for the defense of the Indian Territory. He concluded by saying that for him to advance might subject him to censure. Colonel Snead, who was on the scene, observed:

While this was a very good excuse, it was not McCulloch's real reason for refusing to attack Lyon. He had, in truth, no confidence in Missouri troops and none in General Price or in any of his officers, except Colonel Weightman. Rains he had disliked from the beginning and now he was embittered against him by an open quarrel which had taken place between him (Rains) and McIntosh, for whose opinion and soldierly accomplishments, McCulloch had a veneration which made him distrustful of his own capacity and which often hampered his action.

Neither he [McCulloch] nor McIntosh comprehended the serene wisdom of Price, his unerring common sense, his magnificent courage and those great qualities which endeared him to his troops, nor could they believe that the "undisciplined mob" which Price commanded would, under his eye, fight as well as the veterans of Wellington or Napoleon ever fought. He [McCulloch] had, therefore, determined not to advance except in chief-command of the entire force.

That night, alone in his tent, Major General Price went into executive session with his pride, his patriotism, his conscience, and his courage. The result was that, early in the morning of Sunday, August 4, he went to McCulloch's tent accompanied by Colonel Snead. McIntosh was already there, still grousing about Rains. Again, Price pleaded with the Texan to attack. But the latter, only partially dressed, his long locks dangling to his shoulders, would have none of it. Finally, according to Snead, Major General Price said, in a voice that was rich with poorly suppressed emotion:

"I am an older man than you, General McCulloch. I am not only your senior in rank now, but I was a brigadier general in the Mexican War, with an independent command, when you were only a captain.

"I have fought and won more battles than you have ever witnessed; my force is twice as great as yours; and some of my officers rank, and have seen more service than you, and we are also upon the soil of our own State."

General Price paused, swung his slow glance from McCulloch to McIntosh and back to the Texan again. He cleared his throat as if he had some difficulty in speaking. Then, in a strong, firm voice, he continued:

"But, General McCulloch, if you'll consent to help us whip Lyon and to repossess Missouri, I'll put myself and all my forces under your command. We will obey you faithfully as the humblest of your own men. We can whip Lyon and we will whip him and drive him out of Missouri. And all the honor and all the glory shall be yours. All that we want is to regain our homes and to establish the independence of Missouri and the South."

191

Price paused again as he, for several seconds, looked McCulloch squarely in the eyes. Then he continued:

"If you refuse to accept this offer, I will move with the Missourians alone against Lyon. For it is better that they and I should all perish than that Missouri be abandoned without a struggle."

The major general advanced a short step toward the brigadier general, his eyes grew harder and his voice became coldly formal as he, slowly and softly as always, spoke these words:

"You must either fight beside us, or look on at a safe distance, and see us fight—all alone—the army which you dare not attack even with our aid. I must have your answer before dark, for I intend to attack Lyon tomorrow."

With thumbs hooked into his sword belt and feet placed well apart, Price awaited the answer to his ultimatum.

After some lip-chewing, during which he cast oblique glances toward McIntosh, McCulloch replied in a rather offhanded tone that he expected dispatches that might affect his situation. He promised, however, that he would give Price his decision before nightfall. Whether McCulloch was stalling or not, the fact is that he received word that General Pillow had landed troops at New Madrid toward the end of July. Assuming that Pillow could be moving on Lyon from southeastern Missouri, McCulloch informed "Pap" Price that he was willing to assume the combined command. Without delay, Major General Price published an order that announced the transfer of command. He did, however, reserve the right to resume the command at his own pleasure.

One need not draw deeply upon the well of conjecture to realize the heroic stature of Sterling Price's decision. Only a soldier who held *cause* far higher than *self*, would have had the strength of character to initiate such a surrender of power and prestige. Having made the sacrifice, and having wasted a whole day while McCulloch made up his mind, Price demanded, and received, immediate action.

All three divisions struck camp, ammunition being issued, soon after midnight, on the morning of Monday, August 5. McCulloch marched serenely confident that, come daylight, he would take Nathaniel Lyon by complete surprise at Curran Post Office.

McCulloch's combined armies were well under way when scouts reported that Lyon not only had departed toward Springfield but also had left the encampment almost a whole day earlier.

This information was entirely correct. At break of day that Sunday morning—while Price was offering the High Command to a reluctant McCulloch—Brigadier General Lyon had called a council of war. In his opening statement, he said he was low on rations, with only about one day of bread; that he would necessarily lose the command of the mills from which he obtained supplies of flour, if he moved on; that he would be reduced to salt and fresh beef, of which he could get a sufficient quantity. He added that the enemy had probably been retreating before him to entrap the Union forces in a strongly prepared defensive position. The unanimous vote of the council was that they should fall back on Springfield. This also would avoid a potential trap, through an encircling movement, that might enable the enemy to reach undefended Springfield ahead of them. The foe, according to Lyon's scouts, was about 15,000 strong. This was a fairly accurate estimate if the 2,000 unarmed Missourians were included. Lyon's own force had now dwindled to less than 5,000. It was evident that a general engagement could not be brought on within the limits of time and distance to which Lyon was confined by the state of his supplies. So, back he went.

Lyon's ability to sneak away, so swiftly and so quietly, disturbed Brigadier General McCulloch. Like Lawyer Marks in *Uncle Tom's Cabin*—of which he hated every word—the Texan wanted to be sure of his facts before he went ahead. The way it stood on that August 5, as McCulloch's army marched

193

north over the Springfield Road, the new Commander in Chief had no up-to-date knowledge about Lyon's strength. That night he halted at Moody's Spring near Terrell Creek. Having learned that the Federals were nowhere in sight, and that there were great fields of ripe corn for easy foraging at Wilson's Creek, McCulloch continued on the few miles to Wilson's Creek—or Oak Hills as Confederate records call it—and went into camp.

On August 7, McCulloch, in so many words, informed Major General Price that he would not attack Springfield without knowing the lay of the land and the strength of the enemy. He complained bitterly about his lack of information. He blamed the absence of it on the failure of Rains and other Missourians to collect adequate data. This was a somewhat peculiar attitude for McCulloch to take, especially because he in person had led, or been a member of, several unproductive scouting expeditions. On the afternoon of August 7, he informed Major General Price that "he would order the whole army back to Cassville rather than bring on an engagement with an unknown enemy!"

Unhappy "Pap" Price returned to his headquarters wondering what he could do to salvage the situation. Of one thing he was certain: If McCulloch and Pearce returned to Cassville, he and the Missouri State Guard would not follow. They would fight.

Through his tent flap, Price could look up the slope of a nearby rise of the land. The crimson rays of the setting sun painted it the color of living blood.

Within two days, that stone- and brush-covered rise in the wilderness of Wilson's Creek was to be baptized *Bloody Hill* by the rivers of blood from the 2,500 men who were to die or suffer wounds in the Battle of Wilson's Creek. The Confederates were to call it the Battle of Oak Hills.

And thus, as the sun sank, a darkness spread over the land that was fraught with meaning. A multitude of campfires flickered in the night while thousands of men moved like shadowy figures against the dancing flames.

Lyon's Torments of Indecision

In the forenoon of Tuesday, August 6, after easy marches, Lyon's army returned to its previous encampments on the edge of Springfield. The main body went into camp but remained under arms until a war council decided not to continue the march to Rolla at that particular time. Meanwhile about 2,000 infantry, cavalry, and artillery stood guard—with outflung skirmishers and scouts—some four miles southwest of town. Naturally, tension had been high among Unionists in Springfield and its vicinity as to the outcome of Lyon's sortie. Now, the Army of the West returned empty-handed of victory. And on its heels was a rebel army, at least thrice the size of Lyon's, hovering as a severe threat not only to Springfield, but also to the entire region. There were rumors, too, that the Federals would not make a stand at Springfield but retreat either toward Rolla or march across Missouri to Fort Scott in nearby Kansas. Rumors flew and flashed with the speed and flare of rockets. In the next few days, hundreds of Union families flocked into Springfield as though the only safety in the world remained in the shadow of Lyon's army. Most of these people left their crops in the fields, their possessions standing, their doors unlocked, and their hopes behind them.

Returning to his headquarters, Lyon found the usual vacuum from Frémont. Captain Cavender had caught up with his commander at Terrell Creek that previous week and had told him about his interview with Kelton. He also mentioned the absence of the promised paymaster on the train. Lyon's shrug of indifference had indicated his low expectations.

By now, he had given up hope of receiving reinforcements. He had no way of knowing that Major General Frémont at long last had issued orders on August 5 to expedite help. On August 2, Kelton had wired Frémont at Cairo:

"General Lyon wants soldiers, soldiers, soldiers. So says Colonel Hammer, who has just arrived from Springfield." The same day Frémont wrote General Scott: "Force large in front of General Lyon." Up to then, the Department Commander had ignored Lyon. Now, he extended a delayed and very feeble helping hand. Colonel John D. Stevenson's Seventh Missouri was ordered to Springfield from Boonville "with dispatch." Colonel James Montgomery—one of God's Angry Men —and his Third Kansas Volunteers were ordered from Fort Leavenworth to the Army of the West. That was all very well, but—as was to be pointed out later—if Frémont had made a determined effort to pick reinforcements from faraway places, he could not have done better. When Stevenson finally reached Rolla he was out on a limb. His regiment was unable to move toward Springfield for want of transportation. As for Colonel Montgomery, the Springfield show was over before he even reached Saint Louis. Not to harp on the already overwritten subject of reinforcements—but! The regiments ordered from Kansas and Boonville had been at those locations all along. They could have been expedited to Springfield at any time by Frémont after his long delay in assuming command.

The only cheering light on Lyon's bleak landscape was the long-awaited arrival of Major Mudd's wagon train from Rolla. What with a late start, worn-out animals and many breakdowns, the High Road had been slow as well as long. Mudd's precious caravan brought not only small rations in fair supply but also clothing and, best of all, shoes. As the material was distributed around the various camps, the spirits of the men, which had been downcast, began to soar. The urge to fight, which had become dormant, found swift restoration. Men who had planned to return to Saint Louis changed their minds. On August 1, Sigel had talked the remnants of his dwindling Third Regiment into remaining for eight more days. As for the Iowa boys, they were not going home until they had had a fight or were sure that there would not be one. So far as the Army of the West was concerned, this was certain: From among the volunteers who remained, the timid and the tender had been sifted, leaving a core of men who were tough and reliable.

The following figures of comparative strength, in regiments of volunteers, as of the time of organization in Saint Louis and the rolls of August 8 reveal the great attrition the Army of the West suffered in the loss of 90-day men.

	April	August
First Regiment (reorganized in June)	1,220	900
Second Regiment (First Battalion)	550	200
Third Regiment	1,103	700
Fifth Regiment	926	600
Bischoff's Artillery	253	120
Voerster's Pioneer Company (half in Boonville)	60	60
	4,112	2,580

While this indicates a decline of 1,532, the loss was actually much greater. Many of the gaps in the ranks were filled by local boys who sought more glory than they could hope to find in the Home Guard. Including his regulars, the Kansans, Iowans, and ineffectives, Lyon's force on that date was about 5,400. That total, however, was not the strength of his force subsequently engaged at Wilson's Creek, as shall be demonstrated later.

Those were trying days for Nathaniel Lyon. Despite the high morale of the troops, the spirit of caution was strong among his officers. With but few exceptions, they favored a retreat to Rolla. Among the West Pointers, there was a sharp division of opinion. The younger officers were eager to give battle. But the older grads, such as Schofield and Sturgis, felt that a forced march on Rolla was the wisest course. Lyon kept his own counsel. But, from the few remarks he made to the Unionists in Springfield, one could gather that retreat was not only repulsive to him as a soldier but also as the defender of the Union and those who sought its protection. The complexities of his situation were stirred into swirling emotional turmoil by Frémont's failure to act on repeated requests for reinforcements, plus the low status of his supplies. They changed the general from a decisive, quick-thinking, swiftly acting executive into a nervous and short-tempered person. He paced the floor like a caged animal. Into his usually clear eyes, there had come a haunted look. The burden of responsibility, made greater by handicaps over which he had no control, weighed heavily on his shoulders.

In latter years, this was how Lieutenant General Schofield recalled Lyon during those trying August days in Springfield. Again, Schofield's autobiography is quoted:

Lyon's personal feeling was strongly enlisted in the Union cause, its friends were so emphatically his personal friends and its enemies, his personal enemies that he could not take the cool, soldierly view of the situation, which should control the action of the commander of a National Army.

This was a broad indictment and it represents, of course, only one man's opinion. Still, it reflects a viewpoint that actually did exist at the time although it was never completely vindicated.

Lyon was essentially a man of action. He knew that, once he could break out of the fog of uncertainty that clouded the clarity of his thinking and make a decision, his troublesome internal conflicts would end. On the afternoon of August 8, he called a council of war to be attended by all officers of staff and field rank. Every aspect of the situation was argued from every angle. Regarding the retreat to Rolla—some held that it was both safe and practicable if conducted under strong rear guard protection. Others claimed that highly mobile Confederate cavalry could ride rings around the column and weaken it at leisure. All agreed that Springfield could not be defended.

Well, what then?

Attack the rebels! So spoke Colonel Deitzler and Colonel

Mitchell of Kansas; Lieutenant Colonel Merritt of Iowa; Colonel Sigel of Missouri; and redheaded Captain Sweeny of the regulars. There was every indication, as the constant closing in of mounted patrols revealed, that the enemy intended to move on Springfield. The only effective defense was an attack. It was that or annihilation.

Leading spokesmen for the opposite viewpoint—retreat to Rolla—were Schofield and Sturgis. They said that the topography of the terrain favored a retreat. Besides, there was always the hope that reinforcements, sent by way of Rolla, might meet them on the way.

Throughout the session, Lyon shifted nervously in his chair. Now and then he made as if to speak. However, he would tighten his lips, as with an effort. Thereby he maintained his status as an evaluator who, having heard the arguments for both sides, would weigh them and reach a decision.

After the council broke up, Lyon went to his personal quarters to think things through in solitude. He had barely flung himself on his bed and begun a survey of the ceiling, when Captain Sweeny entered.

The room was small and hot. The two men went out on the back porch of the house where there was a bit of a breeze. Here, speaking as man to man, the two long-time infantry comrades thrashed the situation all over again. Lyon said that even if a retreat were staged, the best way to insure its success would be to stun the enemy's striking force before he could employ it. He was of the opinion that a bold surprise attack would astonish the enemy, disrupt his planning, tire his men, and weaken his strength to pursue. Under such conditions, a retreat could be safe. But, conducted with a strong, fresh enemy on his heels, a run for Rolla would in all probability end in utter disaster. A complete rout for the Army. Loss of artillery, hundreds of wagons, and about a quarter of a million dollars entrusted for transfer to Saint Louis by Springfield's Unionist bankers.

In the course of their conversation, Sweeny urged Lyon not

to attempt a retreat without first having dulled the cutting edge of his enemy's potential onslaught. In fact, if this course was not adopted, Sweeny was for sticking it out in Springfield until reinforcements arrived, hopeless as such expectations might be. When Lyon argued that the town was almost stripped of provisions, Sweeny replied:

"Let's eat the last bit of mule meat and fire the last cartridge before we think of retreating!"

Lyon's face was lit by a grin. Then he laughed heartily and long. Sweeny's remark had reminded him of one fact that he had lost sight of, namely, that his men had shown stamina and the will to fight when the going was really hard and the odds against them. They had all the earmarks of seasoned troops who would stand steadfast under fire. What they lacked in quantity, they made up for in quality. But was that enough?

In the course of that evening, as Lyon still smarted under the spur of indecision, he received his first direct communication from Frémont. The missive came to him by way of Colonel Wyman in Rolla. In a covering letter, the commander of the Thirteenth Illinois sent a copy of a most unusual note he had received by hand from General Frémont on August 6 through Mr. Edward H. Castle of Saint Louis. The major general's note to Wyman read:

I send, by special railroad engine, Mr. Edward H. Castle, for any information you may have of General Lyon's position. Mr. Castle will inform you of the progress Colonel Stevenson has made who, with his regiment, is on his way to General Lyon's camp. Communicate to me, through Mr. Castle, who is instructed to return with any information you may have, all of which you may safely intrust to him. Enclosed letter to be forwarded as immediately as possible to General Lyon.

Only Lyon and Schofield ever read the enclosed letter from Frémont. Through a set of unexplained circumstances, both it and the copy of it in Frémont's files vanished from sight. In referring to it, Schofield commented:

The purport of that letter, which was then of vital importance, is still fresh in my memory. That purport was instructions to the effect that if Lyon was not strong enough to maintain his position as far in advance as Springfield, he should fall back toward Rolla until reinforcements should meet him.

It is difficult to see why General Frémont did not produce a copy of those instructions in his statement to the committee. [Congressional Committee on the Conduct of the War.] It would have furnished him with the best defense he could possibly have made against the charge of having sacrificed Lyon and his command.

But the opinion then seemed so strong and so nearly universal, that Lyon's fight at Wilson's Creek was a necessity and that Frémont ought to have reinforced him before that time at any cost, that perhaps Frémont had not the courage to do what was really best for his own defense, namely, to acknowledge and maintain that he had ordered Lyon to fall back and that the latter should have obeyed that order.

After reading the letter, Lyon's comment to Schofield was to the effect that he would sleep on it. The next morning, as Lyon sat down at his desk, Schofield, as a dutiful Chief of Staff, had a draft of a reply ready for the perusal of his chief. The draft read as follows:

General: I have just received your note of the 6th instant by special messenger. I retired to this place as I have before informed you, reaching here on the 5th. The enemy followed to within ten miles of here. He has taken a strong position, and is recruiting his supplies of horses, mules and provisions by forays into the surrounding country; his large force of mounted men enabling him to do this without annoyance from me.

I find my position extremely embarrassing and am at present unable to determine whether I shall be able to hold my ground or be forced to retire. I can resist any attack from the front, but if the enemy moves to surround me, I must retire. I shall hold my ground as long as possible, and not endanger the safety of my force with its valuable material.

After reading the letter carefully, Lyon stared vacantly for a time at a map on the wall. Then, with a return of his old-time air of decision, Lyon grabbed his pen. He struck out the last line in Schofield's draft—the words reading: ". . . and not endanger the safety of my force with its valuable material." Then he inserted an addition which made the last sentence of the draft conclude with these words:

I shall hold my ground as long as possible, although I may, without knowing how far, endanger the safety of my entire force with its valuable materials being induced by the important considerations involved to take this step. The enemy yesterday made a show of force, about five miles distant, and has doubtless a full purpose of making an attack upon me.

Evidently this definite act of putting his thoughts on paper, served as a booster to blast Lyon out of the doldrums of uncertainty. Quartermaster Mudd was the first to be aware of the return of the smoothly functioning and decisive commander. He entered the office, saluted and asked:

"When do we start back, General?"

The Missouri Yankee fixed his eyes on him—they were blue and bright with purpose. He replied in a firm, pleasant voice from which all irritability had vanished:

"When we are whipped back! Not until then!"

A hurry call went out for an immediate council of war. When all concerned were on hand, Lyon rose and, as recorded by Captain Steele, said:

"It is evident that we should retreat. The question arises, what is the best method of doing it? Shall we retreat without giving the enemy battle before hand and run the risk of having to fight every inch along our line of retreat?

"Or shall we attack him in his positions and endeavor to

hurt him so that he cannot follow? I am decidedly in favor of the latter plan.

"I propose to march this evening [August 9] with all our available force, leaving only a small guard to protect the property which will be left behind and, marching over the Fayetteville [Springfield] Road, throw our whole force upon him at once and endeavor to rout him before he recovers from his surprise."

Following this dictum, the meeting settled down to the task of discussing detailed plans for a surprise attack at dawn on August 10. In the course of these discussions, Colonel Sigel proposed that he should be allowed to take his brigade—about 1,200 infantry, cavalry, and six pieces of artillery—south of the enemy camp while Lyon's main force attacked from the north. The proposal was not regarded with favor. It was not adopted. Lyon made no comment. But later in the morning, Sigel had a private interview with him. This resulted in a new battle order that incorporated Sigel's original proposal.

By virtue of this change, Colonel Sigel was to move, at 6 o'clock that night, with the Third and Fifth Missouri, one company each of cavalry and dragoons, plus Bischoff's six-gun artillery, as a South Column against the enemy. He was to time his arrival at Wilson's Creek so that he would round the enemy's right flank at daylight and be in a position to attack when Lyon's guns began to boom. Sigel's total strength was about 1,200 men.

The Main or North Column, containing the remainder of Lyon's effectives—reduced to about 3,600 men (guards had to be left with the materials in town, many men were sick, others had extra duty)—were to march westward during the night, reach and round the enemy's left flank by daybreak, then launch the attack.

As the detailed orders were drawn, all was hustle and bustle in the camp. Confident that his plan would work, Lyon wanted to be ready to have the wagons roll toward Rolla at the earliest possible moment on his return to Springfield after he

203

had struck his paralyzing blow. He had no illusions about winning a battle. His project was just to hit the enemy hard enough to bowl him over and be on the run before the foe was in fighting balance again. To that end, everything was set for a swift withdrawal from Springfield to Rolla once the attack had been delivered. Tents were struck, wagons were loaded. Horses were ready for harness. All went smoothly and swiftly as sad-eyed and worried Springfield residents and refugees looked on.

Rations, that had to serve as their cold prebattle breakfast, were issued to the men. So were rounds of ammunition. Cartridge boxes were filled. Because of short range in rough country, all cannon were to use canister and shell. Sole exception was DuBois' 12-pounder. This had some solid shot in its ammunition lockers. The march was to begin at 6 o'clock that night of Friday, August 9. There was to be no excess baggage train. Only ammunition wagons and ambulances.

Price Hears of Lyon's Troubles

On August 8, Sterling Price had word at Wilson's Creek from his Springfield grapevine. It was that the overwhelming sentiment among Lyon's officers favored a retreat from Springfield to either Rolla or Fort Scott. Also, that Lyon was so jittery over the instability of his situation that his weary men were virtually under arms at all times and therefore not finely tuned for battle.

Price brought this news to McCulloch and urged him, with all the persuasion at his command, to attack Springfield on Saturday morning. He virtually guaranteed the Texan an easy victory. But Caesar's wreath contained too many Missouri thorns to sit easily on McCulloch's brow. This business of running a large show with a huge untried and untrained element worried him. The best word Price could get from the new Commander in Chief was that he would ride in person toward Springfield to see what he could. On his return to

Wilson's Creek, he would give Price his decision. One thing McCulloch was sure of: he would not, under any circumstances, make a blind attack on Springfield.

Accompanied by McIntosh and several local scouts, the Texan rode off with a large cavalcade. Day passed into night —and still McCulloch did not return. Price waited impatiently in his tent. Finally, at quite a late hour, the Missourian heard McCulloch's party return, but, contrary to his promise, the latter did not call on Major General Price.

That night, "Pap" Price lost his usually urbane calm as he tossed and boiled on his cot throughout the long hours. Friday at sunup, he sent for Snead and directed him to call on Brigadier General McCulloch for his answer. Price was so angry that he virtually spluttered as he spoke. Snead recalls that he barely had arrived at the Texan's tent, when Price rode up at a pounding gallop, threw himself off his mount, and strode into McCulloch's tent with outthrust jaw and blazing eyes. In strictly unparliamentary language, Price demanded that McCulloch should keep his promise to attack. The latter hemmed and hawed but finally agreed to give a definite answer that noon. As they parted, none too friendly, it was agreed that there would be a council of war of all general officers in Price's tent at that hour.

When the meeting convened, McCulloch again repeated his opposition to a blind attack on Springfield.

"If you fail to issue orders, right here and now, for an attack on Saturday at dawn," said Price in a voice that held the echoes of thunder, "I'll resume independent command of the Missouri State Guard and make the attack!"

At this juncture, Brigadier Generals Rains, Parsons, Clark, McBride, and Slack declared that their divisions would be ready to follow Sterling Price in a march on Springfield.

Following some more shilly-shallying on McCulloch's part, the latter at long last agreed to march on Springfield at 9 o'clock that night so as to be in position Saturday morning.

205

In Springfield, Lyon's Army of the West was making ready to pounce on the enemy at Wilson's Creek at sunrise on Saturday morning, August 10.

At Wilson's Creek, McCulloch's Confederate-Arkansas-Missouri forces were engaged in similiar preparations for a surprise blow on Springfield at the identical hour. As matters stood, both movements, if executed, would assume the aspects of a gargantuan game of blindman's buff. Neither side would be on hand to be tagged. Lyon would have the most to lose, were he to find a deserted enemy encampment at Wilson's Creek. McCulloch, on the other hand, would be sitting pretty in Springfield with Lyon out on a limb and the Union wagon train in his possession.

Somewhere, far to the west of Wilson's Creek and Springfield, rain clouds were formed and carried eastward in the hearts of mighty thunderheads. It is possible that the rain, which was to pour from the skies over southwest Missouri after sunset that night, changed the destiny of a Cause and the course of the Civil War.

Chapter 10

Wilson's Creek

Profile of a Battlefield

The place in the wilderness called Wilson's Creek is diminutive and unimpressive when one stacks it up against most sizes and shapes of other Civil War battlefields. But the utter savagery with which that battle was fought—with muskets, rifles, and cannon firing point-blank within shotgun range—places it high among the most hotly contested encounters in the Civil War. Several infantry regiments on both sides had casualties that mounted as high as 38 per cent. The grand total of killed and wounded exceeded 2,500.

One might say that from a military standpoint the Battle of Wilson's Creek was fought in a weed patch only about half a dozen city blocks long and actually only two city blocks wide. Within those narrow confines—hidden by the foliage of the stunted oaks called black-jack, or sheltered by tall grass, dense brush, or thorny thickets—men fought doggedly against each other in a battle that brought neither conclusive victory nor emphatic defeat for either side, but which, nevertheless, served the purpose of the soldier who initiated it.

Wilson's Creek has a total run of about 15 miles. It comes into existence five miles southwest of Springfield. It ends when it merges with the James River. During the first half-dozen miles of its length, the creek meanders westward. Then, in a sweeping curve, it turns to the south and runs—for some eight to ten miles—between sharply rising bluffs and tall hills cut by occasional ravines.

Although the area of Wilson's Creek today is virtually as it was one century ago, there may be enough differences in points of identification to make it necessary for us to look at it through the eyes of those who saw the scene as it appeared on that August 10.

Through this setting ran the Springfield Road. Coming up from the south, the highway passed Sharp's farm—that stood near the edge of a high bluff—and swept down into the valley of Wilson's Creek. After crossing the ford of a small tributary called Skegg's Branch, the road followed the winding course of the creek through a rather narrow valley. This was lined on the east with bluffs that often rose steeply to 80 feet before they leveled off to thickly vegetated tableaux. On the west, fringed at its foot by a grassy expanse known as Skegg's meadow, rose the major eminence that gave the area its name, Oak Hill. From the meadow to the top of this elevation was a distance of about 150 feet. About half of that lifted in gentle slopes cut by ravines and covered by scrub oak, heavy underbrush, and with rocks cropping out near the top. This was to become Bloody Hill.

After following Wilson's Creek for about a mile, the highway swung abruptly eastward, crossed a ford, and headed toward Springfield through a thickly wooded, canyon-like defile. On the plateau just north of this turn of the road, to the east of the stream, lay Ray's cornfield, which was to become the scene of hot fighting. Just beyond it stood Gibson's Mill.

Below the bluff, where the highway dipped down from Sharp's farm, and flanking the west bank of Wilson's Creek, was another large expanse of grassland called Sharp's field. Just south of it stood the Dixon homestead near Terrell Creek.

Commanding this wilderness of rambling creeks, rocky bluffs, and thick vegetation towered Oak Hill. To one who stood on its top, its contour would appear like that of an upturned left hand with thumb and three fingers—index, middle,

208

and little finger—outspread. The palm of that hand, which formed the top elevation of the hill, was about one-quarter mile long and one-eighth mile wide. The thumb, some 70 feet below and to the left, pointed toward Wilson's Creek. The index, middle, and little fingers—formed by ridges cut by ravines—stretched toward the valley of Skegg's Branch. Each finger measured about one-third of a mile in length and the entire spread across the fingers was only about two-thirds of a mile. On this palm, on these fingers, and in these ravines, the major phase of the battle of Bloody Hill was fought.

Distribution of Rebel Forces

With the stage set, it is time to turn attention to the characters who soon would step upon it.

First to appear were McCulloch, Price, and Pearce with their respective armies.

The date—August 9, 1861.

Because of the room afforded there for men and horses, virtually all of the cavalry regiments—Churchill's, Greer's, Major's, and Brown's—were assigned to Sharp's big field south of Sharp's farm. The bay windows, on the heights directly across Wilson's Creek, look right into the field occupied by the horsemen.

In Skegg's meadow, and along the banks of Skegg's Branch, all the State Guard infantry—excepting Weightman's brigade—bivouacked. These included Guibor's and Bledsoe's batteries. Here, too, the armies' combined wagon trains parked in row on row with only narrow walkways in between. Just below the ford on Wilson's Creek, at the foot of Oak Hills, Price and four of his generals—Slack, McBride, Clark, and Parsons—had their headquarters.

Amidst the brush, grass, thickets, and black-jack on the northern plateau east of the creek, McCulloch's Confederates and Pearce's Arkansas were crowded fairly close together with Weightman's Brigade of the Missouri State Guard (Rains). On the bulge of the steeply rising wall that overlooks the ford, where the Springfield Road crosses Wilson's Creek, stood Woodruff's four-gun battery. McCulloch's and Pearce's headquarters were close to the latter. Below and across Wilson's Creek, lay Price's headquarters, almost within hailing distance.

Farther north, on both sides of Wilson's Creek, Brigadier General Rains' Mounted Brigade (Cawthorne)—1,210 strong, well armed, and trained to serve as both cavalry and infantry —was on outpost duty. Although he had incurred the wrath of McCulloch and McIntosh in his luckless encounter at Dug Springs, all seemed to be forgiven. At least, once again, Rains was entrusted with the task of being on the alert against overt acts from Lyon's command in Springfield.

General Rains' own headquarters, and about two-thirds of his brigade, were placed on the Oak Hills terrace identified as the thumb. This camp lies about three-quarters of a mile north of Price's encampment at the ford. The remainder of the outfit, under Colonel Cawthorne, was two-thirds of a mile farther upstream in the vicinity of Gibson's Mill along a trail that runs between Wilson's Creek and Ray's cornfield. The Confederate-Arkansas-Missouri Army on that day, had 10,219 effectives. They were almost equally divided between infantry and cavalry, plus 11 pieces of artillery. (For full listings of the three Southern brigades see Appendix.)

That entire August 9 was one of busy preparation for McCulloch's armies. The orders were to march at 9 o'clock that night against Springfield. The whole encampment was alive with excitement when the orders were issued soon after the midday meal. Not much of a feast, that meal! All grits. No gravy. But who cared, what with a real picnic, like a battle, in the offing.

The troops were drawn up in regiments just before sundown. Ammunition was issued. The men in the Missouri divisions did not have ammunition boxes. They carried their cartridges in cotton bags slung around their necks with pieces of string. This arrangement—while seemingly workable—would be nullified if the black clouds that filled the sky should launch their cargoes of rain. Paper cartridges were notoriously vulnerable to moisture. Because virtually all of the Missouri firearms were smooth-bore weapons of identical caliber, there had been few distribution problems. Most of the cartridges held a ball and six slugs of lead. However, since the majority of their guns were shotguns, and effective only at short range, the Missourians added a bit of extra seasoning to their fusillades. After they rammed their cartridges home, they would drop a handful of buckshot—which they carried in bags or in bulging pockets—into the gun barrels. Such a volley, aimed at breeches buttons at 40 yards, could have devastating effect.

The men stood in ranks when rain began to fall—faster and faster. In an off-the-saddle conference, Price and McCulloch agreed that damage to ammunition by rain would reduce the firing power of the Missourians a full 75 per cent. No sense in going on under those conditions. McCulloch knew that many of his men had only 20 rounds of ammunition and there was no more to be had. Many soldiers were issued only eight rounds, it was revealed later. Orders were given for the men to break ranks and to sleep on their arms in view of a probable order to march when and if the weather cleared during the night.

However, no such instructions were issued as the hours of darkness ticked off toward dawn.

Two Columns March on Wilson's Creek

During the afternoon of August 9, Lyon held a council of war with brigade and regimental commanders. Their only map of the battle area was one sketched by Lyon. It was based on knowledge gained by him on his previous encampment near Wilson's Creek, and Lyon had a well-trained topographical eye. In addition, local men, who were to serve as guides, attended the powwow. They included John Steele and Andrew Adams, for Sigel; Pleasant Hart and Parker Cox, for Lyon. The brigadier general outlined the strategy and tactics of the op-

211

eration. From the top of Oak Hills, he said, the Federals could dominate the encampment below with musketry and cannon fire. This gave McCulloch one of two choices. He could either storm up the hill and into Lyon's missiles, or he could run down the Springfield Road and find Sigel blocking his path.

It was agreed that Sigel's Column would march south about a dozen miles so as to be well below the enemy location at Oak Hills. Then he would turn west on a narrow wagon road, reach Wilson's Creek, and cross it near Dixon's homestead on Terrell Creek. There he was to plant his cannon in the most advantageous positions so as to throw a heavy fire into Sharp's field where, Lyon knew, virtually all of the foe's cavalry was encamped. However, Sigel was to keep under cover and not to open fire until he heard the sound of Lyon's guns about two miles to the north. In rounding the enemy's right flank, Sigel was to use the utmost precaution of secrecy and silence. His second mission was to help bottle-up the enemy at Wilson's Creek and prevent an organized exodus to the south.

As for the Main Column, Lyon's route lay westward six miles over the Mount Vernon Road and then cross-country to the south until he reached the bend in Wilson's Creek. Next he had to cross the valley where stood E. B. Short's farm. After that, he would march up the sheltering northern slope of Oak Hill to the small plateau on its top, get into position, and start the action.

It is virtually impossible to make an accurate estimate of the manpower strength of Lyon's two columns. This because the basic figures of Federal contingents were the muster rolls and not the men actually under arms at the time. The Confederate system, based on effectives actually engaged, is much more reliable. Due to the unreliability of Federal figures, estimates of Lyon's forces vary all the way from an impossible high of 5,400 to a more acceptable 4,800. Of these, 1,123 were in Sigel's column and 3,600 in Lyon's. As previously pointed out, a large contingent of personnel was left in Springfield for various reasons. Lyon could have bolstered his dwindling

Army of the West with a force of about 1,200 well-armed local Home Guards under Captain Marcus Boyd. They were eager to get into the show and confident of their ability to stand up under fire. However, Lyon did not share their confidence. He knew how green troops could trigger avalanches of demoralization under battle pressures and did not want to take any chances.

With respect to the green Missouri Home Guards, Lyon was just as wrong as McCulloch was in regard to his untried Missouri State Guard. Green, gray, or blue—the recruits on both sides fought with the cool tenacity of veterans and stood as steady as rocks.

Union adjutants included all enlisted men and officers present for duty, comprising cooks, clerks, detailed orderlies, wagon guards, farriers, teamsters, hospital details, and helpers of every kind and character; while the Confederate adjutants pursued the better plan of reporting as engaged only those with arms in their hands and actually in the line of battle. For instance, the First Kansas is reported to have had 800 men engaged. Actually the count, just before the battle began, when the column was formed in platoons, was but 644. In the Second Kansas, 600 men were reported as present. Of these, 155 were somewhere else than in the line of battle. (*For full listings of Union forces, see Appendix.*)

The three brigades were constituted as follows:

First—under Major Sturgis: Plummer's Battalion; Osterhaus' Battalion; Totten's Battery; Wood's Kansas Rangers; and Canfield's First U. S. Cavalry.

Second—under Lieutenant Colonel Andrews: Steele's Battalion; First Missouri Regiment of Infantry; and DuBois' Battery.

Third—under Captain Sweeny: Dietzler's First Kansas; Mitchell's Second Kansas; Merritt's First Iowa; Wright's Home Guards (Reserve).

As the council of war broke up, and the participants returned to their respective camps, Lyon stepped out into the street and walked toward the town square. He discovered that Springfield was in utter confusion. Merchandise and household goods were being loaded into wagons, carts, and carriages in preparation for the exodus which everyone knew was at hand. It was all very depressing to Lyon. He felt that, if all had gone as it should, the Union people of the Springfield region would have been wholly secure in their homes. Certainly, he might paralyze the enemy at Wilson's Creek. Still, the foe would be strong enough to swarm over the town and drain it dry of resources after he staged his retreat.

About 6 o'clock, Lyon swung into the saddle on his gray stallion. Accompanied by Major Schofield, his guides, and other aides, he headed toward the camp west of town occupied by his column. Clouds—dark and pregnant with rain—were blanketing the westering sun. Occasional gusts of wind presaged bad weather.

On reaching camp, Lyon noted that the companies were in regimental formations. Starting at the head, he rode slowly down the long lines and came to a full stop before each company. His all-seeing eyes seemed to scrutinize the face of each and every man as he sat erect in the saddle. To each company, he made the same speech and he made it without a lilt or a lift from his ordinary level of intonation:

"Men, we are going to have a fight. We will march out in a short time. Don't shoot until you get orders. Fire low—don't aim higher than their knees; wait until they get close; don't get scared; it is no part of a soldier's duty to get scared."

No hat waving. No flag waving. No cheers. Lyon had no illusions about the inspiring glory of battle. He knew it as a bloody task in which only killing counted and only the lucky and the cool survived. Unfortunately, the young men—who stood on the eve of battle—could not read the thoughts of grave and comradely concern in their leader's mind. In his book, *The Lyon Campaign in Missouri: Being a History of the First Iowa Infantry*, Private Eugene F. Ware, Company E, vividly recalls Lyon making that statement and the letdown it evoked among his comrades. In Civil War days, as before, generals made fiery speeches to their followers before they entered into battle. And the men, in turn, would cheer their generals to the echo. But this night, up and down the line, not a throat vibrated with a hurrah for Lyon.

Sigel Rounds McCulloch's Right Flank

Sigel moved out of camp at 6:30 o'clock and headed down the Springfield Road toward Wilson's Creek for a distance of some four miles. The night was dark and it was raining. Presently, however, the downpour died into a drizzle. From the highway, the column swung straight south over open country. The guides, and Captain Carr's First Cavalry company, had the lead. It required great caution for the vanguard not to lose its way or not to get separated from the main body. Carr's orders were to pick up and hold any person they might come upon; this to prevent information from reaching the enemy.

After trudging some five hours over muddy and rain-sodden country, at the end of which both men and animals were approaching exhaustion, the column rested in a glade of trees, protected from the rain. No fires were lit and all sounds were held at a minimum. At 2 o'clock in the morning, the march was resumed. Nothing untoward occurred during the next two hours. In time the column reached, as expected, the wagon road that crossed Wilson's Creek a short distance to the westward.

Signs that they were approaching the enemy camp appeared about 4 o'clock when, in the lingering darkness, foragers were met going into the surrounding country from the camp. Some 40 were captured by Captain Carr's cavalrymen before they could make outcry or flee.

One of the prisoners said that they were expecting reinforcements from Louisiana and that they had mistaken Carr's cavalry for the reinforcements. In the dark of that morning, Federal coats looked gray.

At about 4:30 o'clock, Colonel Sigel took Lieutenant Farrand and his dragoons to the head of the column and placed his two companies of horsemen ahead and on his flanks. Soon Farrand discovered a small party of men and horses in a ravine—evidently pickets. The men saw him, too, mounted their animals and rode off. Farrand did not capture them but he reported with satisfaction that he had cut them off from their camp. The latter was now in full view, slightly ahead, but mainly on the right.

Luckily for Sigel, at this point the road entered the incline of a ravine. Its walls sheltered his troops from sight. As Sigel held his force briefly under this cover, Carr conducted a swift reconnaissance. It revealed that Wilson's Creek was just ahead and that a large force of rebel cavalry—Churchill, Major, Brown, and Greer—was encamped upstream in Sharp's field on the west bank. Carr also reported that a bluff on the east bank overlooked the site and was a natural selection for the emplacement of cannon. Leaving Carr with his cavalry and an infantry support of several companies as their protective shield, two cannon, under Lieutenant Schuetzenbach, were planted near the edge of the bluff. He was ordered not to discharge a shot until he heard Sigel's fire. Then his guns were to hurl several salvos of canister and shell in among the horsemen who were tending to their animals or preparing breakfast. Carr's position was well sheltered by a curtain of tall weeds.

The rest of Sigel's force crossed Wilson's Creek near Dixon's homestead. Following a rough cattle trail through a thickly wooded area, the column halted when scouts reported sighting the rebel cavalry camp through the edge of the trees.

For Sigel, there was now nothing to do but wait until he heard the opening shots of Nathaniel Lyon's attack from the direction of Oak Hill. The first part of his mission had been performed smoothly and without opposition.

216

Springfield was too far away from Lyon's column for any of its inhabitants to hear when the bugles sounded their lilting summons and when harsh commands set the long line of men, animals, cannon, ammo wagons, and ambulances into motion. The hour hand was creeping toward 7 o'clock when the brigades began to roll. They had not marched far when it started to rain.

When the column had moved far enough from Springfield to stretch out, Lyon halted his horse on the top of a rise in the road and let his troops march past. The night was much too dark to catch even glimpses of faces. But Lyon could hear the talk and laughter in the ranks. He accepted them as signs of high combat morale.

But, even more reassuring to him was the firm, rhythmic cadence of their steps, the solid, earth-shaking impacts with which their boots hit the road. No downhearted dragging of feet here. Even the rain and the mud could not muffle the pulsing tramp—tramp—tramp of their vigorous steps.

Lyon's thoughts flashed back to Boonville where he first had heard his men "Keep Step to the Music of the Union." Now he heard them again.

Tramp—tramp—tramp. The brisk pace of the route step. The taps of company drums.

All was well.

Satisfied, Lyon wheeled his horse down the road and galloped back to the head of the column. As he rode, it is likely that he gave silent thanks for the windfall of shoes that came from Rolla in the nick of time. Even in those hardy days, few men could march to battle in bare feet.

Riding with Lyon, his staff, and guides as an advance guard was Lieutenant Canfield and Company B, First U. S. Cavalry. Then followed Sturgis' Brigade: Captain Plummer's Battalion of regular infantry; Osterhaus' Second Missouri; Totten's Battery; Wood's Kansas Rangers. With but a brief gap, followed Andrews' Brigade: Steele's Battalion of regular infantry;

DuBois' Battery and First Missouri. Next came Sweeny's Brigade of reserves: Dietzler's First Kansas; Mitchell's Second Kansas; Bates' First Iowa; and Wright's Mounted Home Guards.

A description of part of that march was given, with many homely touches, by Albert R. Greene before the Kansas Historical Society in Topeka in 1895. Mr. Greene had marched in the First Kansas on that occasion and he remembered it well. In part, he said, as he spoke about that night of long ago:

The little army was composed of volunteers fresh from the avocations of peace, and regulars who, though long in service, had, with few exceptions, save as to their officers, never engaged in battle or been under fire. The former were officered by old acquaintances and neighbors, who had generally been elected by the men to the positions they held, and who, like themselves, knew little of the science of war. They were from Iowa, Kansas, and Missouri, and the range of their experience in the use of fire-arms comprised the usual exploits of frontiersmen in the game fields of the forest and prairie, with an occasional skirmish against border ruffians in the Kansas troubles. They were marksmen in a general way, and might be said to be handy with the rifle and revolver. A majority were young men or boys; middle aged men with bearded faces were rare exceptions. The few there were had generally seen service in Mexico, a dozen years before, or in European armies when they were boys. . . .

During the three months of service in the Union Army they had been constantly in the field, marching, camping, drilling, foraging, and enduring restively the privations and restraints common to recruits. . . . Now, when a battle was at hand, the enthusiasm manifested itself in copious jokes and ebullitions of song. . . .

The regulars jogged along in comparative silence. Though perhaps no less patriotic, they were nevertheless professional soldiers, at home as much in one place as another, and contented to march a reasonable distance in a day or night in any direction, and fight about so hard and so long whenever called on, as a matter of course.

Between these and the volunteers, there was a mutual feeling

218

of unfriendliness and aversion. Neither party was willing to dignify the other with an admission of jealousy, but each one did envy the other some of their privileges or possessions—the regulars, the roistering style allowed the volunteers; and the volunteers the superior knowledge and better equipment of the regulars.

This feeling of scant civility and offishness was not confined to the ranks; officers shared it to a greater degree than the soldiers, and harbored it more tenaciously. . . . The regular officer, who had devoted his life to the service, had fought in the Seminole and Mexican wars, and hunted Indians all over the plains and mountains, felt an inexpressible disgust at being commanded by a man who had been a farmer or a tradesman a few weeks before, even though he now held a rank several grades higher than himself. . . .

The same feeling existed between volunteers, who had been regularly mustered into the service of the United States, and Home Guards who were in service temporarily. The volunteers persecuted them as they themselves were in like manner persecuted by the regulars.

The proportion of regulars to volunteers in Lyon's army was as one to four, comprised for the greater part of seasoned troops, representing all arms of the service. Two of his three batteries were regulars, and as good as the best. He had privates in his column who wore service chevrons for four terms of five years each. These old soldiers infused a confidence into the ranks of the volunteers which, in spite of all bickerings, was of the greatest value.

It seemed like delegations from Lawrence, Wyandotte, Atchison, Leavenworth, Emporia and a dozen other Kansas towns on their way to a state convention at Topeka. It would never have been mistaken for a funeral procession. Deitzler, Mitchell, Cloud, Sam Walker, Sam Crawford, were moving back and forth along the column giving orders, interchanging views, visiting, chatting with the men, and having a good time generally. John Halderman was working on a series of lurid battle cries which were received with great approval by the hilarious crowd. John K. Rankin, for all the world the size and build of General Lyon, and, although an officer, in rags like the rest. He had an old bayonet for a sword, and tinfoil shoulder straps sewed on with black thread. Officers of higher rank had loaded themselves down with a dragoon sabre apiece, found in the deserted camp of the regulars. They had also appropriated more or less disabled gilt braid, wilted plumes, etc., and, thus arrayed, felt themselves elevated to a plane of unapproachable grandeur. . . .

According to the conflicting statements of eye witnesses, Lyon was dressed in the uniform of a brigadier-general, the uniform of a captain of infantry, and in citizen's clothes, including a linen duster. By the same authorities he wore a forage cap, a yellow wool slouch hat, and a black campaign hat. The men wore government blouses and socks and a miscellaneous assortment of other clothing such as the country afforded. For head gear they had everything, from the range of Jackson's white plug hat at Talladega, to Scott's monstrosity at Cherubusco.

About every other man was sure he would never come out alive. There was much interchanging of messages to be sent to the friends in Kansas, and some were so fully impressed with the belief of their doom that they disposed of their property and made presents, to those who were not so sure of dying, of whatever trinkets they had about them. Lieutenant Jones was one of these; he gave away his pony, and sent word to all his friends in Kansas that they would find him at Wilson Creek! He was shot through the forehead at one of the first volleys. . . .

At the head of the column, mounted on a magnificent dapple-gray horse, rode a man who, if he had lived, would have become commander-in-chief of the army and afterward president, if he had so desired. He would have been the Grant of the war. A man of medium height, slightly built, a full beard of refractory sandy whiskers, blue eyes, deeply set, and a thoughtful, careworn face. . . . Two months before, he had stalked out of the presence of Sterling Price and Claiborne F. Jackson, daring them to a trial of arms. That trial was coming on in a few brief hours. . . .

On this kindly note, let us leave Mr. Greene and his running commentary for the present. Seen from another viewpoint—that of a young private—Brigadier General Lyon does not seem to possess the same striking qualities. Again we turn to Private Ware of Company E, First Iowa. Here is a portrait of Lyon as this teen-age soldier described him:

Lyon was a small man, lean, active and sleepless. He was not an old man although he had wrinkles on the top of his nose. He had a look of incredulity; he did not believe things. He looked like an eccentric man, like an educated "crank." He looked like a man who knew absolutely what he knew. He looked like a man who would be wilfully insubordinate. His hair was sandy red and curly—not kinky but inclined to curl. His beard was worn full; it was a thin, struggling, meager, reddish, unattractive beard, and he pulled on it and jerked on it when he was talking decisively, probably pulling some of it out. . . .

He was not a man that had poise. I think that mentally, he was a good deal of a martinet. He believed in every man knowing his duty and doing it strictly. He was a man, apparently, with whom friendships would not count. He seemed to have no kind word for anybody. He was said to be an uncompromising abolitionist. I think that he was a harsh judge and disinclined to overlook any infraction of duty or military rules. His mental activity must have been intense; he believed in an iron rule.

I never liked him nor did any of us as far as I could ever see, but we did believe that he was a brave and educated officer. He struck us all a man devoted to duty, who thought duty, dreamed duty and who had nothing but duty on his mind.

Could it be that Ware—who tangled with Lyon on several occasions due to his impulsive nature and civilian lack of discipline—drew a fairly accurate picture? But if he did, Ware left out at least one thing, and that was Lyon's deep and abiding love of the Union and his devotion to freedom. One might truly say that the Nation was his mother and that the Army was his wife. With but one single and little known exception in his earlier years, Nathaniel Lyon had (excepting family affections) neither eyes, nor thought, nor love for anything or anyone else.

An interesting glimpse of Lyon, as he saw himself in the early 1850's, is found in the following self-portrait written by him in California. As will be noted, love or women have no place in the picture:

Growing old, but not ashamed of it; proud, perhaps, but not haughty; prudent, may be, in worldly affairs, yet not crafty for wealth; desirous enough for fame but not infuriated with blind ambition—and, in general, taking the world as it comes, enjoying its many blessings, sympathizing with the unfortunate and laughing with the indifference of cool philosophy at the sore disappointments with which selfishness and cupidity are ever torturing their victims.

Well, at any rate, during recent weeks, Lyon had met almost constant needs to draw upon his reserves of "cool philosophy."

In the neighborhood of Little York, the guides reported that the time had come to turn to the south. As the column swung into a straight but narrow wagon road, orders were passed down the line for instant and maximum silence. No more singing. No more loud talking or laughing in the ranks. Somewhere ahead lay the critical zone where complete success depended on complete surprise. The guides, Parker Cox and Pleasant Hart, moved alternatingly forward to make sure that the coast was clear and that the path was right.

After about an hour's silent marching, the column entered a country well wooded and filled with large stone formations. Through timbers and around rocks, the road snaked its lonesome way southward. About 1 o'clock in the morning, the scouts reported that Lyon was now within a few miles of the enemy's camp at Oak Hills. The guides invited him to climb with them to the top of one of the loftier piles of rocks. From this elevation, despite the drizzling rain, the campfires of the enemy were just distinguishable as crimson reflections on the low-hanging clouds. At this particular point, the country was rather open and treeless. The reflected glows were to the east and south. Lyon had succeeded in rounding the enemy's left flank. He felt certain that Sigel had been equally fortunate on the right. Having heard no sound of distant gunfire, Lyon took this as a good sign.

Patrols, sent forth on cautious missions to feel for enemy pickets, returned dumfounded as they reported no contacts. They had no way of knowing that Rains' and Cawthorne's pickets had been withdrawn prior to the contemplated march on Springfield the night before; nor that they had been kept under shelter during the night in order to keep their ammunition dry.

Moving forward at a slow and silent pace, Lyon's column reached an abandoned picket post. Knowing that he must be fairly close to any outposts the enemy might have, Lyon bivouacked his army to wait for daylight. The hour was 4:15 o'clock and on Short's nearby farm early birds among the roosters began their salute to the new day.

Some men dropped in their tracks, others sought shelter among rocks or under nearby trees. Major Schofield discovered a small, cavelike hollow between two boulders which he offered to share with his commander. It was a rocky little lair and Schofield felt rather apologetic about it.

"I'm afraid that you are not very comfortable, sir," said the youthful Chief of Staff. "These rocks seem to be in the way no matter how one turns."

"Think nothing of it," replied Lyon with a chuckle. "I'm quite all right. Back in Connecticut, where I come from, I was born and bred among rocks."

After a few more words, both men dropped into silence. Many minutes slipped by. Schofield, thinking about what the morning might bring, believed that Lyon had gone to sleep. Suddenly, the latter said:

"Schofield—I'm a great believer in presentiments. Somehow, I have a feeling that I can't get rid of, that I'll not survive this battle."

There it was again. That strange compulsive feeling that had seized him before, in Kansas; the feeling that the end of his road lay just around the corner and that he had a vital job to finish before he made the inescapable turn.

Cawthorne's Pickets Make Dawn Patrol

Day had not quite dawned, when Major General Price roused Colonel Snead out of his slumbers and directed him to cross Wilson's Creek to Brigadier General McCulloch's tent with an urgent invitation for the Texan and Colonel McIntosh to join him at breakfast. Price was legitimately annoyed because McCulloch had again failed to advise him with respect to his future plans for attack. The Missourian had made up his mind that this was the end. If McCulloch did not attack this very morning, Price would attack Springfield on his own and McCulloch could go to hell.

As Price dressed, while waiting for Snead's return, the advance camps of Rains and Cawthorne stirred into action. In the former, forage parties were being organized; in the latter, a patrol was being sent out to scout the prairie. Proceeding at a leisurely pace, Cawthorne's patrol was about one and a half miles north of Gibson's Mill when it discovered movement in front and to the left. Careful scrutiny revealed it to be a Federal patrol. Directing his men to take cover and not to fire unless they were attacked, the patrol leader reported. Cawthorne immediately ordered Colonel Hunter, a lanky lantern-jawed hemp planter, to saddle up and, with some 300 men, find out if the enemy were advancing in force. When Hunter reached the patrol about 5 o'clock, the head of the Federal column was in sight. Being under orders not to engage the enemy, Hunter withdrew all of Cawthorne's men and headed back to camp to report.

In the meanwhile, to the west of Wilson's Creek and about half a mile south of Gibson's Mill, Brigadier General Rains received seemingly unreliable reports from foragers that the enemy was advancing in force. He had been seen several miles from camp on the west side of the creek.

To make certain, Rains dispatched his Chief of Staff, Colonel Snyder, posthaste to the north. Snyder, being an excellent as well as fearless rider, took the assignment at full gallop. It seemed that he had hardly left before he returned. He had to waste time finding Rains. When he finally located him, Snyder, without formality, pulled up before his commander and yelled:

"The Federals are coming in great force! Their soldiers and cannon cover the whole damn prairie!"

Following a brief interchange of words, Rains directed Snyder to report to Major General Price.

Union Forces Contact the Enemy

The cocks were really crowing when the sleeping men in Lyon's column were shaken awake by their noncoms who whispered hoarsely as drowsy eyes were opened:

"Get up! Fall in. Keep silent. Not a damn sound, do you hear?"

As the lines were being formed, Brigadier General Lyon rode up to Plummer's Battalion. He directed that Captain Gilbert should take his Company D and move forward to probe for the enemy. The exact position of the latter was ascertained shortly after sunrise. Plummer then was ordered to follow Captain Gilbert with the balance of the battalion, and, uniting with him, cross Wilson's Creek to the east bank to carry forward the left flank of the attack.

Simultaneously, the troops were set in motion in a southeasterly direction. Lieutenant Colonel Andrews received orders to bring his First Missouri up to the head of the column, then still tipped by Plummer's Battalion. Lyon directed that the First Missouri should march parallel with Plummer and at a distance of about 60 yards. Moments later—when Lyon's discovery of enemy pickets and foragers made it certain that his presence would not long remain secret—Andrews was ordered to deploy one company forward as skirmishers. Captain Yates, Company H, immediately executed the command which resulted in the driving in of Colonel Hunter's pickets. This contact with the enemy was followed by an order for the regiment to advance in column of companies. A few shots had been exchanged by skirmishers and pickets. Lieutenant Colo-

225

nel Andrews looked at his watch. The hour was 5:10 o'clock.

The element of surprise having been torn to shreds, Lyon stepped up his pace and the column moved ahead as rapidly as the soggy ground and tangled vegetation would permit. All regiments now marched in column by companies, the batteries by section.

McCulloch's Breakfast Incompleted

Price, McCulloch, McIntosh, and Snead were having breakfast—soggy cornmeal, tough beef, weak coffee. There was no conversation. Chomping that meat down to swallowing size took all the jaw-power the four could muster.

Then, after being announced by an aide, Colonel Hunter entered the tent to deliver the news of his contact with the enemy in force.

McCulloch gave Hunter a piercing look, swallowed hard, and remarked coolly:

"Another one of Rains' scares!" He waved a hand at Hunter in dismissal.

The Texan just had had time to take a hunk of cornbread and slosh it around in the meat juice on his plate, when there was another interruption. This time Colonel Snyder rushed into the tent. He fixed his flashing dark eyes on Sterling Price and, without preliminaries, shouted:

"'Pap,' I've seen them! They're coming! The Federals! By God! 20,000 men and 100 pieces of artillery!"

Without waiting for a reply, Colonel Snyder ran out of the tent, climbed on his horse, and headed back to his outfit to be ready for the battle he knew was close at hand.

McCulloch shook his head in disbelief. Price rose from his camp chair and walked toward the tent flap.

Lyon Speeds to a Position of Attack

Passing to the west of Short's farm—infantry on the double, cavalry at a jog, caissons and cannon thumping and jumping over the rough ground—Lyon's column rushed southward.

Plummer, on the left flank across the creek, with Wright's Mounted Home Guards on his own left flank, was maintaining visual contact and keeping pace with the main force on its southward dash. The captain had wallowed into trouble before he had a chance to catch up with Gilbert and Company D. In his report, Plummer said:

I overtook Captain Gilbert in a deep jungle, said Plummer in his report, where he had been checked by an impassable lagoon. Much time was consumed in effecting a passage of this obstacle. The battalion, however, finally emerged in good order into a cornfield. . . .

Across Spring Branch and its valley, Lyon rode impatiently at the tip of his troops. On his right and left were his guides. To the fore were his First Missouri skirmishers. To the immediate rear were Andrews and his First Missouri with Totten and his six cannon almost stepping on their quickly moving heels.

Up the slope to the first plateau. The thumb of the hand. And there was the enemy. Not in force. But in sufficient numbers to give pause. After crossing a ravine and ascending a high ridge, they came in full view of a considerable force of Rains' skirmishers. Major Osterhaus' battalion was at once deployed to the right, and two companies of the First Missouri Volunteers, under Captains Yates and Cavender, were deployed to the left, all as skirmishers. The firing now became very severe. It was evident to Lyon that he was approaching the enemy's stronghold, where the rebels intended to give battle. A few shells from Totten's battery assisted his skirmishers in clearing the ground in front.

What actually happened was that: On the east side of Wilson's Creek—below Gibson's Mill—Plummer's Battalion had tangled with Cawthorne's outpost and, after a hot but brief encounter, driven it back. The dismounted Missourians made a short, futile stand with shotguns against the rifled muskets of the regulars.

On the west side of Wilson's Creek, the Federal forces had come upon the portion of Cawthorne's brigade encamped under Rains. Here, too, the resistance was of short duration. The outpost on the thumb crumbled as it had at Gibson's Mill. In short order, there was a wild retreat of horses, wagons, and riders down the hill, despite heroic efforts of sturdy individuals of all ranks—from Jimmy Rains himself to cabin-bred privates—to stop the flow. But the rain of missiles, large and small, solid or exploding, was too much for mortal men to take without a chance really to fight back.

In a very short time, Rains' encampment was a deserted space dotted with empty tents and a few scattered wagons. With those of his men still on hand, Rains regrouped his forces under the brow of the hill. There, in thick underbrush, hidden and out of range of Totten's guns, he soon established a foothold which Lyon was unable to dislodge.

Sigel's Cannon Begin to Bark

In his position south of Sharp's field, just north of Terrell Creek, Colonel Sigel had been waiting with eager impatience for the roar of Totten's guns. On the heights across Wilson's Creek, two hidden cannon stood ready to hurl their shot into the camp of enemy cavalry. His force at hand, equally well shielded, was ready to sustain the bombardment with additional cannon and musketry fire.

The morning was as quiet as the proverbial grave. The chill air and overcast sky did not encourage birds and insects to give voice to their usual chirrupings. From the nearby enemy camp came the occasional sounds of horses, the calls of waking men, and the odors from cooking fires. The peaceful morning scene was a good omen to Colonel Sigel. The silence proved that the rebels had not the slightest inkling of the unpleasant and painful surprise that he held in store for them.

Now, muted by distance, came the roar of a cannon. Another blast. And still another. Totten's iron dogs were barking and it was time for Sigel to join their chorus.

"Fire!" he shouted at Captain Schaefer.

The four-gun section exploded charges of canister into the cavalry encampment. A split-second later, Schuetzenbach's two guns on the opposite heights slammed out their case shots. Unfortunately, the aim was high and most of the missiles crashed harmlessly into the woods. The battery's original gunners, all 90-day men, had returned to Saint Louis. They had been replaced by green recruits who did not know a touch-hole from an elbow. Loading and firing the guns excited these youngsters to a point where neither Schuetzenbach nor his noncoms could make them take time out to aim their pieces. It was bang—bang—bang! Great fun and to hell with where the shots went.

Still, even if the artillery fire was poorly directed, its psychological impact on men and horses was heavy. There was a headlong exodus from the camp. Chores were left undone and breakfast uneaten as men rushed for shelter. Many left their frightened horses to their own devices. But, from habit or otherwise, most of the mounted riflemen swept up their arms and ammunition.

Price Halts a "Panic-Stricken Drove"

"Pap" Price had not had time to cross the stamped-down grass that constituted the carpet of his tent when claps of man-made thunder seemed to crash all about him. As he emerged into the open, he looked up the gentle slope to the top of Oak Hill. There, silhouetted against the skyline, he saw Totten's cannon spewing flame and dirty gray smoke. Seconds later came the explosion of shells. From Rains' and Cawthorne's camps on the heights along each side of Wilson's Creek, living streams of men poured with the turmoil of flash floods. Snead, who stood at his general's side at this breathtaking moment, describes it:

229

Looking up, we could, ourselves, see a great crowd of men on horseback, some armed, and some unarmed, mixed in with wagons and teams and led horses; all in dreadful confusion, scampering over the hill, and rushing toward us—a panic-stricken drove.

We saw the flash and heard the report of Totten's guns, which had gone into battery on the top of the hill, not more than 1,000 yards away, and were throwing shots into the flying crowd.

And then—in quick response—came the sound of Sigel's guns as they opened upon Churchill, Greer, Brown and Major and drove them in confusion out of the valley in which they were encamped and into the thick woods which fringed the banks of Skegg's Branch and covered the hills that rose on either side of that little stream.

In a moment McCulloch, followed by McIntosh, was on his way to take command of the troops on the eastern side of the creek; Price, ordering his infantry to follow, galloped up Bloody Hill to take command of Cawthorne's Brigade. With it, Price hoped to hold Lyon in check until the rest of his Missourians could come up.

With truly amazing swiftness, discipline, and coolheaded response to orders, Price's "unregimented rabble" formed into companies and regiments on the Springfield Road between the fords on Wilson's Creek and Skegg's Branch. Any commander would have been proud of their stouthearted behavior. Green and untried troops—whom McCulloch did not have the nerve to trust—fell into line and awaited marching orders as bullets bored into their ranks and solid shot, shells, and canister howled and whooped all around them.

Presently, up the hill they marched—up the slopes of Bloody Hill—which they were to baptize with their own blood. Price, Rains, and Cawthorne began to establish their slowly reorienting troopers just under the tip of the index finger and toward the west bank of Wilson's Creek. Up came Slack with Hughes' Regiment and Thornton's Battalion to form its line of battle to the left of Price-Rains; Clark, with Burbridge's Regiment, formed on the left of Slack; Parsons, with Kelly's Regiment, took his place to the left of Clark; McBride came up with Wingo's and Foster's Regiments to fall into the extreme left.

Guibor's four-gun battery (Parsons) and Bledsoe's three-

230

gun battery (Slack) had been limbered the night before. In minutes, the horses were harnessed, the mounted cannoneers in their saddles—and the artillerists ready—for a swift run to position. Guibor's pieces were thrown into battery between Slack and Price; Bledsoe's were hauled to the top on an elevation to the rear of Slack near Skegg's Branch.

Meanwhile Colonel Richard H. Weightman, commanding the infantry brigade of Rains' Division, led his men on the run from their encampment on the plateau east of Wilson's Creek to the battle line his fellow Missourians were forming on the slope of Bloody Hill. Weightman, who had distinguished himself at the Battle of Carthage, was well along in years. Yet he set the younger men who followed him a fast pace through heavy and continuous musketry fire. Suddenly, Weightman plunged forward, mortally wounded. His post at the head of the column was immediately taken by Colonel John R. Graves. Here, too, among the many who fell, was Colonel Benjamin Brown, leader of the mounted riflemen who bore his name.

As the rebel fire gained volume and tempo on Bloody Hill, Captain William E. Woodruff, of the Arkansas Light Artillery, took the initiative on the northern plateau that faced Bloody Hill from east of the ford on Wilson's Creek. He rushed his four pieces to the rounding turn of the northern bluff, ran them into battery, and began to heave shot and shell at the Federal forces. Woodruff's, unlike the other Southern batteries in this engagement, had a good supply of regular U. S. artillery shells obtained from Little Rock Arsenal. There is little doubt but that quick action, well-timed shell fuses, and good sighting on Woodruff's part had a great deal to do with checking Lyon's advance as well as in enabling Price and his generals to get into position and form their line of battle.

Plummer Marches Through the Corn

Covering Lyon's left flank, Plummer was pushing south through the stubble of harvested wheat in Ray's field when he heard the sound of gunfire from straight ahead. In moments, he caught sight of smoke from Woodruff's Battery south of Ray's field and on the other side of the Springfield Road. Although remnants of Cawthorne's outpost subjected him to musketry fire at this time, the fire was light and easily quelled. Plummer pushed forward, intent on storming the battery, should the opportunity offer.

However, that opportunity was not to come to pass. Woodruff discovered Federal troops in Ray's field as they moved through the wheat stubble and before they reached the sheltering corn. He gave the alarm, and McIntosh—who heard it first—issued some snappy orders that produced immediate results. As good fortune would have it, McIntosh's second-in-command, Lieutenant Colonel Benjamin T. Embry had moved in the right direction when cannon fire broke out on Bloody Hill and Woodruff made ready to reply. At the call of the bugle, the regiment—Second Arkansas Mounted Riflemen—mounted and formed in line of battle in good order. Embry marched the regiment to a timbered spot near Woodruff's Battery to shield men and horses from the Federal guns on Bloody Hill. The regiment had dismounted when McIntosh returned from his incompleted breakfast conference with Major General Price. Learning that the enemy was in the cornfield, McIntosh led the way, but first he issued orders to Colonel Hébert, whose Third Louisiana Infantry was already formed, to follow him.

Their path led down the bluff and up the Springfield Road for a short distance. Then they entered a narrow byroad that crossed Ray's valley and climbed the slope to the cornfield. The road was flanked on both sides by the thickest kind of underbrush. On one side almost hidden, stood a rail fence. On the other side of the fence was Farmer Ray's tall corn. There was nothing in sight but stalks of corn; no movement but that of lightly weaving top leaves. The Confederate troops, about 1,000 strong, came to a halt preliminary to entering the cornfield.

At the moment of deploying into the line of battle (reported Colonel Hébert) and when only two companies had reached their positions, the enemy opened their fire on our front, within 15 paces at the most. Deploying the other companies, an advance was ordered, led gallantly by McIntosh to whom I owe all thanks for assistance. The enemy was posted behind the fence and in the cornfield. The companies moved up bravely, broke the enemy, pursued them into the cornfield and routed them completely.

A great deal of time and hotly contested ground are covered by that simple statement. The battle in the cornfield raged for the better part of an hour as the two lines swung back and forth among the stalks. The Confederates had superior numbers, but the Federal regulars had superior arms. The dice were thrown when Captain Plummer, and other key officers in his battalion, were wounded. They staged a slow retreat which McIntosh and Hébert were quick to follow up with the heavy pressure of fire power. Once out of the shielding corn and in the open wheat stubble, the Federals were exposed to a torrent of fire. Fortunately for them, Lieutenant DuBois—whose battery was in position on Bloody Hill and almost opposite Ray's field—discovered Plummer's predicament. His four guns gave the Confederates such a heavy shelling that they thought it best to withdraw. At the same time, Captain Steele, with his reserve of regulars, came to Plummer's assistance. He enabled the latter, with his heavily mauled battalion, to reach the relative safety of Spring Branch Valley on the western side of Wilson's Creek.

The battle midst the ripening corn took a total of 127 casualties. On the Federal side, 19 were killed, 52 wounded. Confederate losses were: 10 killed, 44 wounded. Captain Wright's Home Guards took no part in the action. Horsemen would be too easy targets in a cornfield.

McCulloch Takes Effective Measures

Now that the time for talking was over and the moment for action was at hand, Brigadier General McCulloch showed no reluctance. On the contrary, he revealed the fighting qualities and combative instincts that had made him famous in Texas, Mexico, and California. While Price formed and stabilized the lines of his State Guard on Bloody Hill and McIntosh, with Hébert, rushed to stop Plummer's advance toward Woodruff's Battery through Ray's cornfield, McCulloch moved quickly and effectively to deal with the surprise attack (Sigel's) that was developing to the south. From Price's tent he rode, as swiftly as his horse could carry him, back to the plateau on the eastern side of Wilson's Creek. There, as will be recalled, his own Confederate Brigade as well as Pearce's Army of Arkansas were encamped. The booming of cannon and the crackle of musketry had alerted the two contingents before McCulloch reached their camps. Woodruff's guns were in battery and firing. McIntosh and Hébert had already started toward the cornfield.

Having no information to go on, except that the bombardment (by Sigel) had come from the south, McCulloch had to think fast. He concluded that, owing to the nature of the terrain, any enemy coming up from the south would have to enter the Oak Hills arena by way of the Springfield Road. He would have to march down the steep hill from Sharp's farm to Skegg's Branch. He might try to infiltrate through the thick stands of trees and underbrush along Wilson's Creek south of Sharp's farm. But either way, the enemy, to storm Bloody Hill and attack Price in the rear, must cross Skegg's Branch. Acting on this conclusion, McCulloch made the following disposition of his then available forces.

Reid's Battery was rushed to the plateau south of Manley's Branch where he occupied one of the bay windows formed by the bluff. Much later, Bledsoe's three guns were posted only a few dozen yards north of the spot where two of Sigel's guns had once been placed. Reid's four pieces were pointed so that they commanded the Springfield Road, as it ran past Sharp's hilltop farm, and also the ford over Skegg's Branch. Walker's Fourth and Dockery's Fifth Arkansas Infantry, with

Brigadier General Pearce, were assigned to support the two batteries. McRae's, Dockery's, Gratiot's, and Carroll's (dismounted) Arkansas regiments were placed along the western edge of the bluff to overwhelm any enemy who might be foolish enough to venture down from Sharp's farm to Skegg's Branch. The First and Second Arkansas Cavalry were hidden, ready to surge forth, in Manley's Valley.

Having issued his orders, McCulloch did not remain to make sure of their execution. Renewed cannon and rifle fire to the south had engaged his attention. Dashing down to the highway level, he found himself in a hectic flow of more than 1,000 horsemen. These, on having organized to give Sigel battle, had descended on their former camp only to be driven off by well-sustained fire. McCulloch, anxious to find McIntosh and Hébert—in order that they might deal with the situation to the south—fought his way through the disordered ranks toward Wilson's Creek ford and the byroad that led to the cornfield.

Chapter 11

Bloody Hill

———◄◆►———

Long-Time Enemies Come to Grips

As Price's Missourians marched up the slopes of Bloody Hill, Lyon took his position on the small platform that constituted its summit and placed his troops, as the human wall of enemies took form below him. In order to make a clear picture of a somewhat complicated setup, it is best to resort to the device of the open palm. With this aid, one may hope to describe the line-ups of the opposing sides.

The North:

Lyon, with his staff, occupied the center of the palm on the summit. In front of him spread the index, middle, and little fingers and, of course, the ravines that separated them. Behind Lyon, partly on the palm and partly to eastward on the lower plateau of the thumb, stood the reserves in three staggered lines. From west to east, they were: Second Kansas, First U. S. Cavalry, Kansas Rangers, First Iowa, Second U. S. Infantry, and DuBois' Battery. In front of Lyon, on the palm, stood Totten's guns. Two pointed down the slope toward Wilson's Creek, between thumb and index finger; four dominated the ravine between index and middle finger. Below the levels of these guns were, from left to right, the Second Missouri (on the little finger), the First Missouri (on the middle finger), and the First Kansas (on the index finger).

The South:

Major General Price's State Guard infantry—only State

Guards were engaged during the early phases of the Battle of Bloody Hill—stretched in a rough half-circle below and upon the points of the fingertips. Rains' Division covered the ground from Wilson's Creek westward to a point just below the tip of the index finger. Continuing westward was Guibor's Battery, four guns facing up the very ravine at the top of which Totten had four guns posted. Next came Slack's Division, also facing up the ravine. Then Clark on the tip of the middle finger, Parsons on the tip of the little finger, and McBride to the west, covering the left flank.

Although the opposing lines were not very far apart, there was considerable cover for both sides. During the period of organization, there had been almost continuous musketry fire up and down the slope. Just prior to this time, Lyon had heard the sound of cannon from the point where Colonel Sigel was expected to launch his attack. All was going according to schedule, he concluded, and the South's advantage of mere numbers would be vastly reduced. But, to Lyon's great amazement, from then on Sigel's column was neither seen nor heard from until much later in the morning. However, Sigel's doings were secondary for the moment.

Lyon ordered his entire line of battle to advance. This was done with energy and enthusiasm. With equal zest, the State Guard met them more than halfway. The firing, which was just spirited for the first half hour, soon increased to a continuous and crackling roar during which bullets flew like hailstones. The regulars were either in reserve or in Ray's cornfield at this time. The Arkansas and Confederate troops were elsewhere. On the hill, it was Missourian against Missourian and Kansan against Missourian—two lines of hot-tempered, fiercely fighting, hotly hating antagonists who neither sought quarter nor had the slightest intention of giving it. It was a tug o' war with the South having an uphill disadvantage. However, Price's infantrymen thought nothing of it. As the hated Dutch and the detested free-soilers pressed forward, so the secessionists surged up the slope to come within shotgun range. What with bushes, grass, thickets, and trees, it was really a large-scale game of blindman's buff. Enemies could be almost face to face and still not catch sight of each other. Once, the Southern line seemed to yield. One of Lyon's staff officers said:

For a few moments, I thought we had won the fight almost before we had begun it, but just then I saw the rebel camp fairly vomiting forth regiment after regiment, until it seemed as if there was no end of men coming against us; they were coming on the left and right and in front of us, in some places in three lines, all on the double-quick, and then I changed my mind.

During this curtain raiser on the first act of the drama of Bloody Hill, Totten's Battery again came into action. Ably aided by Lieutenant Sokolski, the artillery captain played his pieces with the skill of the virtuoso he was. Totten had a feeling, an instinct, for the handling of his round-mouthed monsters similar to that of a great chess player. He had an uncanny instinct for just when and where to place his pieces. That morning he bellowed orders, always ending with his stentorian, "God damn you, sir!" that brought his guns into action by the battery, by the section, or by the piece. He worked under great handicaps. This was not artillery country—too small a field of fire; too many trees; too much underbrush. Still, he played on the enemy's lines with telling effect.

The second half of the first act, lasted another long half hour. During it, the Federal troops were driven back two or three times in more or less disorder. Still, these retreats seldom covered more than a dozen yards. Then the lines would re-form and press forward with increased vigor. On the last rally, the enemy gave way and retreated to his base lines down the slope of the hill.

Following this recession, there was an interlude of inaction —like that of wrestlers trying to regain their breath after a strenuous set-to. Then Slack's and Clark's Infantry hurled themselves at the First Missouri in a determined effort to

238

break through. Although Andrews and his men were offering strong resistance, Lyon brought up support by way of the Second Kansas. Mitchell came up just in time to stem the upswelling rebel tide. The First Missouri was on the point of being flushed into oblivion, when the Kansans put their trigger fingers into the dike and brought their comrades a new lease on life.

At this point, the firing became general as the rebels, shouting, screaming, and yipping, rushed toward the center. It soon became obvious that Major General Price was planning to swamp Totten's Battery, a very active thorn in his side. To support Totten, Steele and his battalion of Second U. S. Infantry were sent into the firing line. Hardly had the regulars taken their positions, when a veritable torrent of flying lead broke loose. It did not seem possible, but actually the State Guard made lunges more ferocious than before against Lyon's entire line.

Lyon had to handle his small reserves with great care, but the aggressive attacks by the State Guard left little room for caution. In fact, overcaution could readily become fatal. The First Missouri and the First Kansas—fighting like veterans—showed signs of giving ground as they manfully stood up against a galling holocaust of fire. On the double, the First Iowa came to their support.

Up and down the line raged the crackle of musketry and the roar of cannon. The enemy came on, often in three or four ranks. They threw themselves against the Federal lines like a raging surf to stop short at 40 yards or less. Standing, kneeling, or prone on the ground, they fired, reloaded, and fired their weapons. The pressure was especially high about Totten's guns. Time and again, attacking waves would come within 30 yards of the cannon. Each time to be driven back by the machine-like firing maintained by the regulars or mowed down by Totten's canister. The very earth shook as his guns blasted and rocked.

Suddenly, as if someone had turned off a tap, the attack

ceased. The enemy withdrew to his previous position. Again, there was a lull in the battle.

Half an hour later, the rattle of guns was resumed. The opening gambit was a move against Steele's Second U. S. Infantry on the left. DuBois, who had been assisting Totten in trying to silence the enemy's cannon, had just received orders to move from the center to the right. While DuBois was limbering, Steele was driven back by an overwhelming force on the left (Major's Riflemen, dismounted), who, during their advance, had swarmed into great clusters. This tactical error was swiftly punished by Lyon. He ordered DuBois to swing his guns on Major's outfit. This enfiladed the forward moving mass. Round upon round of shell and canister from DuBois' guns drove them back with heavy slaughter. The broken regiment rallied behind a house or a barn on the right of the line. Aiming the battery's solitary 12-pounder, Captain Gordon Granger slammed a couple of solid shot into the building. He was just about to fire a third, when a hospital flag was displayed from the door of the structure. Granger ceased firing, and the would-be attackers retired.

All along, Woodruff's Battery had been laying down a wicked barrage. Now a new battery, Hiram Bledsoe's, opened up from an opposite hill. Having a plunging fire, it did great execution. All the shot that passed over the battle line fell among the wounded who had been carried to the rear of DuBois' position.

There are many incidents related of the Union troops at this stage of the battle. They were more than willing to fight. In fact, they could not be restrained. Mainly, the only service performed by the officers, after the battle lines were formed, was to keep the men from unnecessarily exposing themselves. Most of the regiments were lying flat on their faces, the line officers sitting on the ground a few paces in the rear. Everybody was cool after the first volley. Desultory conversations sprung up, liberally sprinkled with jokes. Captain Cracklin, of the First Kansas, took out his old briar-root pipe. After fumbling for tobacco in every pocket, he got up, borrowed a fill from one of his men, and smoked as unconcerned as if it were a sham battle.

When the men were ordered to lie down, a tall German by the name of Henry Neukampf refused to do so. He kept walking back and forth along the rear of the line, picking off the Johnnies as the opportunity offered. For a time, the soldier seemed to bear a charmed life. He escaped injury where the bullets were flying so thick that a gun or ramrod held up a few feet above the ground was sure to be hit.

To all entreaties of his comrades, Henry stoically replied, "Oh, vell, it makes me no difference out."

Neukampf was hit in the head after an hour of exposure and a mortal wound inflicted.

"Now I vas mad," he shouted. Dropping to his proper position, he fought like a tiger to the end of the battle. He died 12 days afterward in Springfield.

An Indian sharpshooter, who fought with the South, had climbed to the crotch of a tree between the lines and wounded two men in Cracklin's company with one shot. Bob Schuyler drew a bead on him and the Indian tumbled to the ground stone dead.

Throughout the action, Lyon had been riding back and forth behind the shifting lines to lend moral support when he could and physical assistance where he could spare it. All the time, he was listening with one ear and looking with one eye toward that southern point of the theater where Sigel should be operating. If nothing else, Lyon hoped to hear the boom of Sigel's guns. In that respect, he was very much in the position of one who sought to listen to a plumbing leak in a stamping mill.

And yet, wonder of wonders, he caught it; the sound of cannonading below and beyond Bloody Hill. The general glanced at his watch. It was well past 7 o'clock. About two hours had passed since the battle began, and still there was nothing decisive in sight. The casualties had been heavy. The wounded and the dead lay in great windrows along the line of combat. Lyon was rather astounded by Price's capacity to return to the fray after receiving heavy casualties. He did not know about "Pap's" unarmed reserves—shadowy men who stole up the slopes by the hundreds during the lulls between attacks to gird themselves for combat by picking up the weapons and ammunition of dead or disabled friends and foes.

Sigel and His Boys in Clover

After hurling their missiles into the enemy cavalry encamped in Sharp's field, Lieutenant Schuetzenbach's artillerists limbered their pieces and, with their infantry escort, crossed Wilson's Creek to join Sigel's main force. Lieutenant Carr and his cavalrymen remained on the bluff. It was an excellent observation post in that it gave a wide view of the Wilson's Creek area north to Skegg's Branch.

Schaefer's pieces had done such an excellent job of driving the enemy out of the camp that Sigel moved into it without meeting one whit of resistance. Lieutenant Farrand reported:

As we passed through it, I saw many dead bodies and quantities of arms of all description lying on the ground. Many of the latter I caused my men to destroy. There were in their camp a wagon load of Maynard rifles, one of regular rifled muskets, and several boxes of U. S. regulation sabers, all new.

Colonel Sigel did not know it at the time, but, contrary to his expectation, the cavalrymen he had put to flight had not sought escape by taking to the road and heading toward Cassville. Also, they were hindered from rushing north on the Springfield Road by the swirling flood of humanity which thronged the highway, after having poured down the sides of Bloody Hill from Rains' and Cawthorne's camps under the pressure of Federal guns and muskets. Instead of leaving the battle scene as intended, the men driven out of Sharp's field sought shelter in the valley of Skegg's Branch. There, those

242

who were armed and mounted were presently reorganized for a counterattack.

Carr, from his perch on the bluff, saw the new group of horsemen being formed. He sent word to Sigel as he, too, made ready to join the latter's column which was now in the center of the enemy's encampment. The Federals just had time to throw their guns into battery, and brace their infantry in support, when enemy cavalry swept down upon them. Whooping and yelling, they rushed toward the men and the guns. On this occasion, however, the cannon were better served. The battery opened with shell and canister. The spray of speeding missiles from six guns delivered at such short range virtually pushed the attackers back, as if they were hit by a battering-ram. Musketry supported this formidable blow. The charge was over before it was even well begun. A large body of dismounted enemy cavalry, who had deployed into the bush on the south side of the field, also was driven back and in such a hurry that they were obliged to leave their horses. Carr remembers that the attackers fled "although their officers raged and stormed and tore their hair in trying to make their men advance."

After this double victory, Sigel's men not only regarded themselves as victorious but also proceeded to practice the creed that, to the victor belong the spoils. They broke ranks, started to pillage the enemy's tents, and set out to capture and appropriate his horses.

However, this browsing in the clover of easily gained loot was not to be of long duration. From his position on the eastern bluff, with the Fourth and Fifth Arkansas in support of Reid's Battery, Brigadier General Pearce had noticed the melee in Sharp's field. Before the encounter, he had seen Sigel's cavalry, artillery, and infantry march onto the pasture. Due to the distance, he was unable to determine the character of the column. It did not display a flag until it was in position and its artillery had fired several rounds. Only then, through a glass, he saw the Stars and Stripes unfold.

By now, the attacking rebel cavalry was in the way. Even so, Pearce would have been unable to fire at the enemy just then, since Reid's guns had not as yet been placed in battery. By the time Reid's pieces could be brought to bear, the looting was in full swing. Shells and solid shot from the Arkansas battery on the bluff drove the Federals out of the encampment into the woods to the west of the field. Along the field, into the woods and up a hill, ran a rough road in a northerly direction. Sigel's guides informed him that it joined the Springfield Road just west of Sharp's farm.

In his new situation, Sigel's thoughts turned to what he considered the second and most important phase of his operation: to cut off the enemy's retreat. This naturally was based on the assumption that Lyon's attack succeeded as planned. Sigel's optimism in this regard is expressed in his post-battle report:

The firing toward the northwest was now more distinct and increased until it was evident that the main corps of General Lyon had engaged the enemy along the whole line. To give the greatest possible assistance to him, I left position in the camp and advanced toward the northwest to attack the enemy's line of battle in the rear.

Marching forward, on the wagon road, we struck the Springfield Road, making our way through a large number of cattle and horses, until we arrived on an eminence used as a slaughtering place and known as Sharp's farm. On our route, we had taken about 100 prisoners who were scattered all over the camp. At Sharp's place, we met numbers of the enemy's soldiers who were evidently retiring in this direction and, as I suspected that the enemy, on his retreat, would follow in the same direction, I formed the troops across the road, by planting the artillery on the plateau and the two infantry regiments on the right and left across the road, while the cavalry companies, extended on our flanks.

At this time, and after some skirmishing along the front of our line, the firing in the direction of our northwest, which was during an hour's time roaring in succession, had almost ceased. I, thereupon, presumed that the attack of General Lyon had been successful, and that his troops were in pursuit of the enemy, who moved in large numbers toward the south along the ridge of a hill about 700 yards opposite our right.

When Colonel Sigel straddled the Springfield Road, and settled down on a thick pink cloud of optimism for the coming of the victorious Lyon, the hands of the clock stood at 8:30 o'clock.

Bewilderment in the Wilderness

The placing of what appeared to be a well-supported enemy artillery position across the Springfield Road on the top of Sharp's hill, was promptly reported to McCulloch. Equally promptly, he decided to lead a head-on attack on it with the aid of the first battalion First Arkansas Mounted Riflemen—dismounted and acting as infantry under Lieutenant Colonel Dandridge McRae—and the first battalion of Hébert's Third Louisiana Infantry under Lieutenant Colonel S. M. Hyams. McIntosh, who had returned fresh from his hard-won victory in the cornfield, placed himself in position next to Hyams. Several companies of Major's and Brown's dislodged Mounted State Guard joined these contingents under Captain Thomas Staples. Bledsoe's Battery was rushed across Wilson's Creek and planted on the bluff south of Reid's position.

The rapidly assembled column was headed by Captain John P. Vigilini of the to-be-famous Pelican Rifles (Baton Rouge) and the equally noted Iberville Greys, both of the Third Louisiana. These companies, like those of the First Iowa Zouaves, were long established marching organizations. Although the regiment was part of the Confederate Army, its uniforms were not the Confederate gray. They were, as the long arm of coincidence arranged the matter, almost the exact shade of blue gray as the blouses worn by the Iowa lads. The Pelicans and the Iberville Greys also marched with the same rhythmic dress parade swing and shouldered their rifles as straight as if they were drawn on a string.

The Pelicans and the Iberville Greys strode with more than their usual snappy stride as they led the procession of Louisianans, Arkansans, and Missourians across Skegg's Branch toward the hill where Sigel's artillery had been planted. Brigadier General McCulloch rode in the van with Captain Vigilini. In his report on that attack, which had a truly unique finale, the captain wrote:

General McCulloch, finding that Colonel Sigel had placed his batteries in a position where they were doing terrible execution in the ranks of the Arkansas and Missouri troops . . . determined that it must be taken. Accordingly, he ordered the Louisiana regiment to do so, he leading us in person. We started with about 300 men. . . . The Pelican Rifles and Iberville Greys, under my command, were on the right, and thus marched until we were within 30 or 40 yards of the battery, which was on a steep hill. When within the above-named distance a man appeared on the edge of the hill.

The General then ordered us to halt, and asked the man whose forces those were.

He replied, "Sigel's regiment!"

At the same time, he raised his rifle to shoot. But ere he had time to execute his design, the sharp crack of a Mississippi rifle carried a messenger of death to him. Thus to Corporal Henry Gentles, of my company, belongs the honor of having saved the General's life. The General then turned to me and said:

"Captain, take your company up and give them hell!"

I then ordered my company forward, and was followed by the remainder of the regiment.

When near the top of the hill I ordered a halt, went up to see the position of the enemy, and was followed by Sergeant William H. Tunnard. I was much surprised to find myself in front of and about 15 feet from the battery. I asked them who they were, when Tunnard answered:

"Look at their Dutch faces."

We immediately fell back, and they fired two guns over us.

I then ordered, "Fire!"

All fired and charged the battery, the enemy falling back and retreating into a cornfield, where they were followed by our men and shot down as they attempted to escape. We then returned to the battery we had taken and found the guns all in good order. A fire from Reid's battery (which was ours) made us give way once, and killed Captain Hinson and his brother-in-law, Private Whetstone, of the Morehouse Guards.

As previously established, in those early days of the war—when blue for the North and gray for the South had not as yet been stabilized—it was frequently difficult to distinguish between friend and foe. Under the conditions of poor visibility that existed at Wilson's Creek, due to heavy vegetation, this was particularly true. Many mistakes were made through lack of swift identification. But since tne game was played for keeps without any ground rules whatever, those who made mistakes, and did not recover from them in time, had to pay the price. Colonel Sigel, on that morning, became a victim of misidentification that cost him dearly. The best way to present this highly unusual incident is through his own words. His story begins as he stands near his artillery planted across the Springfield Road on Sharp's hill on the morning of August 10, awaiting the coming of a victorious Lyon. He begins:

This was the state of affairs at half-past eight o'clock in the morning, when it was reported to me by Dr. Melchior, and some of our skirmishers, that "Lyon's men were coming up the road."

Lieutenant-Colonel Albert, of the Third, and Colonel Salomon, of the Fifth, notified their regiments not to fire on troops coming in this direction, while I cautioned the artillery in the same manner.

Our troops in this moment expected, with anxiety, the approach of their friends, and were waving the flag, raised as a signal to their comrades, when at once two batteries opened their fire against us, one in front, placed on the Springfield Road, and the other upon the hill (eastern bluff) upon which we had supposed Lyon's forces were in pursuit of the enemy, while a strong column of infantry, supposed to be the Iowa regiment, advanced on the road, up the hill, and attacked our right.

It is impossible for me to describe the confusion and frightful consternation which was occasioned by this important event. The cry, "They [Lyon's troops] are firing against us," spread like wildfire through our ranks; the artillery men, ordered to fire, and directed by myself, could hardly be brought forward to serve their pieces; the infantry would not level their arms until it was too late. The enemy arrived within 10 paces of the muzzles of our cannon, killed the horses, turned the ranks of the infantry and forced them to fly. The troops were throwing themselves into the bushes and by-roads, retreating as well as they could, followed and attacked incessantly by large bodies of Arkansas and Texas cavalry.

In his retreat, Sigel lost five cannon, of which, he reports, three were spiked, and the colors of the Third Missouri. The color-bearer was wounded and his substitute killed. The flag was captured by Captain Staples. He boldly dashed into the cluster of men who were trying to protect Old Glory, captured it, and displayed it proudly. Emblazoned in gold on the standard was the word: *Lyon.*

Sigel's column was completely splintered. Seeing that it was each man for himself, without hope of reorganizing the infantry or artillerists, Sigel sent staff officers to Carr and Farrand with orders to retreat. He also sent Artillery Sergeant Froelich with instructions to make his way as best he could to Lyon's position and report Sigel's retreat. The cavalry and the dragoons had been so far off on the flanks as to be out of sight and the encounter had terminated so swiftly that there was no time to call them into action. Captain Carr reported:

After retiring about one and a half miles, during which we were fired on from a bushy hillside by a body of men whom I repulsed, but who caused the loss of one of our remaining guns by killing a wheel horse, I saw Colonel Sigel at the spring where we camped the first night when returning from Dug Springs (August 4–5). It was then decided to move south on the Fayetteville (Springfield) Road until we could go out and circle around the enemy toward Springfield. We then had my company, 56 men;

about 150 infantry, badly demoralized, one piece and two caissons.

After retiring about one and one-half miles, a large body of cavalry (Major's Mounted Riflemen—Clark) was discovered in front of us. I was sent to the front, where I observed a column of horse at least a quarter of a mile in length moving toward the south on our right and filing into the road in front of us. . . . I watched them for a few moments, when Colonel Sigel sent me word to take the first left hand road. One, luckily, happened to be just at that point. While retreating along this road, Colonel Sigel asked me to march slowly, so that the infantry could keep up. I urged upon him that the enemy would try to cut us off in crossing Wilson's Creek and that the infantry and artillery should march at least as fast as the ordinary walk of my horses. He assented and told me to go on, which I did at a walk.

Upon arriving at a creek, I was much surprised and pained to find that he was not up. As, however, I observed a great dust coming from the enemy's camp, which was not far off, I concluded that it was no time for delay and moved on, after watering my horses, till I arrived at a spot where I thought I could venture to halt and wait for Colonel Sigel. This I did for some time, and then pursued my march to Springfield. It turned out that the Colonel was ambuscaded [by Major's horsemen], as I anticipated, his whole party broken up, and that he himself narrowly escaped.

It is a subject of great regret with me to have left him behind, but I supposed all the time that he was close behind me till I got to the creek. However, it would have done no good for my company to have been cut to pieces also. As it was, four of my men were lost who had been placed in rear of his infantry.

Orders for retreat had also been passed to Lieutenant Farrand beyond the left wing of the Fifth Missouri. His report runs as follows:

Upon finding myself with my company alone, I retired in a southerly direction, and accidentally meeting one of the guides who had been employed in taking us to the enemy's camp, I detained him until I could collect some of the troops whom I found scattered and apparently lost. I halted my company and got quite a number (about 150–175) together. I directed the guide to take us to Springfield by way of Little York.

To close the incident, let it be recorded that Colonel Sigel reached Springfield during the late forenoon with a small escort and that stragglers kept drifting into town during the rest of the day and night. The casualties of the units engaged were 297 of a total of 1,123, or 28 per cent. Killed were 35; wounded, 132; and missing, 130. Carr and Farrand were not engaged.

On reaching Springfield, Colonel Sigel headed for his quarters and went to bed.

Lyon, the Target of Full Rebel Strength

With the menace of an attack in the rear removed, McCulloch was now free to throw his Confederates and Arkansans into line to fight shoulder to shoulder with Price's State Guard on Bloody Hill.

First to respond was Colonel Gratiot's (Arkansas) infantry regiment. He had served under Price in the Mexican War and was genuinely happy to be under arms with "Pap" again. Major General Price's face, usually the clear pink of vin rosé was now, due to heat and exertion, a deep, dark Burgundy. The clouds had cleared away and the day was stinging hot. For hours, Price, wholly disdainful of danger, had been galloping back and forth from flank to flank, directing the movements of his troops. For reasons known only to the gods of war, he had not even been wounded. Still, bullet rips and holes in his coat testified that he had had many a close shave. So far, even his horse had survived unscathed. Still, Price's losses in the high command had been heavy. Weightman and Brown were mortally wounded early in the battle. Cawthorne and his adjutant also died of wounds. Brigadier General Clark was shot in the leg. Brigadier General Slack was terribly slashed by musket bullets. Burbridge, Foster, and Kelly, although badly wounded, carried on despite their injuries. In that, they set examples of fortitude to run-of-the-line soldiers who, with wounds more or less bandaged, still fought the Federals at every turn.

Led by Price and Gratiot, the Arkansas infantry rushed up Bloody Hill to the position they were to hold between Parsons and Clark, slightly west of the center of the State Guard's line. The position was, as someone observed: "Warmer than the hottest corner of hell!" The point was right under Totten's guns and they were spewing missiles as fast as their artillerists could serve them.

"You'll be in a pretty hot place, men," shouted Price as he drew up to let the infantry pass. "But I'll be near you and I'll take care of you. Keep as cool as watermelons and give 'em thunder!"

They waved their free arms and cheered. Turning to Gratiot, who had reined his horse at the general's side, Price continued:

"This is your position, Colonel. Take it and hold it, whatever you do. I will see that you are not too hard pressed. Don't yield an inch!"

At that moment, Totten's guns hosed the position with a heavy stream of canister. The front of the column escaped the torrent, but the rear of the column was swept of its regimental field and staff officers. However, the survivors, including the slightly wounded, marched on. Soon the remnants of the regiment were in position. They held their place under a fire so furious that, in half an hour, 109 of its 500 men were either disabled or dead.

Price, who was watching the trials of the outfit with deep concern, suffered a painful bullet wound in his side.

"That isn't fair," he stated wryly. "The fellow who hit me would have missed me completely if I were as skinny as General Lyon."

During this interval, other rebel regiments went into line.

They included McIntosh's, Dockery's, Churchill's, and Mc-Rae's, as well as Reid's four-gun battery. Hébert's Louisiana boys had not as yet returned from the ruin that had been Sigel's column on Sharp's hill. As McCulloch reported later:

A terrible fire of musketry was now kept up along the whole side and top of the hill upon which the enemy were posted. Masses of infantry fell back and again rushed forward. The summit of the hill was covered with the dead and wounded. Both sides were fighting with desperation for the day.

Having, so to speak, a royal flush, McCulloch decided to play his pat hand to the hilt. He now had plenty of artillery, cavalry, and infantry. He would make a full-out assault on Lyon's position and use Greer's Mounted Riflemen (800) and Carroll's Mounted Company (40) as a diversion on Lyon's right flank. Unobserved during the heat of the battle, the horsemen swung to the far left out of sight across the rolling prairie. Soon they paralleled the battle ground as they rode north and formed below the crest of a hill. With loud shouts of "Texas" the charge descended on Lyon's unprotected rear. This was how Colonel Greer remembered the assault:

The enemy was thrown into considerable confusion. Some of them left without firing their guns; others stood still until we had nearly ridden upon them, then fired and fled; others concealed themselves in the bushes and shot at us as we passed. Several of my men were killed and wounded in this charge.

I would have attempted to charge the main body of the enemy's force still farther to our right, but for the fact that we would have been exposed to the fire not only of the enemy but of our own guns.

It was very evident that they were embarrassed by the cavalry force, which still flanked them and were at a loss what to do. This gave our army encouragement and enabled them to strengthen their position. The enemy moved several wagons and a portion of their force back. Soon they showed themselves beyond us in considerable numbers, supported by what I took to be three pieces of artillery. They were intimidated and were never brought into action.

Captain Totten saw the encounter through entirely different eyes. After referring to the onrushing horsemen, he continued:

Fortunately, some of our infantry companies (led by Captain Madison Miller, Company I, First Missouri, with units of the First Iowa) and a few pieces of artillery from my battery were in position to meet this demonstration, and drove off their cavalry with ease. This was the only demonstration made by their cavalry and it was so *effete* and ineffectual in its force and character as to deserve only the appellation of child's play. Their cavalry is utterly worthless on the battlefield.

After the charge had run its course, some of the men saw a Confederate flag on the ground. Before one of them could venture forth to pick it up, one of Greer's cavalrymen galloped into view. When some of the lads brought their muskets to shooting position, a great cry went up among the Union infantrymen:

"Don't shoot him!"

When he came within about 60 feet of the flag, the solitary rider spurred his horse. As the animal thundered forward, the Southerner leaned gracefully down from his saddle, scooped the flag up from the ground, and held the banner high with a great show of gallantry. Then he gave voice to a long, loud Texas yell that cut to the bone, sharp as a razor's blade.

The Federals responded with a rousing cheer. There was another, less lighthearted flag incident.

Captain Cary Gratz, commanding Company F, First Missouri, was advancing at the head of his men when he discovered a body of the enemy approaching. They were led by a mounted rebel officer carrying a Union flag. Captain Gratz, drawing his revolver, fired and knocked him off his horse. But, upon reaching the ground, the rider immediately arose and rushed forward. At that instant, Captain Gratz fired a second shot, pitching the rebel headlong out of sight. The enemy now opened fire and Captain Gratz fell, pierced by five shots.

McCulloch's massive frontal and left flank attack, the third of that crimson morning, began about 9 o'clock and lasted an hour, more or less. To meet it, Lyon was compelled to throw every last one of his units into action. There was neither time nor opportunity to give badly decimated troops a chance to rest or to re-form. As matters now stood, Price had more regiments available than Lyon had companies. This, the third act of one of the bloodiest "little" fights this nation has ever staged, took a terrible toll of lives on both sides. Musket flares blazed like prairie fire up and down the slope of that battle-scourged hill. Above the humming of rifle bullets were the more terrifying sounds made by raking fires of case shot and shells. To illustrate the quantity of the carnage, DuBois found that, in order to move his guns from one position to another, he had to send men ahead to open a road through the wounded and the dead.

As the day grew older, and the sun's heat increased, the morning breeze died down. Soon the visibility, poor enough because of the dense vegetation, became even worse. Dirty gray gunsmoke drifted in lazy clouds around the hill. To it was added the thick black smoke that rose from the Southern wagon train parked along Skegg's Branch. Totten's and Du-Bois' shells had hit the vehicles so constantly that many were smashed and some were burning.

What with Reid's artillery to assist Guibor's, the firepower on the Southern side had doubled. Not only that, but these batteries, like Sigel's, used 6-pounder ammunition. This meant that Sigel's shell-filled caissons and limbers could be turned to good account against the Federals—and they were.

"What Has Become of Sigel?"

During this particular phase, the First Missouri was again sorely pressed. Reported Lieutenant Colonel Andrews:

The enemy would undoubtedly have forced us back had not the First Iowa, led on by General Lyon and Major Schofield, arrived at the critical moment together with a battalion of the Second Missouri Regiment led by Major Osterhaus. . . .

As the fire slackened, I met General Lyon and asked him "Have you seen or heard from our other column (Sigel)?"

To this inquiry, the General shook his head. I now noticed that he appeared to be suffering and found he had just received a shot in the leg.

As a matter of fact, Lyon and his officers were becoming increasingly jittery with respect to the whereabouts of Sigel's column.

"What has become of Sigel?" was a question that was frequently asked among staff officers on the summit of Bloody Hill, when the rattle and roar of firing died down to volumes so that they could hear themselves talk. Sigel's regiments wore uniforms of nearly the same gray as that used by McCulloch's Confederate troops. The latter were several times mistaken for Sigel's men. Therefore, on two distinct occasions, they escaped severe punishment at Federal hands. During the opening phase, DuBois' Battery had been raising great havoc among the Louisianans (in Ray's cornfield), when Major Sturgis informed DuBois that he was slaughtering Sigel's men, and ordered him to cease firing. At another time, one of the Louisiana battalions marched by the flank in front of the Union line within musket range. They were allowed to pass unharmed, being mistaken for Sigel's column.

Suddenly, an inkling of an answer was given with respect to the fate of Sigel's column. It came in the guise of a shell that howled just head-high over Totten's artillerists.

"K-rist on a caisson! That's one of our basket-shells!" shouted Sergeant Armstrong. "I can tell by its whistle!"

All knew that Bischoff's Battery was the only one to have drawn this type of shell from the ammunition stores at the Saint Louis Arsenal.

"Captain Totten!" yelled young Lieutenant Sokolski, excitedly—he had only been out of West Point one month since his graduation in June—"They're shooting Sigel's ammunition at us!"

The captain, glowering darkly through the smoke of the enemy lines, replied in his usual voice, that of a slightly muted bugle:

"Silence those guns, God damn you, sir!"

From this point, when tragic events followed in quick succession, Mr. Greene of Kansas provides a concise, graphic and on-the-spot narrative. To be sure, his is only one of many versions. However, since none of the versions agrees, his observations merit consideration because he went to considerable trouble to check on his findings. Said Mr. Greene in part:

At 10 o'clock both sides were occupying the ground they had taken four hours before. The lines were within shotgun range. Neither line was more than half a mile in length, but the rebel forces were more than five times the deepest. They extended in masses away back into the valley, and across the creek and to the crest of the hills beyond. There was a lull in the firing, and as the smoke cleared away all this could be seen. The men as well as the officers knew what was coming. It was the calm before the storm. No wonder the sight of the swarming hosts appalled even the brave heart of Lyon, and made him fear the day was lost.

There was a rush on the left. Schofield led the First Iowa to meet it; Lyon rode with the file-closers at the right of the battalion. His favorite horse was killed under him, and at the next moment he received a shot in the leg and one in the head. He staggered a few paces to the rear and met Sturgis, who begged him not to so recklessly expose himself.

[It was at this point when Lyon—according to Major Schofield —is supposed to have said: "I fear that the day is lost."]

A lull of half an hour ensued. Again the field officers gathered about Lyon on the crown of Bloody Hill. There was no enemy in sight. What did it mean? Conjectures were various, but the men believed they had won a great victory. Lyon was giving orders for extending the line on the right, and the Second Kansas, which had come up meantime, was clamoring to be assigned a place.

At this instant a line of men was seen at right angles to the column of Lyon, and a question arose as to who they were. There was a possibility of their being Sigel's men. Lyon, Mitchell, and an orderly rode out toward them. (This was near the very tip of the index finger.) Three officers at the same time advanced from their lines and asked, "Who are you?"

Nathaniel Lyon Is Killed in the Charge

For some reason, Lyon at once saw that they were rebels. Perhaps he recognized them as Old Army associates, at any rate he turned to his bodyguard which had come up and roared:

"Shoot them! Shoot them!"

Instantly there was a volley from a thicket a few rods away. (It was delivered by Dockery's Fifth Arkansas Infantry.) Lyon received a bullet in the heart. Mitchell was hit in the thigh at the same time, but caught Lyon as he was falling and lowered him from his horse to the ground.

To his orderly, Albert Lehman, the general muttered: "I am killed; take care of my body."

This simple recital is gathered from personal interviews with soldiers who witnessed the event, officers within speaking distance of Lyon when he fell, numerous letters, and lastly, the official records of the battle. It differs from the popular accounts which have given inspiration for the cheap pictures, the only representations extant, of the death of Lyon.

There was none of the impetuous dash and wild clamor of war, "peal on peal afar"; no leaping steed, frenzied with the clash of arms; no fluttering pennants, nor host of aides in brilliant uniforms to signalize the event; none of the stock accessories of the death that came to Nelson and Packenham. Simply a quiet, unassuming soldier, bareheaded, and bloody from crown to foot, sitting on a jaded horse with a few comrades at his side.

In this way Lyon fell; the first great sacrifice of the war; the only leader who had rightly interpreted secession, and the only one who had seized it by the throat or seriously threatened its overthrow. At the time of his death there was no general in the Union Army worthy to be compared with him. What he had done and attempted to do had already endeared him to the whole North. Suddenly elevated from a captain to a general, he at once disclosed the qualities of leadership, roused the hopes of his countrymen by his tremendous energy in pursuing—and sublime audacity in fighting—overwhelming odds. He crowded into two months a career as brilliant as it was brief, and as precious to the Cause as its ending was bloody and pathetic.

There was more fighting, more prodigies of valor, more heroic dying on the stricken field, but the battle culminated with the death of Lyon.

He had ceased to fear that the day was lost since the repulse of the impetuous attacks on the left and right and the lifting smoke had revealed a field unquestionably his own. That he was not permitted to survive the moment of victory, and that his successor, either through incompetence or overcaution, fled the field, cannot detract from his glory or dim the luster of his great name. All Union authorities agree that at 11:30 o'clock the enemy had been driven from the field. Half an hour after the firing ceased, he burned a portion of his trains and set the remainder in motion toward Fayetteville. The Union forces were withdrawn to a new position a short distance in the rear, and a new line formed facing the field. This line remained there so long that discipline was relaxed, and the men sat down on the ground to rest and play cards and talk over the battle.

Everybody, but Major Sturgis, now in command, believed the Union forces had won a great victory. The men were exulting, and, although they had marched all night and fought for six hours in thirst and hunger, were impatient to pursue the enemy. Sturgis was importuned to do so by the highest officers in his command. Sweeny insisted on following up the victory and making it complete. So did the brave Surgeon-

General Cornyn, who kept his gun ready near the surgeon's table, and whenever opportunity offered ran to the front to pick off a rebel or two.

Gordon Granger, who rode up to Sturgis, after making a reconnaissance of the field alone, remarked that there was not an enemy in sight and that he ought to be pursued and cut to pieces.

To this Sturgis replied:

"I order you to leave the field."

"But," said Granger, "they have burned their train."

"I order you to leave the field!" said Sturgis sharply. . . .

Discussing Sturgis' retreat many years later, the then Lieutenant General Schofield expressed himself as follows:

This retreat was undoubtedly an error and the Battle of Wilson's Creek must be classed as a defeat for the Union Army. The error was a failure to estimate the effect it must have produced upon the enemy, as well as upon ourselves, by so much hard fighting. It was only necessary to hold our ground, trusting to the pluck and endurance of our men, and the victory would have been ours.

Had Lyon—who was in front of the line of battle when wounded as well as when killed—appreciated this fact, and acted upon it, instead of throwing his life away, it is safe to say he would have won a brilliant victory.

Schofield's assertion, that "Lyon threw his life away," is based on an earlier observation by him dealing with Lyon's remark to the effect that "all is lost." After referring to General Lyon's two wounds, Schofield said:

General Lyon became more despondent than before, apparently from the effect of his wounds, for there appeared nothing in the state of the battle to dishearten a man of such unbounded courage as he undoubtedly possessed.

A portion of our troops had given away in some disorder. Lyon said:

"Major, I am afraid the day is lost!"

I looked at him in surprise, saw the blood trickling down his face, and divining the reason for his despondency, replied:

"No, General; let's try it again!"

He seemed encouraged and we then separated, rallied and led forward the only troops then not in action—two regiments. Lyon was killed at the head of these regiments while exposing himself with utter recklessness to the enemy's fire.

But that recklessness in battle was not a by-product of wounds or Bloody Hill. It was Lyon's way of leading his troops, from Mexican combats to Indian warfare. He was always at the tip of his column.

Samuel J. Crawford, a captain in the Second Kansas and later Governor of Kansas, was within ten paces of General Lyon when he fell. Side by side with Lyon was Colonel Mitchell, of the Second Kansas. Crawford did not notice any recklessness in Lyon's behavior. Nor is it likely that Colonel Mitchell would have participated in any overly foolhardy or suicidal act. The two officers were just showing the way for the regiment to follow. Wrote Crawford in his book *Kansas in the Sixties:*

The two were leading straight toward a thicket of underbrush and a scattering of oak trees when a volley was fired from the thicket.

Lyon was killed and Mitchell wounded.

The same volley struck Captain Tholen's company on the flank and threw it into confusion. The next two companies (Russell's and Mitchell's) also swayed back for a short distance. My company came next; and I, being farther from the concealed enemy, and having more time to steady the men, wheeled the company into line, facing the ambuscade and sent a volley into the bushes where the enemy was concealed.

We fired over Lyon's body and three or four of Captain Tholen's men, as they lay wounded. As soon as the enemy was driven out, . . . Lieutenant Gustavus Schryer of Tholen's company, took a detachment of his men and removed General Lyon's body and all the wounded to the rear.

Major Sturgis, who inherited the mantle of command on the death of Nathaniel Lyon, did not learn about his general's death until about half an hour after it occurred. The tragic and shocking news was conveyed to him by Major Schofield during a lull in the fighting. He told Sturgis that he (Sturgis) was the senior officer on the scene and, therefore, in command. All colonels and lieutenant colonels were either dead or wounded. Certainly, the situation Sturgis acquired from Lyon was far from enviable. Moreover, the cavalryman's training for his sudden increase in responsibility had not been adequate. And yet, he discharged his duty as a soldier, as he saw that duty, and did it well. No one can say for certain, but Sturgis may have done what he subsequently did on the strength of Lyon's own objective. Remember: Lyon was not in quest of victory. He sought to dull Southern strength so as to insure the safety of his retreat. Sturgis' report, although it covers some of the ground presented by Mr. Greene, deserves more extensive recognition. Among other things, Sturgis makes it clear that the Union forces were almost out of ammunition. He said in part:

After the death of General Lyon, when the enemy fled and left the field clear, so far as we could see, an almost total silence reigned for the space of 20 minutes, Major Schofield informed me of the death of General Lyon, and reported for orders. The responsibility which now devolved upon me was duly felt and appreciated.

Our brave little army was scattered and broken; over twenty thousand men were still in our front; and our men had had no water since five o'clock the evening before, and could hope for none short of Springfield, 12 miles distant; if we should go forward, our own success would prove our certain defeat in the end; if we retreated, disaster stared us in the face; our ammunition was well nigh exhausted, and should the enemy make this discovery through a slackening of our fire, total annihilation was all we could expect.

The great question in my mind was, "Where is Sigel?" If I

could hope for a vigorous attack by him on the enemy's right flank or rear, then we could go forward with some hope of success. In this perplexing condition of affairs I summoned the principal officers for consultation. The great question with most of them was, "Is retreat possible?" The consultation was brought to a close by the advance of a heavy column of infantry, advancing from the hill where Sigel's guns had been heard before.

Thinking they were Sigel's men, the line was formed for an advance, with the hope of forming a junction with him. These troops wore a dress much resembling that of Sigel's brigade, and carried the American flag. They were, therefore, permitted to move down the hill (toward the ford of Skegg's Branch) within easy range of DuBois' battery, until they had reached the covered position at the foot of the ridge on which we were posted, and from which we had been fiercely assailed before, when suddenly a battery, planted on the hill in our front, began to pour upon us shrapnel and canister. . . .

At this moment the enemy showed his true colors, and at once commenced along our entire lines the fiercest and most bloody engagement of the day. Lieutenant DuBois' Battery on our left, gallantly supported by Major Osterhaus' battalion and the rallied fragments of the First Missouri, soon silenced the enemy's battery on the hill, and repulsed the right wing of his infantry. Captain Totten's battery in the center, supported by the Iowas and regulars, was the main point of attack. The enemy could frequently be seen within 20 feet of Totten's guns, and the smoke of the opposing lines was often so confounded as to seem but one.

Now, for the first time during the day, our entire line maintained its position with perfect firmness. Not the slightest disposition to give way was manifested at any point; and while Captain Steele's battalion, which was some yards in front of the line, together with the troops on the right and left, was in imminent danger of being overwhelmed by superior numbers, the contending lines being almost muzzle to muzzle, Captain Granger rushed to the rear and brought up the supports of DuBois' Battery, consisting of two or three companies of the First Missouri, three companies of the First Kansas, and two companies of the First Iowa, in quick time, and fell upon the enemy's right flank, and poured into it a murderous volley, killing or wounding nearly every man within 60 or 70 yards.

From this moment a perfect rout took place throughout the rebel front, while ours—on the right flank—continued to pour a galling fire into their disorganized masses. It was then evident that Totten's battery and Steele's little battalion were safe.

A few moments before the close of the engagement, the Second Kansas, which had firmly maintained its position on the extreme right, from the time it was first sent there, found its ammunition exhausted. I directed it to withdraw slowly and in good order from the field, which it did, bringing off its wounded, which left our right flank exposed. The enemy renewed the attack at that point, after it had ceased along the whole line; but it was gallantly met by Captain Steele's battalion of regulars, which had just driven the enemy from the right of the center. After a sharp engagement, he drove the enemy precipitately from the field. Thus closed, at about half-past eleven o'clock, an almost uninterrupted conflict of six hours.

The order to retreat was given soon after the enemy gave way from our front and center, Lieutenant DuBois' Battery having been previously sent to occupy with its supports the hill in our rear. Captain Totten's battery, as soon as his disabled horses could be replaced, retired slowly with the main body of the infantry, while Captain Steele was meeting the demonstrations upon our right flank. This having been repulsed, and no enemy being in sight, the whole column moved slowly to the high, open prairie, about two miles from the battleground. Meanwhile, our ambulances passed to and fro, carrying off our wounded.

It should be here remembered that—just after the order to retire was given, and while it was undecided whether the retreat should be continued, or whether we should occupy the more favorable portion of our rear and await tiding of Colonel Sigel—one of his non-commissioned officers (Sergeant Froelich on a foam-flecked horse) reported that the Colonel's brigade had been totally routed and all his artillery captured, Colonel Sigel himself having been either killed or taken prisoner. Most of our men had fired away all their ammunition, and all that could be obtained from the boxes of the killed and wounded. Nothing, therefore, was left to do but to return to Springfield, where Home Guards, with two pieces of artillery, had been left to take care of the train. On reaching the Little York road, we met Lieutenant Farrand, with his company of dragoons and a considerable portion of Colonel Sigel's command, with one piece of artillery. At five o'clock, we reached Springfield.

Thus ended Major Sturgis' report. A wholly different story, about the closing phase of the Battle of Wilson's Creek, is told by Southern combatants in their reports.

Major General Sterling Price, in discussing the fourth and final phase of the conflict, says:

The action now became general, and was conducted with the greatest gallantry and vigor on both sides . . . when the enemy retreated in great confusion, leaving their commander-in-chief, General Lyon, dead upon the battlefield, over 500 killed, and a great number wounded.

The forces under my command have possession of three 12-pounder howitzers, two brass 6-pounders, and a great quantity of small arms and ammunition taken from the enemy; also the standard of Sigel's regiment, captured by Captain Staples. They have also a large number of prisoners.

The brilliant victory thus achieved upon this hard-fought field was won only by the most determined bravery and distinguished gallantry of the combined armies, which fought nobly side by side in defense of their common rights and liberties with as much courage and constancy as were ever exhibited upon any battlefield.

Colonel Gratiot, too, tells how his Third Arkansas was in at the kill:

I advanced until we came near the enemy. We then faced toward them, and marched, in line of battle, about 50 paces, when we were attacked by a large force of the enemy in front and on the left flank.

At this moment, a battery commenced playing on our left flank, enfilading the entire regiment with grape, canister and shell. So terrific was the fire that my regiment was obliged to lie down, and then commenced firing in that position. We remained in this atti-

tude for about 30 minutes, firing with deadly effect, silencing the
fire of the artillery and infantry upon our left and driving the
enemy in front. We remained upon the ground long after the enemy
had fled and all firing ceased.

To cap these Southern victory reports, of which there are
many, comes that of Brigadier General McCulloch. After a
general description of the battle, he adds:

Nothing could withstand the impetuosity of our final charge.
The enemy fled, and could not again be rallied, and they were
seen at 12 M. fast retreating among the hills in the distance. Thus
ended the battle. It lasted six hours and a half. The force of
the enemy, between nine and ten thousand, was composed of well-
disciplined troops, well armed, and a large part of them belonging
to the Old Army of the United States. With every advantage on
their side they have met with a signal repulse.

The casualties on both sides were heavy. The grand total
was 2,653—of these 539 were killed, 1,938 injured, and 186
missing. (For full listing of casualties see Appendix.)

The North suffered 258 killed, 873 wounded, 186 missing.
Total: 1,317.

The South suffered 281 killed, 1,055 wounded, 000 missing.
Total: 1,336.

Among Northern units that received casualties in excess of
10 per cent as based on muster rolls (computed on actual effectives, the percentages would be much larger) are the following: First Missouri, 38 per cent; Second Missouri, 37 per
cent; First Kansas 35 per cent; First U. S. Infantry, 28 per
cent; Third Missouri, Fifth Missouri, Bischoff's Battery, 27 per
cent; Second U. S. Infantry, 22 per cent; First Iowa, 19 per
cent; Totten's Battery, 13 per cent; Second Kansas, 12 per cent.

Starting with McCulloch's Brigade, Southern regiments
with more than 10 per cent casualties were: Churchill's Regiment, 33 per cent; McIntosh's Regiment, 13 per cent; Pearce's
Army of Arkansas, Gratiot's Regiment, 22 per cent.

Price's Missouri State Guard: Burbridge's Regiment (Clark), 38 per cent; Kelly's Regiment (Parsons), 30 per cent; Wingo's and Foster's Regiments (McBride), 24 per cent; Guibor's Battery (Parsons), 24 per cent; Hughes' and Thornton's Regiments (Slack), 22 per cent; Weightman's Brigade (Rains) 13 per cent. The accuracy of these State Guard statistics may be challenged on the ground that there is no way of knowing how many of the unarmed State Guard entered its ranks during the conflict.

Incidental, but interesting, is the fact that the loss of junior and senior officers on both sides was conspicuously heavy. From early in the battle, sergeants and corporals took command of companies and platoons when their officers were either killed or incapacitated by wounds. On the Federal side, near the finish of the contest, Sturgis—by no means an over-age major —was the ranking officer. All those senior to him had given their blood to Bloody Hill. Some, like Brigadier General Lyon, died; others, like Captain Plummer, recovered.

From time to time, during the telling of this story, mention has been made of various officers in Lyon's forces who reached the grade of general officers. Among those not mentioned so far are Captain Steele, Captain Carr, Captain Plummer, and Colonel Mitchell. Among Southern veterans of Bloody Hill who reached the military summit were: Colonel McIntosh, Colonel Churchill, Captain Shelby, Colonel Hébert, Lieutenant Colonel McRae, Colonel Greer, Captain Colton Greene, Colonel Gratiot, and Colonel Dockery.

Chapter 12

Aftermath of Wilson's Creek

———◆———

Dead End on the Road to Glory

Where the truth actually rests between the conflicting claims to victory is anybody's guess. However, one thing is sure:

By the time Major Sturgis received word that the remains of Nathaniel Lyon had been left unrecognized and unguarded on the open prairie just north of Bloody Hill, the Southern forces were in occupation of the battlefield.

In life, Brigadier General Lyon always had sought to be the spearhead of the lead. Through a series of tragic blunders, he was relegated to a place far behind the rear soon after his death. One of those who saw the shaping of the closing chapter of the life of Nathaniel Lyon at first-hand was Major (then Lieutenant) William M. Wherry, USA. He was an aide-de-camp to Lyon that day at Wilson's Creek. In a speech before the Missouri Historical Society in March, 1880, he said:

General Lyon's body was brought to me through the ranks by his servant, Albert Lehman and a party of soldiers. Lehman was crying and making a great noise. Apprehensive that the troops might be unduly influenced by the knowledge of the death of their General, I ordered the face to be covered and that secrecy should be observed as to Lyon's death. The body was placed in safety and I went to find Schofield. When he and I got back, several other officers had gathered about the body which was taken to a place selected as a hospital. Here it was placed in an ambulance, with

267

positive orders that, in no case, was it to be removed from the vehicle.

By somebody's order, it was taken from the ambulance and left on the ground. When the battle was ended, and we had moved back about a mile and taken a new position, it was discovered that General Lyon's body had been left. Lieutenant Canfield was sent back with a company of cavalry under a flag of truce to get the remains. I do not think that there was any necessity for a flag of truce as, from the best information I have, the enemy—unless it may have been a few stragglers—was further from the field than we were.

The body was recovered and brought into Springfield about 9 o'clock that night. It was decently laid out in the house which he (Lyon) had occupied as his headquarters. When the army moved the next day, it was left there through another unfortunate oversight. However, Mrs. Phelps (wife of Congressman John S. Phelps) looked after it in the kindest and tenderest manner and had it temporarily interred in her garden [as a measure against vandals].

McCulloch Snubs Price's Follow-Up Plan

According to Southern sources, it was a good thing that Lieutenant Canfield returned to Bloody Hill under a flag of truce. He did, they maintain, find Price's and McCulloch's forces in possession of a field they had never left. According to this version, Price did not know that Lyon had fallen until Canfield told him and described the circumstances. The State Guard leader immediately issued a pass, asked the lieutenant if he could be of any service and even rode with him to the spot where Lyon's body—his eyes as blue and wide as the August sky—was lying near a clump of bushes and without any covering. In death, Lyon looked even smaller than he had appeared in life. His face, seamed by sun and weathered by wind, had lost its careworn look. If it had not been for the unblinking gaze of the deep-set eyes, he could have been asleep. The body was wrapped in a blanket and placed in an ambulance Canfield had brought along.

"Pap" Price was not in a very happy state of mind that afternoon when he saluted the going of Nathaniel Lyon. He had had another run-in with McCulloch. Price wanted the Southern Army to fall in and attack the retreating Federals. In fact, he claimed that now was the time to recapture all of Missouri and chase the Union forces east of the Mississippi. But McCulloch, who at first had been receptive toward the idea, changed his mind. In his own words, this was his reason:

Immediately after the battle was over, and, in truth, before all my forces had returned from pursuit of the enemy, orders were issued for the wounded to be brought from the battlefield, the dead to be buried and the Army to be ready to march after the enemy that night.

We did not march and for the want of ammunition. Several of my officers informed me, when they heard of the order, that some of their men had fired their last cartridge at the enemy as we had only twenty-five rounds to the man before the battle began and no more within hundreds of miles.

Price, on the other hand, thought that the Federals were as depleted with respect to ammunition as they were. He maintained that the issue could be won with cold steel—swords swung by cavalry, bayonets thrust by infantry would put the "invaders" to utter rout. Pointing out that the Union had barely 3,000—if that many—weary and disheartened men, Price went on to declare that between them—he, McCulloch, and Pearce—had nearly twice that number of fresh troops.

While "Pap" harangued, McCulloch remained obdurate. He would not budge. Thomas Snead flatly lays the Confederate brigadier general's attitude to his distrust of the Missouri State Guard. While McCulloch said that such an invasion would be contrary to the policies of the Confederate Government, Snead countered with:

McCulloch would perhaps have pursued, even at the risk of displeasing his own government, had he not by this time become even more prejudiced against the Missourians. The distrust that he conceived the first moment that he saw their unorganized condition, and which had been increased by the behavior of a few of them at Dug Springs, reached its height on the morning of the battle of Wilson's Creek when his army was completely surprised by Lyon and Sigel.

Snead calls attention to McCulloch's report to the Secretary of War of the Confederacy:

The fault was theirs. The two extremes of the camp were composed of mounted men from Missouri, and it was their duty to have pickets on the roads on which the enemy advanced.

It seems that, according to this remarkable statement, General McCulloch completely forgot that his right—the point attacked by Colonel Sigel—was largely composed of the First Regiment Arkansas Mounted Riflemen—600 under Colonel Thomas J. Churchill; and the South Kansas–Texas Mounted Regiment—800 under Colonel E. Greer. And, as Snead observed:

It was his [McCulloch's] own duty to keep his camp properly guarded and he unjustly attributed the blunder to the Missourians alone. The result was that he disliked them more than ever.

Nor could he [McCulloch] keep [from] contrasting their condition with that of his own well-organized, well-disciplined, well-equipped and finely uniformed brigade. . . . Many of them (the Missourians) had not even enlisted but had only come out to fight; thousands of them had not been organized into regiments; many of them were unarmed; none of them were uniformed and very few of them had been drilled. . . .

McCulloch was not wise enough to see that they were, in spite of all these drawbacks, true soldiers, as brave as the bravest and as good as the best, and he still distrusted them, even after they had unflinchingly borne the brunt of the battle for five hours and, with the aid of Churchill, Gratiot, and Woodruff, had won the main fight on Bloody Hill.

To be sure, McCulloch and Pearce marched to Springfield with Price after the Army of the West was well on its way to Rolla. But that was as far as he went. When Price, about August 22, left Springfield for Lexington on the Missouri River, McCulloch—with Pearce—remained encamped at Pond Spring. Two days later, he wrote Brigadier General Hardee the following letter with a pen that was dipped in the bitter gall of prejudice:

I am in no condition to advance, or even to meet an enemy here, having little ammunition or supplies of any kind. Will in consequence shorten my lines by falling back to the Arkansas line near the Indian territory.

We have little to hope or expect from the people of this State. The force now in the field is undisciplined and led by men who are mere politicians—not a soldier among them to control and organize this mass of humanity. The Missouri forces are in no condition to meet an organized army nor will they ever be while under their present leaders. I dare not join them in my present condition, for fear of having my men completely demoralized.

We lost at least 300 stand of arms in the battle on the 10th taken by their camp followers from my killed and wounded. Before the engagement, they borrowed of General Pearce 600 more, none of which they would return after the fight was over.

They stole the tents my men left at Cassville (to facilitate their march) and brought them after us the next day on the same road. In a word, they are not making friends where they go, and, from all I can see, we had as well be in Boston as far as the friendly feeling of the inhabitants is concerned.

Since this is our point of departure with the Southern forces, it is also the place to establish that neither McCulloch, nor McIntosh, would live to see the splendid record made by Major General Price's Missourians under the Confederates' Stars and Bars during the remainder of the Civil War. Both were to die of bullet wounds during the Battle of Pea Ridge, Arkansas, on March 7, 1862. A few months later, Governor Jackson died in Little Rock of cancer.

Three days after the Federals reached Rolla, Major General Price began his march on Lexington on the Missouri River. Here Frémont was to repeat his tragic failure to reinforce badly pressed Federal commanders in Missouri. If the Great Pathfinder had helped Colonel Mulligan in time, it is questionable if Price could have starved Lexington into surrender in September. The air blew out of this victory when Price, a week or so later, marched south toward Arkansas and the Confederacy.

After Appomattox, "Pap" Price, with Joe Shelby and others, went on a quixotic errand into Mexico to support the tottering empire of Maximilian. Finding that he was supporting a hopeless cause, Price returned to his Chariton County home where he died in 1868.

The Federals Retreat to Rolla

When the regulars of Plummer's Battalion, spearhead of the returning Federal column, entered Springfield, the town was in the utmost confusion. Civilians of all ages, with as many of their belongings as they could transport or carry, crowded not only the streets but cluttered the road toward Rolla. The Army of the West had, itself, a wagon train that stretched more than two miles from first lead mule to last tail gate. Plummer entered Springfield about 5 o'clock. Steele's Battalion, which brought up the rear, did not pull in until after dark.

On their arrival, Sturgis and Schofield learned of the safe return of Colonel Sigel and Colonel Salomon. On instructions from Sturgis, Schofield rode to Colonel Sigel's quarters to find out what had happened and to inform him that Major Sturgis had called a meeting of such officers as were physically able to attend. However, now that the safe return of Sigel was known, Sturgis would turn the command over to him as the senior officer in the command.

During the meeting at Lyon's old headquarters, with Sigel presiding, it was assumed that McCulloch's forces would attack the following morning. Deciding not to make a stand at

Springfield, it was agreed to start the retreat toward Rolla at 2 o'clock in the morning. By making this early start, the officers hoped that the column, with its long train of 370 wagons, could mount a favorable defense posture at dawn.

Just before the close of the meeting, Colonel Sigel arranged the order of march. The remnants of his own brigade and the Iowa Regiment would form the advance guard, followed by the wagon train, then the main body of the army, and, lastly, Major Sturgis' brigade of regulars. Schofield gave the necessary instructions for the movements of the various portions of the train and of the different commands. Provision also was made for the transportation of such of the wounded as could be carried along and for the care of those who had to be left behind. Four surgeons were detailed for this duty. In his capacity as Chief of Staff, Major Schofield went to the various camps, except Colonel Sigel's, and saw that all possible preparations were made. He reported later:

At 1:30 o'clock, I went to Colonel Sigel's camp, and found his wagons not loaded, his men apparently making preparations to cook their breakfast, and no preparations to march. I could find no officer to execute my commands nor any one to pay the slightest heed to what I said.

I rode at once to Colonel Sigel's quarters, arriving there at 2 o'clock, and found him asleep in bed. I aroused him, told him the hour for marching had arrived and that all were ready except his brigade. I urged upon him the importance of marching at once if at all. He said, "Yes, I will move at once." I started the train immediately, and sent the Iowa regiment ahead, directing it to halt about a mile from town. In this condition the column was delayed more than two hours while waiting for Colonel Sigel's brigade, so that the rear guard could not leave town till about 6 o'clock.

Schofield could make neither head nor tail of this tardiness. Sigel himself had been one of the most vociferous among the officers who believed that the Southerners would descend on

273

them, come morning, with the flaming swords of avenging angels. And here Sigel was, not only asleep but also without preparations for departure. Moreover, the Army of the West could not get rolling until Sigel and his outfit took their places in the vanguard.

That morning, Sigel brought quite a headache to Sturgis, Schofield, and their fellow officers. But there was more—much more—to come.

Serving as rear guard of a slowly moving column in retreat— and being constantly on the alert against potential enemy strikes—is an exhausting assignment. And yet, during the first three days of the march, the regulars performed rear guard duties. They expected but little out of Army life, but even they began to mutter in the ranks. Schofield urged Sigel to change the order of march. But the snippy little German professor would merely adjust the gold-framed pince-nez on his thin-bridge nose and freeze his Chief of Staff with a schoolmaster's glare. It said, plainer than words: "Who's running this class?"

There were other complaints. For instance, although the column made daily marches of only ordinary length, long halts were made in the middle of the day. This meant that, while Sigel's advance guard would reach camp at sunset—early enough to obtain and cook provisions—the rear guard would be marching or waiting wearily in the road till long after dark. In the vast confusion, that resulted from the attempt to encamp a large force with an immense train in an extremely rough and wooded country in a dark night, entire companies would go without food. Any attempt to find their wagons and get them in position was just too much for foot-weary regulars. Many of the men thus went for 24 hours without a morsel, and some much longer.

The dissatisfaction came to a climax on the morning of the third day. The whole column was detained three hours while Colonel Sigel's brigade had beef killed and cooked for breakfast. Members of less privileged regiments made their breakfast on such as they had. With the exception of the Iowa Regiment, they also marched six miles before the killing of beef for Colonel Sigel's breakfast commenced. After that, they stood in the road, marked time, and matched profanities. Noted Schofield:

By now the clamor for relief became such that almost total anarchy reigned in the command. At length, after numerous entreaties from officers of the command, Major Sturgis resumed command of the Army. He gave as his reason, for so doing, that—although Colonel Sigel had been for a long time acting as an officer of the Army—he had no appointment from any competent authority since the expiration of the 90-day service period.

Colonel Sigel protested against this assumption. But Sturgis was sustained by the great majority of officers of the Army. So Sigel submitted.

Colonel Salomon proposed that the question of title to command be put to a vote by the officers. Sturgis objected on the grounds that the vote, by fellow Saint Louisians, might possibly be in favor of Colonel Sigel. He added, slowly and with feeling:

"Then, some of you might refuse to obey my orders, and I'd be under the necessity of shooting you!"

There was no more talk about balloting.

On August 19, nine days after the battle, the Army of the West reached Rolla. Aside from occasional annoyances—such as rocks and trees obstructing the road and infrequent shots from ambush delivered by Southern sympathizers—the column's progress had been undisturbed. Advices from Springfield were that while McCulloch's, Price's, and Pearce's armies were camped about the town, they were too exhausted, too badly mauled, and too short of ammunition to stage any effective pursuit. Also, the wholesale lootings expected in Springfield did not materialize.

Frémont Locks the Barn Door Too Late

News of the battle on Bloody Hill reached Saint Louis by train from Rolla on August 13. Information about the defeat or the victory at Wilson's Creek—no one knew for sure what was what—did not appear in the Eastern press until the following day. While the outcome of the battle was uncertain, one certainty rang throughout the nation with the dull tones of a sadly tolling bell: Nathaniel Lyon, one of the North's first and greatest Civil War heroes, was dead. In every Union State, from New England to the Pacific, flags were lowered to half-mast and mourning crape was displayed on homes, business and public buildings. A large part of the press, in praising Lyon, turned to the condemnation of Frémont. In a matter of days, he was, justly or not, singled out as the one man responsible for Lyon's demise and defeat. In Washington, among those loudest in their condemnation of the major general were the Blair brothers. Frank, who was still in the Capital, decided to return to Saint Louis at the earliest possible moment.

As for Frémont.

Now that Lyon was dead, the man who replaced him as Department Commander could, overnight it seemed, do more toward the acquisition of troops than he attempted to do while Lyon was alive and shouted for "soldiers, soldiers, soldiers!"

He sent the following telegram to the governors of Ohio, Wisconsin, Iowa, Illinois, and Indiana:

"Severe engagement near Springfield reported; General Lyon killed; Sigel retreating in good order on Rolla. Send forthwith all disposable force you have, arming them as best can for the moment. Use utmost dispatch."

Fearing all sorts of dire consequences on the heels of Sigel's retreat, Frémont's aides almost hysterically jammed the panic buzzers. In addition to the telegrams just mentioned, other messages, as follows, went to state executives:

To the Governor of Iowa: "Order Warren's cavalry here at once!"

To the Governor of Ohio: "Have the Groesbeck regiment ordered here forthwith!"

Within the hour, Frémont wired the Secretary of War at great length about the Battle of Wilson's Creek and pleaded for assistance from State and Federal manpower sources. Then he shot off additional telegrams with the speed of rockets on a Fourth of July.

To President Lincoln: "Will the President read my urgent dispatch to the Secretary of War?"

To Montgomery Blair: "See instantly my dispatch to the Secretary of War."

To Thomas A. Scott, Assistant Secretary of War: "Will you order company of regular artillery at Cincinnati to report to me forthwith together with the battery at Bellaire?"

To Brigadier General Prentiss: "I am sending reinforcements to Rolla."

To Honorable T. A. Scott: "I require this week $3,000,000 for quartermaster's department."

On that day, the next and the following days, Army telegraphers worked their fingers to the bone clicking out and ticking in the telegraphic words that reached and departed Saint Louis in a seemingly endless stream. From Washington and elsewhere came reassuring replies. All the help requested by Frémont was on the way. Soon troops would pour into Saint Louis like a veritable flood.

And still, Frémont wrote telegrams even faster than he could read them. On August 15, he received the following mild reprimand by wire from the White House:

"Been answering your messages ever since day before yesterday. Do you receive the answers? The War Department has notified all the Governors you designate to forward all available force. So telegraphed you. Have you received these messages? Answer immediately. A. Lincoln."

From Montgomery Blair, the same day:

"Every available man and all the money in the public chest

277

have been sent. We will send more money immediately, our financial arrangements at New York having been perfected. Let our fellows cheer up. All will be well."

One cannot help but wonder why these currents of productive energy were not released by Frémont before Lyon—as some put it—was sacrificed. It is vain to speculate; history does not provide the answers.

Considering Frémont's previously announced attitude, namely that southwest Missouri was unimportant, it is truly amazing that its fall assumed such stature in his mind as a menace to the safety of Saint Louis. He also disclaimed all responsibility for Lyon's disaster.

On August 20, Major Schofield arrived in Saint Louis from Rolla. He had orders from Major Sturgis to call on Major General Frémont at the earliest possible moment. His mission was to deliver a verbal report on the contest fought on Bloody Hill. Schofield first of all went to the Arsenal to pick up a change of clothing. There he met Frank Blair who had just returned from Washington. Schofield, being a major in the Volunteers but only a lieutenant in the Regular Army, expressed doubt about being able to reach Frémont's ear in anything short of a week. Blair replied that he thought he could fix it so that they could meet with the department commander the following morning. Telling about this meeting in his *My Forty-Six Years in the Army,* Lieutenant General Schofield writes:

The headquarters palace was surrounded by a numerous guard, and all ingress by the main entrance appeared to be blocked. But Blair had some magic word or sign by which we passed the sentinels at a basement door. Ascending two flights of stairs, we found the Commanding General with a single secretary, or clerk, occupying the suite of rooms extending from front to rear of the building.

The General received me cordially, but, to my great surprise, no questions were asked, nor any mention made, of the bloody field

278

from which I had just come, where Lyon had been killed. I was led at once to a large table on which maps were spread out from which the General proceeded to explain at length the plans of the great campaign for which he was then preparing.

Frémont spoke for more than an hour about his plans and himself. As soon as the explanation was ended, Blair and Schofield were invited to take their departure. Neither one had been permitted to complete a single sentence about Lyon or Wilson's Creek! As they walked down the street, too baffled for words, Blair, at length, broke the silence and said:

"Well, what do you think of him?"

Schofield replied (as he observes in his memoirs), "In words rather too strong to repeat in print, to the effect that my opinion as to him [Frémont] was the same as it always had been."

To this, Schofield added that, in the course of the visit, he had "learned much in confirmation of the opinion of the character and ability of General Frémont which had been very generally held in the Army."

Blair replied: "I have been suspecting that for some time."

Martial law was proclaimed and with this abrogation of the rights of civilians came censorship and/or suspension of newspapers. It was not even safe to be critical of Frémont in speech or in correspondence. Colonel Blair, so charged Frémont, had been guilty of both. Frank had referred to the California contingent of the general's army of hangers-on as "obscene birds of prey," and, so Frémont charged, the colonel had been disloyal to him in letters to Postmaster General Blair. As a result, the general staged an outstanding example of his inferior administrative judgment by charging Blair with insubordination. He was placed under arrest and confined to quarters at Jefferson Barracks. Frank's roars of anger resounded from the banks of the Mississippi to those of the Potomac. So great were the reverberations that Frémont canceled the order of arrest. But Frank vowed that he would remain under arrest until he had been vindicated. The deadlock was only solved when Montgomery, for the sake of precious Union unity, stepped in as an intermediary.

Meanwhile Frémont's frantic search for military security assumed the patterns of geometric doodlings by a distraught mathematician. He seemed to move in circles, squares, and triangles in his feverish efforts to defend Saint Louis against onslaughts by enemies who were nowhere near at hand. Heavy guns were planted and regulars were encamped near the city's reservoir. On the heights south of the Arsenal, strong posts with howitzers were established. All five original Home Guard Regiments were paid off and reorganized for extended service. Captains Voerster's and Genter's Pioneers were assigned the task of construction fortifications around the city. For this job, laborers were employed by the thousand. The forts, incidentally, were never manned nor prepared for defense.

Ulysses Grant, like Nathaniel Lyon, was to run head-on into Frémont's reluctance to make firm and swift combat decisions. And, like Lyon, he met an emergency with action without awaiting Frémont's consent. On September 5, Grant, now a brigadier general, was at Cairo, Illinois. On learning that Confederates at Columbus, Kentucky, planned to seize Paducah, strategically located at the mouth of the Tennessee, he realized that he must take Paducah without delay to thwart the Southern plan. He wired Frémont that he was taking steps to anticipate the enemy in the occupation of the town and asked for orders. When utter silence met his inquiry, Grant telegraphed his Commanding General that, unless he received other orders, he would start for Paducah at dawn of September 6.

Getting no reply, Grant, with characteristic initiative, occupied the town the next morning, thereby anticipating the enemy by half a dozen hours. After he had garrisoned the town and placed Brigadier General Smith in command, Grant returned to Cairo. There he found a telegram from Frémont who straddled the issue by authorizing Grant to take Paducah "if he felt strong enough."

Week by week, Frémont's Saint Louis position was becoming weaker. Complaints against his administration grew in the fall when Colonel Frank P. Blair, Jr., took the leadership in a drive to have Frémont removed from his command. In charges brought against the general, the latter was accused of extravagance and waste of public moneys, despotic and tyrannical conduct, plus disobedience of orders. These charges were sustained by many specifications. Remembering that when Blair went into a fight, he went out for a funeral, the colonel's vitriolic accusations were not wholly free from personal animosity and partisan prejudice. On the other hand, the charges against Frémont contained so much truth that the War Department felt that they could not be ignored. As for Saint Louis, the Unionists in the city were now divided into two new camps. One for, the other against, the general. As the Reverend Galusha Anderson observed in his *Story of a Border City During the Civil War:*

The situation was so grave that the Secretary of War himself came to make an investigation. He evidently found much that he did not approve. He went out into the State to Tipton and had an interview with Frémont, who was then on the march; and when, on October 14th, he was about to return from St. Louis to Washington, the Secretary instructed Frémont to correct certain irregularities in his disbursement of military funds, to discontinue the erection of earthworks around our city, as wholly unnecessary, and of barracks near his own headquarters. He also declared that no payments would be made to officers, other than those of the volunteer forces, who had been commissioned by Frémont without the President's approval.

Such deliverances from the head of the War Department betokened reprehensible, even if it were thoughtless, insubordination, and contained a pretty clear hint of incompetence. In fact the evidence of his incompetence was startling and cumulative. When at Jefferson City, he ordered his army to march without sufficient means of transportation. He did the same at Tipton. His ammunition was wet; the Belgian rifles that he bought in Europe were nearly useless.

It soon leaked out that Frémont had appointed general and staff officers without the authority of the general government; that those constituting his bodyguard had been commissioned primarily to serve him personally rather than the United States; and that often ignoring his adjutant-general, he had sent in bills payable, approved simply by himself. At a later day, a committee appointed by the House of Representatives, after thoroughly investigating these alleged misdemeanors, in the main confirmed the conclusions reached by the Secretary of War.

When the Secretary arrived at Washington and made his report, the removal of Frémont from his command soon followed. He was apprised of it on November 2d, and immediately took leave of his army. To most of us, this seemed at the moment a calamity. Not that we could justly find fault with the decision reached by the government, but we keenly felt that the time for promulgating this decision was most inopportune.

The General was apparently on the eve of a great battle; his army glowed with enthusiasm; the prospect of complete victory was unusually bright; he had in fact, with the smallest modicum of fighting, nearly driven the rebel army from our State. [Major General Price's State Guard had moved toward Arkansas from Lexington.] The strong, instinctive feeling of the great body of loyal men and women of our city was that he ought to have had the chance to finish the campaign so auspiciously begun. But the authorities at Washington had, with apparently abundant justification, decreed otherwise. There was only one thing to be done; that was to submit without murmuring.

So far as charges that Frémont failed to give proper and available support to Nathaniel Lyon are concerned, the Joint Committee on the Conduct of the War whitewashed this human storm center of culpable responsibility. Briefly, the committee held that Frémont was pushed into his command so suddenly "that even if he had failed to do all that one under the circumstances might have done, still, your Committee can discover no cause of censure against him."

The Lincoln Administration, the United States Senate, and the House of Representatives went unqualifiedly on record, on December 24, 1861, as declaring, in a joint resolution, that the Battle of Wilson's Creek was a Federal victory won under the leadership of Brigadier General Lyon. It also authorized the regiments engaged to bear the word "Springfield" in gold on their colors. Since then, the verdict of history has been that, because they occupied the battleground, McCulloch's forces were the victors. But, as a Southern victory, it was both hollow and expensive. The Confederate-Arkansas-Missouri combination was too exhausted in manpower and too expended in matériel to pursue the retreating Union forces. Moreover, Lyon's success in paralyzing his opponents made it impossible for them to mount an offensive against the entire State. The long-range result was that Missouri remained in the Union. This course of destiny gave great moral encouragement to Unionists who fought to, and succeeded in, keeping Kentucky among Northern States. The resources, as well as strategic locations of those two commonwealths, would, had they joined the Confederacy, have weighed heavily in favor of the South. With his small, almost homemade army, Nathaniel Lyon contributed greatly from making those twin menaces to the Union cause come to pass.

The Nation Pays Homage to Lyon

Danforth Knowlton of New York City and John B. Hasler of Webster, Massachusetts—respectively cousin and brother-in-law of the late Nathaniel Lyon—arrived in Saint Louis on August 18 to take the body for interment in the Lyon family plot in the Phoenixville, Connecticut, cemetery. To their surprise, they found that the remains, so far as anyone knew, were still in Springfield. The Union commander had forgotten to attend to them. The two reached Springfield a few days later, secured the body—which Mrs. Phelps had had placed in an oaken box inside a zinc casket—and returned to Saint Louis. There a funeral train had been prepared to take the body eastward with all the stately and melancholy pomp that the era could produce. The Honor Guard, composed of regulars from Lyon's old company in the Second Infantry, was commanded by Captain Plummer, who had known Nat Lyon since they were West Point plebes. En route, the body lay in state in Cincinnati, Pittsburgh, Harrisburg, Philadelphia, New York City, and Hartford. Lyon's last, long and dreary journey came to an end in a newly dug grave in Phoenixville cemetery. This lies two and a half miles from Eastford where Nathaniel Lyon first saw the light of day in 1818.

He was home again. Home, in the place where he was born and bred among the rocks, and of which he had seen so little during the years of his active life. The rural cemetery was small, ill kept, and surrounded by a rusting iron fence. Here and there, grass grew rank among untended graves of men, women, and children long forgotten. Over Lyon's grave, in time, was placed a simple headstone that gave his name, rank, and years of birth and death.

Somehow no one saw any necessity for inscribing an epitaph. And why? Was not his name inscribed in the hearts of all the people of that region as well as throughout the Union?

But, just in case one should seek an epitaph for this Yankee soldier who fought so valiantly to retain Missouri in the Union, its text is to be found in the following summary by one who fought and lived wholeheartedly for the South—Colonel Thomas L. Snead:

Lyon had not fought and died in vain. Through him, the rebellion (sic) which Blair had organized, and to which he (Lyon) had given force and strength, had succeeded at last. By capturing the State Militia at Camp Jackson and driving the Governor from the Capital, and all his troops into the uttermost corner of the State, and by holding Price and McCulloch at bay, he had given the Union men of Missouri time, opportunity and courage to bring their State Convention together again; and had given the Convention an excuse and the power to depose Governor Jackson and Lieutenant Governor Reynolds, to vacate the seats of the members of the General Assembly, and to establish a State Government which was loyal to the Union and which would use the whole

284

organized power of the State, its treasury, its credit, its militia and all its great resources to sustain the Union and crush the South.

All this had been done while Lyon was boldly confronting the overwhelming strength of Price and McCulloch. Had he abandoned Springfield instead, and opened to Price a pathway to the Missouri [River]; had he not been willing to die for the preservation of the Union, none of these things would have then been done. By wisely planning, by boldly doing, and bravely dying, he had won the fight for Missouri.

In the Army—be the time peace or war—one does the best one can with what one has. That is the Army way. It was Nathaniel Lyon's way.

Appendix

Casualties and Contingents

———◆———

UNION FORCES AT WILSON'S CREEK

	Killed	Wounded	Missing	Total	
Bloody Hill					
1st Missouri Volunteers	76	208	11	295 of	775
Osterhaus Battalion	15	40	0	55 of	150
1st Iowa Infantry	12	138	4	154 of	800
1st Kansas Infantry	77	187	20	284 of	800
2nd Kansas Infantry	5	59	6	70 of	600
Steele's Battalion, regulars	15	44	2	61 of	275
Totten's Battery	4	7	0	11 of	84
DuBois' Battery	0	2	1	3 of	66
Total on Bloody Hill	204	685	44	933 of	3,550
Left Wing					
Plummer's Battalion, regulars	19	52	9	80 of	300
1st Cavalry, Company D, Kansas Rangers, Home Guards Mounted (Total)	0	4	3	7 of	350
LYON'S COLUMN (Total)	223	741	56	1,020 of	4,200
Sigel's Column					
Infantry & Artillery, Volunteers	35	132	126	293 of	1,075
1st Cavalry	0	0	2	2 of	65
2nd Dragoons	0	0	2	2 of	60
SIGEL'S COLUMN	35	132	130	297 of	1,200

Grand Total Union Casualties: 1,317
258 killed; 873 wounded; 186 missing
Total Union Force: 5,400

SOUTHERN FORCES AT WILSON'S CREEK

	Killed	*Wounded*	*Total*
McCulloch's Brigade			
3rd Louisiana Infantry	9	48	57 of 700
McRae's Battalion	3	6	9 of 220
Churchill's Regiment	42	155	197 of 600
McIntosh's Regiment	10	44	54 of 400
Greer's Regiment	4	23	27 of 800
	68	276	344 of 2,720
Pearce's Brigade			
Gratiot's Regiment	25	84	109 of 500
Walker's Regiment	0	0	0 of 550
Dockery's Regiment	3	11	14 of 650
Carroll's Regiment	5	22	27 of 350
Carroll's Complement	0	0	0 of 40
Woodruff's Battery	3	0	3 of 71
Reid's Battery	0	1	1 of 73
	36	118	154 of 2,234
Missouri State Guard			
(Major General Price)			
Rains' Brigade			
Weightman's Brigade	40	121	161 of 1,327
Cawthorne's Mounted Brigade	21	66	87 of 1,210
	61	187	248 of 2,537
Parson's Brigade			
Kelly's Regiment	11	38	49 of 150
Brown's Mounted Regiment	3	2	5 of 320
Guibor's Battery	3	11	14 of 61
	17	51	68 of 531
Clark's Brigade			
Burbridge's Regiment	17	83	100 of 279
Major's Battalion Mounted	6	5	11 of 272
	23	88	111 of 551
Slack's Brigade			
Hughes' & Thornton's			
Regiments, Infantry	37	107	144 of 656
Bledsoe's Battery	2	4	6 of 45
Rive's Regiment Mounted	4	8	12 of 284
	43	119	162 of 985

	Killed	Wounded	Total		
McBride's Brigade					
Wingo's & Foster's					
Regiments, Infantry	32	114	146	of	609
Campbell's Company	0	0	0	of	40
	32	114	146	of	649
Major General Price and Staff	1	2	3	of	12
Missouri State Guard:	177	561	740	of	5,265

Grand Total Confederate Casualties: 1,336
281 killed; 1,055 wounded; 0 missing
Total Confederate Force: 10,219

Bibliography[*]

ABBOTT, JOHN C., *History of the Civil War in America* (Norwich, 1883).

ANDERSON, GALUSHA, *The Story of a Border City During the Civil War* (Boston, 1908).

BLAIR, FRANCIS P., JR., *Frémont's Hundred Days in Missouri* (*Congressional Records*, 1862).

CONFEDERATE MILITARY HISTORY (C. A. Evans, ed.) (Atlanta, 1899).

CONFEDERATE REPORTS ON THE BATTLE OF WILSON'S CREEK:

   Colonel T. J. Churchill, First Arkansas Mounted Riflemen, CSA,

   Colonel John R. Gratiot, Third Arkansas Infantry, AOA,

   Colonel John R. Graves, 2nd Division, Missouri State Guard,

   Colonel E. Greer, South Kansas–Texas Mounted Riflemen, CSA,

   Lieutenant Colonel Benjamin T. Embry, Second Arkansas Mounted Riflemen, CSA,

   Colonel Louis Hébert, Third Louisiana Infantry, CSA,

   Lieutenant Colonel S. M. Hyams, Third Louisiana Infantry, CSA,

   Colonel James McIntosh, Second Arkansas Mounted Riflemen, CSA,

   Brigadier General Ben McCulloch, CSA, Commanding Confederate Brigade,

   Lieutenant Colonel D. McRae, Second Arkansas Riflemen, CSA,

   Brigadier General N. B. Pearce, AOA., Commanding Army of Arkansas,

   Major General Sterling Price, MSG., Commanding Missouri State Guard,

   Brigadier General James S. Rains, MSG., Commanding 2nd Division Missouri State Guard,

   Captain J. G. Reid, Light Artillery Battery, AOA,

   Captain John P. Vigilini, Third Louisiana Infantry, CSA.

ESCOTT, GEORGE B., "History and Directory of Springfield, Mo." (Springfield, 1878).

GREENE, ALBERT R., "On the Battle of Wilson's Creek" (Kansas State Historical Society, 1895).

[*] Articles in popular periodicals and newspaper accounts not included.

291

Holcombe, R. I., "History of Greene County Missouri" (1885).

Hulston, John K., "West Point and Wilson's Creek," Civil War History (1955).

Kansas State Historical Society, Transactions of (Topeka, 1895).

Lyon, Albert W., family archives.

Lyon, Nathaniel, official reports and personal papers.

Lyon, Rolfe N., Lyon Family Genealogist.

Meador, Dr. L. E., "History of the Battle of Wilson's Creek" (Springfield, 1938).

Missouri Historical Society Bulletin, Saint Louis, Mo.

Missouri (State) Historical Society Review, Columbia, Mo.

Monahan, Jay, "Civil War on the Western Border" (Boston, 1955).

Moore, Frank, "Rebellion Record" (New York, 1867).

Nevins, Allan, "Fremont, the West's Greatest Adventurer" (New York, 1928).

Peckham, James, "General Nathaniel Lyon and Missouri in 1861" (New York, 1866).

Rombauer, Robert J., "The Union Cause in Saint Louis in 1861" (Saint Louis, 1909).

Scharf, John T., "History of Saint Louis and County" (Philadelphia, 1883).

Schofield, John M., "Forty-Six Years in the Army" (New York, 1887).

Sherman, William T., "Memoirs" (New York, 1875).

Snead, Thomas L., "The Fight for Missouri From the Election of Lincoln to the Death of Lyon" (New York, 1886).

Union Reports on the Battle of Wilson's Creek:

Lieutenant Colonel George L. Andrews, First Missouri Infantry, Commanding 2nd Brigade,

Lieutenant Colonel Charles W. Blair, Second Kansas Infantry, Captain Eugene A. Carr, First U. S. Cavalry,

Lieutenant John V. DuBois, U. S. Light Artillery Battery,

Lieutenant Charles E. Farrand, First U. S. Infantry,

Major General John C. Frémont, Commanding Department of the Missouri,

Major John A. Halderman, First Kansas Infantry,

Major General H. W. Halleck, Commanding Department of the Missouri,

Lieutenant Colonel William H. Merritt, First Iowa Infantry,

Captain Joseph Plummer, First U. S. Infantry,

Major John M. Schofield, Acting Adjutant General, Army of the West,

Colonel Francis Sigel, Commanding Southern Column,

Captain Frederick K. Steele, Second U. S. Infantry,

Major S. D. Sturgis, First U. S. Cavalry, Commanding 1st Brigade, Captain James Totten, Second U. S. Artillery.

VIOLETTE, EUGENE M., "History of Missouri" (Boston, 1918).

WARE, EUGENE F., "The Lyon Campaign In Missouri: Being a History of the First Iowa Infantry" (Topeka, 1907).

WHERRY, WILLIAM M., "The Campaign in Missouri and the Battle of Wilson's Creek" (Saint Louis, 1880).

WOODWARD, ASHBEL, "Life of General Nathaniel Lyon" (Hartford, 1862).

RESEARCH ACKNOWLEDGMENTS

CALIFORNIA STATE LIBRARY, Reference Department, Sacramento, California.

CONNECTICUT HISTORICAL SOCIETY, Hartford, Connecticut.

CONNECTICUT STATE LIBRARY, Reference Department, Hartford, Connecticut.

HULSTON, JOHN K., Springfield, Missouri.

KANSAS STATE HISTORICAL SOCIETY, Reference Library, Topeka, Kansas.

LIBRARY OF CONGRESS, Reference Department and Photo Collections, Washington, D. C.

LOCKWOOD, CHARLES A., Vice Admiral, USN, Ret., formerly of Lamar, Missouri.

MAULDIN, HENRY, Lake County Historian, California.

MEADOR, DR. L. E., President, Wilson's Creek Battlefield Foundation, Springfield, Missouri.

MISSOURI GEOLOGICAL SURVEY, Rolla, Missouri.

MISSOURI HISTORICAL SOCIETY, Reference Library and Photo Collections, Saint Louis, Missouri.

MISSOURI (STATE OF) HISTORICAL SOCIETY REFERENCE LIBRARY AND PHOTO COLLECTIONS, Columbia, Missouri.

MISSOURI STATE HIGHWAY COMMISSION, Department of Information.

NATIONAL ARCHIVES, Early Wars Branch, Washington, D. C.

SAN FRANCISCO PUBLIC LIBRARY, Reference Department, San Francisco, California.

SIXTH U. S. ARMY RESEARCH LIBRARY, Presidio, San Francisco, California.

SMITH, JOHN H., Phoenixville, Connecticut.

SPRINGFIELD PUBLIC LIBRARY, Reference Department, Springfield, Missouri.

SUTRO BRANCH, CALIFORNIA STATE LIBRARY, Reference Department, San Francisco, California.

Subject Index

⎯⎯⎯◆⎯⎯⎯

295

296

297

299

Key to Abbreviations in Index

AAG—Acting Adjutant General; **ACdr**—Army Commander; **AG**—Adjutant General; **AoA**—Army of Arkansas; **BGen.**—Brigadier General; **1-BUSRC**—First Brigade U.S. Reserve Corps; **1-BUSV**—First Brigade U.S. Volunteers; **Cmdg**—Commanding; **CSA**—Confederate States of America; **Kan-Vol.**—Kansas Volunteers; **LCol.**—Lieutenant Colonel; **LGen.**—Lieutenant General; **Lou-Inf.**—Louisiana Infantry; **MGen.**—Major General; **MSG**—Missouri State Guard; **MSM**—Missouri State Militia; **Mtd**—Mounted; **QMG**—Quartermaster General; **UCPS**—Union Committee on Public Safety (St. Louis); **1-USRC**—First U.S. Reserve Corps; **VAdm.**—Vice Admiral; **Vol.**—Volunteers